Governing by Contract

Public Affairs and Policy Administration Series

Governing by Contract

Challenges
and
Opportunities
for Public
Managers

Phillip J. Cooper
University of Vermont

CQ PRESS

A Division of Congressional Quarterly Inc.
Washington, D.C.

CQ Press
1255 22nd Street, N.W., Suite 400
Washington, D.C. 20037

202-729-1900; toll-free, 1-866-4CQ-PRESS (1-866-427-7737)

www.cqpress.com

∞ The paper used in this publication meets the minimum requirements of the American National Standard for Information Sciences—Permanence of Paper for Printed Library Materials, ANSI Z39.48-1992.

Printed and bound in the United States of America

07   06   05   04   03   5   4   3   2   1

Cover and interior designs: Karen Doody

Library of Congress Cataloging-in-Publication Data

Cooper, Phillip J.
  Governing by contract : challenges and opportunities for public managers / Phillip J. Cooper.
     p. cm. — (Public affairs and policy administration series)
Includes bibliographical references and index.
  ISBN 1-56802-620-X (pbk. : alk. paper)
 1. Public contracts.   I. Title. II. Series.
  HD3860 .C666 2002
  352.5'3—dc21   2002008776

For Virginia French.

Every writer needs someone to be the first to say

he or she could write and to provide

the encouragement to try.

Contents

Foreword

Even experts in public policy often make a huge mistake. When they look at puzzles like contract management, they race past the details to get to what they see as the "real" issues. They seem to do so for two reasons. One is that they prefer to focus on what they view as the big policy problems, the decisions that shape grand strategy. Should the Pentagon buy a new-generation fighter plane or refit the existing models? Should state governments hire charitable organizations to run welfare reform? Should local governments contract with private companies to manage public schools? For many experts the grand design is the only issue. Details about how to manage contracts are unimportant, to be left to third-level administrators to sort out.

The other reason is that, quite frankly, they regard the details of contract management as dull and boring. It is the stuff of legal language, administrative law, monitoring and oversight, and the nitty-gritty of front-line management. For the grand designers, the issues seem arcane and the fine points seem dry. The same is true for policymakers and policy analysts. It's sometimes hard to get them to stifle a yawn.

The enormous contribution of Phillip J. Cooper's *Governing by Contract* is how powerfully he demolishes each of these false presumptions. He has written a gripping, lively book that proves the subject of contract management is interesting and entertaining. The volume is chock full of lively examples and spins a tale that anyone interested in how public policy really works will find fascinating. That is no mean feat. But a genuine adventure awaits readers who flip the pages past their prejudices to what Cooper has charted and discover what they have been missing.

Cooper's contribution goes far beyond demonstrating how interesting contract management truly is. He makes the critical, and often overlooked, point that American governments rely increasingly on contracts with for-profit and nonprofit organizations. The quality of our public services depends on the quality of our contract management. Indeed, as Cooper points out, reformers tend to turn to private and nonprofit partners when they seek reform of public programs. Elected officials have also discovered that they can make political hay when contracts go bad or when government managers fail to oversee them well. For example, exactly six months to the day after the September 2001 attacks on the World Trade Center and the Pentagon, the Immigration and Naturalization Service delivered student visas for two of the terrorists who died in the attacks. The foul-up generated enormous political outrage. And it demonstrated what happens when government policymakers and private contractors, who managed some of the paperflow, fail to build a system that works. At the core is a fundamental paradox that, in turn, is the foundation of Cooper's book: Why have we come to rely so much on contracts without paying more attention to how to make them work?

Indeed, as Cooper points out, the interorganizational, interjurisdictional, and intergovernmental dimensions of public contracting have quietly formed one of the very pillars of American democracy. The explosion of contracting out not only raises critical issues of contract management. It also raises fundamental questions about who makes the big decisions in American government, how political influence flows, how the responsiveness of public programs works (or doesn't), and how, if we seek to put the enduring dreams of American democracy in a twenty-first-century setting, we must understand the implications of government contracting. That is why Cooper's book is so aptly titled *Governing by Contract*. It's not a book focused narrowly on management. It's a book on how we govern ourselves—and what we need to do the job better.

That makes *Governing by Contract* a valuable addition to CQ Press's Public Affairs and Policy Administration Series. It joins other books by Beryl A. Radin and Anne M. Khademian in charting the important issues of governance and public policy. The aim of this series is to produce short, lively, and provocative books that explore the cutting-edge issues in the field. Cooper's book breaks new ground in demonstrating the central role that contracts—both contract management and contract governance—play in American government. Anyone who skips past his message because they wrongly think it might be dull is missing a terrific yarn.

Donald F. Kettl
University of Wisconsin–Madison
Series Editor

Preface

If contracting out is such a good idea, then why does the government so often seem to get a bad deal? What does it mean to get a good deal for the public? For that matter, why are so many public managers and citizens uncomfortable debating the subject, even if the discussion is about doing well for the taxpayer? And if contracting out for government services is such an effective way to save money, why does the press uncover cases of excessive spending, such as when the U.S. Department of Defense spent $150 for a hammer and $250 for a toilet seat? If relying on the marketplace for public goods and services is so efficient, why does the Pentagon spend $44 billion for bombers that do not perform as advertised?

If these examples of defense expenditures are alarming, consider the more than $275 billion per year that state and local governments spend on goods and services.[1] No longer possessing the internal capacity to deliver services themselves, virtually every state and many local governments are now utterly dependent on contractors. The federal government's domestic agencies are, in turn, dependent on state and local contract operations to implement federal programs.

Given these developments, why has every major study of the subject found that no government at any level has developed an adequately trained and supported contract management capability? Furthermore, why is so little attention given to the intergovernmental and interjurisdictional nature of government contracting? Why is there so little concern for the relationship between government organizations and nonprofits with respect to contract management? After all, these are the groups with which state and local governments often contract, particularly for the delivery of public services.

The broad answer to all these questions is, at least in part, that too much attention has been focused on the ideological debates over privatization. Whereas policymakers have decided to use contractual instruments to do the people's business, the reform tradition dating back to the party spoils system has caused us to devote most of our attention to bid processes and to attempts to keep them clean. Yet bid procedures and the decision to use a contractor form but a fraction of the larger subject of public contract management, which includes forming, operating, and terminating or transforming the relationships needed to acquire goods and deliver services.

This book advances two general arguments. First, it asserts that what makes public contract management complex and challenging is that the public manager operates at the intersection of a vertical, authority-based model and a horizontal, negotiation-driven one. The vertical model draws its authority, resources, and influences from the constitutional and political processes at the heart of governing. The horizontal model operates on negotiations between two or more presumptively equal participants who create individual relationships governing their behavior and decide which parties will handle certain discrete functions. The horizontal relationship is based on the concept of contract, which differs greatly from the vertical, authority-based approach and is in many respects in tension with it. Second, this volume proposes, therefore, that the move from governance by authority to government by contract is not merely a technical matter. Anyone who truly seeks to govern well in the contemporary, and indeed the future, public setting must move beyond the general debate over privatization to the more specific set of challenging questions raised earlier.

Governing by Contract seeks to address these questions. The book explores what happens when public sector organizations form working relationships with other agencies, communities, nonprofit organizations, or for-profit firms through contracts. It focuses on key elements of the formation, operation, and termination or transformation of these relationships and seeks to do so from the perspective of the generalist manager rather than from a narrow, technical view. The purpose is not to debate whether government at all levels should do more contracting or less but to assess what happens when public managers decide to use contractors to perform services or provide materials.

Toward that end, the book approaches the subject in five ways. First, the volume uses, as I do in my courses and have done in my research, an intergovernmental and intersectoral approach that is not focused on one level of government or type of policy. Second, although the purchase of goods and systems is certainly an important topic in these pages, a purchase agreement is but one kind of contract and usually not the most complex. Rather than focusing only on purchasing, the book considers the full range of contracts, particularly service agreements, in the context in which they are developed and operated. Many contracts today operate under grants that are funded by federal government programs through state agencies and that flow to nonprofit and for-profit organizations at the point of service. Thus successful and competent public contract management at the state and local levels, as well as within nonprofit organizations, is as critical to the success of policies made in Washington as is anything done by federal officials.

Third, the book sheds light on one of the often ignored topics in this field, the significance of interjurisdictional agreements. Today such agreements are increasingly common and important, ranging from interstate compacts to agreements between school districts and towns to build and operate multiple-use recreational and educational facilities. Fourth, this volume asserts that public managers must be alert to new issues that pose different kinds of challenges while trying to understand what is not new and where lessons can be learned from the history of contracting. Finally, public law perspectives are integrated throughout the book. Most studies of individual contracts or broad discussions of privatization almost completely ignore public law issues despite the fact that contracts are legal instruments developed in a complex web of statutes and within the constraints of the Constitution.

As these premises suggest, the book draws on research across the spectrum of contracting, from the many federal studies on particular government programs to those on the wider policies governing contracts, including such critical investigations as the *Report of the Federal Procurement Commission,* the Office of Management and Budget's SWAT team analysis of civilian contracting, and numerous analyses done by the U.S. General Accounting Office. The volume also incorporates a variety of state and local case studies, ranging from the contracting out of public school management in Baltimore or senior citizen programs in Kansas to the use of competition between city departments and external contractors in Phoenix. Although analysts have conducted many individual investigations of particular contract operations, they have not done enough to draw important and more generalizable lessons from these studies. A critical emphasis of this book, then, is to find and explore the linkages and common issues that unite the lessons learned from these individual cases.

ACKNOWLEDGMENTS

Even small books sometimes owe a lot to many colleagues. This volume is an example. Early in my course of study at the Maxwell School of Citizenship and Public Affairs at Syracuse University, I frequently visited Washington to work with James Carroll and the other members of the Committee on Acquisitions and Assistance of the National Association of Schools and Public Affairs and Administration. With the encouragement of Jim and other members of that committee, such as Nicholas Henry and Augustus Turnbull of Florida State University, I pursued the subject of government contracting and published my first piece on it in *Public Administration Review.* Dwight Waldo was a mentor who encouraged my work in public law and public administration as well as my interest in crossing sectors and levels of government. He also prompted me to study the corporate form of organization and other private sector organizational designs to understand their relationships to and conflicts with public sector organizations. John Clarke Adams took me through a broad range of European theory on the jurisprudence and politics of authority. Many years passed before I understood just how much influence he had had on my understanding of public and private legal, political, and economic relationships. Over the years I continued to discuss the connection between public law and public budgeting and finance with my colleague Thomas Lauth of the University of Georgia. Thanks, too, to Donald Kettl of the University of Wisconsin for encouraging me to do this project and to Charisse Kiino of CQ Press for her encouragement, patience, and flexibility.

Last but by no means least, my work with Claudia Vargas on nonprofit organizations in sustainable development and in refugee services administration became a critical feature of my understanding of public sector contracting in its contemporary manifestations. The manuscript also benefited from Claudia's editorial skills and all the love and support that she gives each day.

As always, while those acknowledged can claim credit for the positive attributes of the project, I alone bear responsibility for its shortcomings.

Phillip J. Cooper
Burlington, Vermont

Note

1. Peter A. Harkness, "Dollars and Discipline," *State and Local Sourcebook 1998,* a supplement to *Governing* magazine, February 1998, 8.

1

Getting a Good Deal for the Public: Moving past Advocacy and beyond Bidding

Consider the following scenario. Suppose that a southwestern state is about to enter into a contract for the administration of some of its programs designed to serve needy families. This would be a large contract, amounting to some $600 million per year. It is a new program design that the state is seeking to implement under federal legislation and rules permitting innovative social service delivery programs, subject to approval by the U.S. Department of Health and Human Services (HHS).

An invitation for bids (IFB) has been issued and bids received (Table 1.1). The low bid came from a large national corporation best known as a major aerospace manufacturer. The firm has seen the wave of contracting out for human services around the nation as a major business opportunity and has created a corporate division to enter this field. The high bid comes from a consulting unit of one of the nation's largest accounting firms. The next highest bidder is a national nonprofit organization that has long been involved in a variety of social service contracts and grants. In addition to its hands-on service delivery work, the organization is also an active advocacy group at the national level for improved social services and more effective delivery aimed at ensuring that all those who ought to be served are enrolled and effectively and efficiently assisted.

The next-to-the-lowest bidder is a well-known nonprofit social service group that has operated within the state for years, although on much smaller projects under some contracts and several federal and state grants. (Nonprofit organizations are usually referred to internationally as nongovernmental organizations, or NGOs, and that term will be used in this book.) The group began nearly twenty years ago as a volunteer service agency and has evolved steadily. It prides itself on

1

Table 1.1 The Competitors for the Contract

Bidder	Type	Over low bid (%)
"Big Five" consulting firm	For-profit	10
National social service association	National nonprofit	8
Electronic systems/state human services dept.	Public/private venture	6
Southwest aid association	Local nonprofit	2
Aerospace Inc.	For-profit	0

its familiarity with and sensitivity to the state's people, including their special needs. The bid for this contract represents a major step up in size and scope of activity, but one that the organization is convinced will both improve its management of existing programs and provide better service to clients.

The next-highest bidder is another for-profit firm, but one whose past work has focused largely on information systems. Developed by someone who has been politically active on both the state and national levels, the firm has decided to bid in cooperation with a state agency that wants to be part of the competition for the contract. The state agency is convinced that the knowledge and experience of its personnel in delivering the services required and the strengths of its private sector partner make a winning combination.

Assuming that the bid process did not require selection of the lowest bid and based on the information provided, which bidder should prevail and why might the other bidders not be selected?

Traditionally, the public assumption is that the low bidder should receive the contract. After all, if the point of the contract is to save money over the costs of existing state agencies and employees, then why not select the lowest price? Of course, that statement assumes that the low bidder, and all the other bidders for that matter, have submitted bids that address all the work requirements and specifications included in the IFB, known as bid responsiveness. The selection of any other bidder would, by definition, mean that other values are as important as cost or at least that they can narrow the difference among bids. What sorts of considerations might cause one to elect such alternatives?

When presented with this scenario, it is common for an audience to raise serious doubts about the aerospace firm. After all, what does that firm know about delivering social services? For one thing, its supporters answer, it is large and can mobilize extensive resources very quickly. The firm did that in this case as part of its decision to invest in creating a new enterprise to compete in this emerging social services marketplace. Part of that investment involved hiring a highly regarded welfare reformer from a midwestern state to lead the effort and buying talent elsewhere around the country as well. But questions still arise about whether this new business is a truly viable service provider, what is termed a responsible bidder. It may be responsible in the sense of its level of capitalization and its corporate infrastructure, but is that all that is involved in determining whether the firm is really likely to be able to deliver on its promises? And what about its staying power? Will the parent aerospace firm be willing to support the new venture as a central part of the corporation, or will it treat this unit as an experimental start-up business that will receive little continuing support and may be closed or sold off if it fails to meet profit expectations quickly?

At the other extreme, it is common for those queried to reject the high bidder, but not solely because that firm presented the highest price tag for the same proposed work. Actually, at least as important for many respondents is the question whether the consulting unit of the national accounting firm will make profits more important than the services that the state is seeking to deliver. For many, that is a particularly important question because in this proposed operation the contractor would be responsible not only for operating the program but also for determining eligibility for services. Would the firm take a draconian attitude toward eligibility determinations as a way to maximize its own profits under the contract and also to curry favor with state politicians? The firm obviously rejects what are in its view unfounded assumptions, pointing to its long-standing reputation in the accounting and consulting fields. Still, respondents have doubts.

The idea of a government agency bidding on the contract and competing with other bidders holds an attraction for some evaluators. After all, these are people who presumably know what it takes to deliver the services and who are nevertheless prepared to compete with private sector bidders, both for-profit and nonprofit. In addition, these public servants would presumably be accountable both under the contract and according to regular public official statutes and regulations, which suggests far greater accountability than would likely be true for purely private sector contractors and their employees. Moreover, the fact that the agency was willing to work in a joint venture with a private sector organization suggests an openness and willingness to innovate, which some find attractive. Still, if a state agency can do the work so well and efficiently, why did state officials feel the need to put the services out to bid in the first place? Was it because of failures in the agency or simply to test the possibilities for innovation and efficiency?

The local nonprofit organization is also attractive, but for different reasons. This is a group that has a local track record and that has been successful through the dedication of its people and its ability to deliver programs effectively. It has also demonstrated a capacity to attract federal grants, adding resources to the state. One attractive feature of the local group is its knowledge of the local culture and of the special requirements of serving some of the communities within the state. In this instance, the organization is used to working with multicultural and multilingual groups. All these factors are attractive, and the price is one of the lowest offered to the state. Nevertheless, there may be a serious question whether this growing but still relatively small organization can make what would be the very large jump in size and capability required to run the state's programs without losing the very qualities that have made it successful to this point. The question whether it will be a truly responsible bidder is not based on any assumptions about ill intentions or deception but out of concern about possible overconfidence and overreaching. For one thing, is the organization sure that its cost analyses are really accurate, given that this project would be so much wider and more complex in scope than its activities to date? Has it really taken into account the full costs of the infrastructure that will be needed to deliver the services and manage the organization?

Finally, the national nonprofit is also very attractive. It has some of the attributes of the local NGO, but it clearly has more experience playing in a larger arena. The bid was clearly not the lowest, but there seems to be some question whether the lower bids will turn out to be realistic. This is a group with broad and deep knowledge of social service programs and what it takes to provide them, even if it has never worked with this particular program design before. It has some degree of political clout in Washington and knows the federal agencies that provide most of the funds on which the state services are based. However, it has no real experience in this state and it certainly is not favored by many of the political players in the state.

A SET OF CRITERIA AND INEVITABLE TRADE-OFFS

Given this information, what would it mean to get a good deal for the public in this case? Three observations jump out from this case study and apply in many contract settings.

It seems obvious that a good deal means something more than simply obtaining the lowest price. Indeed, audiences who have been given this example have rarely opted for the lowest bid or chosen it simply to save money. Even private sector organizations that purport to be focused solely on the bottom line take a range of factors into consideration before they enter into an agreement that will make their success dependent upon a contract supplier of goods and services. That is why both public and private discussions of contracting have come to emphasize best value rather than lowest price.

The kinds of factors raised with respect to the welfare program contract discussed above also clearly suggest that a serious assessment of what constitutes a good deal for the public really only begins with the decision about the bids and the awarding of the contract. Most of the concerns expressed as to the choice of contractor in the example involved fears about difficulties that may arise after the agreement is signed and throughout the operation of the contract. Even in their private lives, most people have learned that the deal that appeared to be a great opportunity when they entered into it turned out to be very different. By definition, then, making the best deal for the public lies not simply in deciding whether

to contract or to whom the contract is to be awarded but in the entire administration of the contracting process from beginning to end. And, in fact, the vast
majority of that process takes place after the advocates debate whether to contract
and well beyond the bidding.

The best deal is not measured by any one criterion. Although price is a factor,
other critical issues include efficiency, effectiveness, equity, responsiveness, and
responsibility. Furthermore, because these different criteria are frequently in conflict, a determination as to what constitutes a good deal requires a process of
working through a set of trade-offs among these factors.

Modern public management traces a significant part of its heritage to what
was known as the "double E" movement, short for economy and efficiency.[1] It is
still true that the primary argument most often given to support contracting out
by government for goods and services is that it will save money. This sales pitch
often comes out after a scandal in which there is an indication that outrageous
amounts of public money have been expended for something available at a much
lower price in the local economy. Perhaps just as often, however, the claims about
the likelihood of obtaining more economical services by contracting out come
not from clear evidence but from a set of assumptions. These assumptions are often grounded in ideological principles that government is too large and costs too
much and that private firms can provide the same or better services at lower
prices. However, private sector firms have a long history of cost-overruns and
other misbehavior, both in their dealings with the government and with other
private sector organizations. That history raises the question whether they really
do things more economically or can be trusted to do things for the public at
lower cost than the government can.

For all these reasons, economy claims are usually paired with efficiency arguments. In its most common usage "efficiency" simply refers to the amount of out-
put per unit of resources invested. But efficiency is a very complex concept and
one that has myriad uses, including political purposes. Indeed, during the era of
scientific management, the leaders of the emerging public administration profession termed efficiency, "axiom number one in the hierarchy of administration."[2]

The call for efficiency often becomes a kind of mantra along with the assumption that there is one best way to achieve that efficiency. Donald F. Kettl
has termed that formula the "competition prescription." It is the idea that because competition is the key to efficiency in the private sector marketplace, it
can provide the same benefits in the public arena.[3] To be sure, there certainly are
advantages to be achieved from competition in public contracting. Indeed, the
history of public contracting has often revealed that the lack of competition—
either because of a lack of contract bidders or because public decision makers
were partial to particular contractors—has been at the heart of many scandals
and failed contracts. Long ago, however, Dwight Waldo warned that, for all of
its attractiveness, "efficiency" is a term to be used with care and certainly not to

be employed as the sole deciding criterion for public policy decisions or public management.[4] In addition, Kettl has explained that many of the common assumptions about the competition prescription in public contracting are uninformed or oversimplified.[5]

Beyond these sophisticated critiques of the use and abuse of efficiency in discussions of contracting, there is a relatively simple problem that requires that additional criteria be included in decision making. To the degree that economy and efficiency are used primarily as measures of quantity, they may miss important issues of quality. Thus, commonly used, seemingly contradictory criticisms are found in the marketplace. Although Americans show great frustration with public agencies that appear to be buying "Cadillac"-level goods and services, in their private lives and businesses many of them tend to believe that "we get what we pay for." The bottom line is not simply about quantity but also quality. Cheap goods or very efficient services are not always the most effective. Effectiveness is an assessment of the degree to which a contract actually delivers the services needed at a high level of quality.

Another potential area of tension is between effectiveness and responsiveness. The best-quality services may take longer to provide than many impatient citizens will tolerate. In an era in which those citizens have been conditioned to view themselves as customers, they often show little patience with delays in service delivery, even if that means that a public agency is pressured to prefer speed in responding to demands over the best quality of service and lowest price.

The effort to be as responsive as possible can, in turn, conflict with demands for public responsibility. Responsiveness, efficiency, economy, and sometimes even effectiveness can be limited by the many demands for political and legal accountability. There are many such demands for enhanced responsibility in contracting, ranging from criticisms of classic pork-barrel politics, in which a legislator seeks to acquire or preserve jobs for constituents, on one end of the continuum to a public desire to ensure that government is doing business with firms that use acceptable labor practices to pressures for public organizations to maintain transparent and vigorous efforts at enforcement in the case of a default by a contractor. The tools used to obtain information and ensure accountability can cost money and take time, with litigation or administratively imposed disciplinary actions but the most obvious examples.

One other very important criterion is critical to the mix of standards governing public contracts; but, like the others, this one can also present tensions. That is the need for equity. The term "equity" is used very loosely in contemporary public policy discussions, as if it meant the same thing as equality. However, "equity" means more than that. It requires not only that government not discriminate in its provisions of public services or programs but also mandates that agencies address a variety of special needs for different communities. Indeed, in its formal uses, equity is deliberately unequal treatment in the interest of justice.[6]

In recent decades, such discussions about equity have immediately brought to mind controversies over affirmative action in contracting. However, there are many circumstances apart from race or gender in which public agencies must address special needs. Common examples include special challenges required for the delivery of services in rural communities, in poverty-stricken areas, in areas affected by natural disasters, and in communities with unique or varied cultural traditions. Thus, the federal government has for years required agencies to ensure access to services for persons with limited English proficiency.[7] There are also special service needs for persons with disabilities.

Certainly, such requirements increase costs to some degree and affect efficiencies that would otherwise come from the wide use of standard operating procedures. Even so, those savings would be of doubtful legitimacy if they meant that the services were not being effectively delivered in a manner responsive to the needs of the target population. Further, although issues of equity in contracting may involve important legal issues, they are much larger than that and are becoming more important as society becomes increasingly diverse. The 2000 census demonstrated that that change is occurring even more rapidly than most Americans might have anticipated.

Clearly, then, obtaining a good deal for the public requires an effort to maximize each of these criteria in order to produce contracts that are economical, efficient, effective, responsive, responsible, and equitable, not only at the bidding stage but throughout their operation. Even though the goal is to maximize all these criteria, public contract management inevitably entails a continuing effort to address the trade-offs that must be made along the way.

IS "DEAL" A FOUR-LETTER WORD?

Although these criteria for describing what public contracts ought to achieve are certainly reasonable, if complex, many people still find something troublesome about the very idea of making a deal. The language seems vaguely illegitimate somehow, as if it implies a kind of corruption. Even experienced professionals often react in a surprisingly similar fashion to discussions of deal making. That is true even though they know from experience that "doing good deals" for the public is but a slightly hard-edged way of stating precisely what they are employed to do every day. This unease suggests some important tensions and assumptions that are worthy of attention before we move on.

First, much of the discussion of public contract management is conditioned by a fear—and to some extent, unfortunately, a history—of corruption. Whether it is war profiteers who have gouged the public in every conflict since the American Revolution; the corrupt city machines that have used contracts and associated graft as basic tools to build and maintain their power; suppliers who have delivered shoddy merchandise at inflated prices, buying off inspectors in the process;

or modern medical care providers padding their bills or double-billing and then threatening to withdraw from service if their actions are not tolerated, the sad fact is that public contract abuses have always been a problem. It is equally regrettable that these abuses have sometimes been possible because of corrupt officials willing to tolerate or even to exploit them deliberately. In fact, the effort to combat such corruption has been one of the important forces driving the development of the profession of public administration since the Progressive Era at the end of the nineteenth century and in the early decades of the twentieth. For example, the creation of city management is directly traceable to those efforts.[8]

Much of the concern with corruption has overwhelmingly focused on the awarding of contracts, the process leading up to the bidding and selection of the contractor. The result has been a great deal more effort spent to combat corruption at that stage of the process as compared to the real need to take a more positive approach to the management of the entire process. However, the evidence over the years consistently shows that many of the most important difficulties that arise in public contracting happen after the bidding process during contract administration.[9]

Another factor that has reinforced the focus on the front end of the process and has also discouraged discussion of good deals for the public is the highly charged set of debates about whether to privatize or not. The emphasis has often been about whether government should be providing a service or whether the work should be done by the private sector, either on its own or as a contractor supported by government funds. Thus, a large literature has emerged concerning privatization and whether to contract out; as if, once that decision is made, the rest is easy, or at least more or less mechanical.

This privatization approach has been limited and in many respects unhelpful. In the first place, most of the discussion has not really been about privatization properly so called. Some consideration has been given, particularly in developing countries and in the republics of the former Soviet Union, to divesting publicly held assets like industrial plants and equipment and shedding services by simply removing government from responsibility for delivering them. Most of the time, however, no real question arises about whether government will continue to be responsible for action; rather, the debate centers on whether government will deliver the services directly, using public servants, or indirectly through contractors. In the latter situations, government continues to be responsible for the functions and most often continues to pay for them, although contractors are sometimes permitted to recover some of the costs through user fees.

Even voucher programs such as those advocated to support parental school choice[10] that are often touted as classic examples of marketizing services are not really privatization. The responsibility for basic service delivery remains with the public sector, and taxpayer funds are used to support the market choices. In these

cases, parents are simply contracting on behalf of the government as they determine whose services to purchase with public dollars. This is true even where tax
credits or deductions are used to fund the choice. In such cases, government has
decided to fund a program by forgoing tax revenue it would otherwise receive
from the taxpayer. Someone else must be required to pay more taxes, or other
programs must be cut to make up the difference. Such an approach is known as a
tax expenditure and still involves a decision to support a purchase of services.
Thus, except in real decisions about whether government should divest itself of
services or functions, the discussion about privatization is both a misnomer and
generally unhelpful.

The other side of the so-called privatization debate is the argument for more
contracting and less direct service by government, although the issue is not really divestiture. That is still not a particularly helpful discussion because, as
Kettl and others have noted, the public sector has long contracted out a wide
variety of functions and has continued to expand the range of contracted operations over the years. That was true long before contemporary advocates put
the argument as if any resistance to contracting was a conspiracy to protect civil
service jobs. In fact, at a conference in the early 1990s, just as the Clinton administration adopted David Osborne and Ted Gaebler's *Reinventing Government*[11] as a guiding spirit of its approach to management,[12] a city manager
made the point in strong terms. A corporate executive asked this manager of a
substantial-sized city whether he was at last convinced that he should start contracting out. The manager answered that the executive should come to his city
and if he could find anything that was not already contracted out that should
be, he should share the information. As far as the city manager was concerned,
reinventing government and its prescription for contracting out was very old
news indeed.

In truth, most of the privatization discussion, in the United States at least,
has been more concerned with ideology or supporting the marketing efforts of
consulting firms than with ensuring a good deal for the taxpayer.[13] It has focused
more on assumptions about the virtues of the private sector and the presumed
weaknesses of the public sector than it has on providing the capacity needed to
ensure not only that good contracts are developed but also that they will be effectively administered to achieve all the essential values at stake in public contracting.[14]

Some business people find all the fuss about "doing deals" to be more than a
little confusing and very countercultural. After all, "doing deals" is what business
is about, and the expression itself is treated very positively in the marketplace. After all, a deal is a transaction that the parties to the agreement think is to their
mutual advantage. A good deal is often described as a "win/win" or a "non-zero-
sum" situation in which both parties not only benefit from the current agreement
but will be inclined to work together in the future in mutually beneficial arrange-

ments. Concluding bigger, better deals is a business executive's key to promotions and increased income.

Of course, it is also true that some executives in the private sector take a less cooperative and more combative approach to deal making. For those who see business as combat, a good deal may carry a definition that includes beating the people on the other side of the table such that the deal is a victory rather than an agreement. Many years ago, William O. Douglas, then chairman of the Securities and Exchange Commission, referred to such executives as "financial termites" who, he said, were engaged in a destructive process he called "predatory finance."[15] Douglas argued that such hostile practices were destructive of the very markets upon which those businesses relied and that were so important to the life of the nation. (This chapter was written before the Enron debacle unfolded.)

Unfortunately, those lessons of the Great Depression have been forgotten by some contemporary market players. Even more disturbing is the fact that some people in the public sector take just such a combative view. Thus, in the case of a Texas contract for operating a credit card–style social service benefits program, political figures congratulated themselves on crafting a contract that placed the private firm delivering the program in the position of losing millions each year.[16] It would be unfortunate and bad for business in the future if a good deal for the taxpayer were broadly defined as taking advantage of contract partners.

Even assuming that such a negative approach was not involved, it nevertheless becomes clear that those in the culture of politics and public management often perceive "doing deals" differently from those in the private sector. The assumption may be that the deal is an arrangement concocted through the back door in which the public may be made to suffer rather than benefit. Indeed, the concept of the "sweetheart deal" is often used to describe an arrangement in which government representatives intentionally award a high-profit contract to a firm that will not be required to perform well.

Far less sinister are difficulties in regard to who is at the table and whose interests are served. In standard business practice, the parties at the table are obligated only to represent themselves, but when public officials enter the relationship the interests of the contractor, the agency, and the public come into play. And the people directly involved will not always regard the public interest in the same way as they will their own concerns. Contemplating the importance of the public interest as compared with narrower interests in government, Woodrow Wilson warned that "[b]usiness-like the administration of govt. may and should be—but it is not business. It is organic social life."[17]

These features of public contracts begin to suggest some of the many ways in which the public and private sectors converge and diverge. They also indicate some of the ways in which we think about public contract relationships and point to the foundations of some of the fears and frustrations related to those arrangements.

A 300-POUND GORILLA CANNOT BE IGNORED: THE REACH OF CONTRACTING ISSUES

Many people, even those who should know better, consider government contracts to be rather arcane technical matters that are most concerned with defense agencies and are best left to government watchdog agencies like the U.S. General Accounting Office (GAO). Such assumptions are not only wrong but dangerous.

First, the scope and scale of contracts mean that neither public officials nor citizens can afford to ignore them. The federal government spends some $200 billion each year through contracts. As large a figure as that is, state and local governments expend even more, roughly $275 billion annually, through contracts.[18] Thus, nearly half a trillion dollars are expended through contracts each year.

Second, notwithstanding the huge size of some major defense acquisitions, other kinds of contracts affect many more citizens in far more direct ways on a day-to-day basis. Many services, from health care to housing to juvenile justice, are operated by federal grants to state and local governments, which, in turn, contract with nonprofit organizations or private firms for the actual service delivery. Beyond that, state and local agencies purchase every kind of service from road construction and repair to building maintenance to computers. They contract with firms to do data processing, to evaluate public programs, and to operate school buses. Government purchases have long served as catalysts to help launch or build industries, from the airline industry (dependent on technology developed with government contract dollars and on air mail contracts for its early rise) to what are now known as the new economy firms, based on computer hardware and software (much of the development of which grew directly out of government contracts). It is difficult to think of any aspect of modern life that is not significantly affected by government contracts coming not only from the Department of Defense but from agencies as diverse as the National Aeronautics and Space Administration (NASA) and local school districts.

Third, the increased pressure for more contracting, even as public agencies have been called on to shrink their size and role, has created a situation in which we not only use government contracts for many purposes but are dependent on them. Whatever may have been true in an earlier period, today, federal, state, and local agencies do not have the capacity to deliver directly the services and perform the tasks with which they are charged by law. Both the agencies responsible for public policies and citizens who rely on them are forced to depend on contractors. The likelihood that this will change back to the old modes of service delivery is nonexistent, and there is considerable reason to think that, contemporary political pressures as they are, the dependency will grow.

Finally, people often forget that the purchase of goods, even the large systems bought through the big defense contracts, is but one type of contracting. In addition to contracts for goods and services, personnel contracts are made within government, and interjurisdictional agreements are formed between different levels of government or different jurisdictions for the various kinds of services. Here again, growing service demands and limited resources require the use of such devices to get the public's work done.

By virtually any measure, then, government contracts touch our lives in countless ways every day. Public officials who create public policy and public managers who administer it must rely on contracts to meet their responsibilities. Finally, the sheer scope and scale of government contracts mean that public contracts shape everything from employment practices throughout the marketplace to the operation of the economy as a whole. It makes no sense to speak of effective public policy or of professional public management, or even informed citizenship, without an awareness of the nature and operation of public contract management.

LIFE ON THE BUBBLE: THE PROBLEM OF THE VERTICAL AND HORIZONTAL MODELS

Despite their importance, public contracts are means and not ends in themselves. They are policy tools available to decision makers to achieve public purposes, from wide national actions to local service needs. The decisions as to the ends to be served and whether to employ particular means to implement them are political judgments made by a democratically driven constitutional republic. As Woodrow Wilson's quote about the difference between business and government suggests, despite their important relationships, the political process and the businesslike relationships it operates present important differences.

The political process that produces the decision to contract, the appropriations to be used for that purpose, and the techniques of accountability to be employed to maintain oversight of contract operations come from a vertical, authority-based process starting from the Constitution and flowing down through legislative processes and administrative agencies to the point where contracts are made and managed. It is governed by the constitutions, statutes, executive directives, treaties, regulations, and judicial precedents that are together known as public law. As the supremacy clause of Article VI of the U.S. Constitution provides, "[t]his Constitution, and the Laws of the United States which shall be made in Pursuance thereof; and all Treaties made, or which shall be made, under the Authority of the United States, shall be the supreme Law of the Land; and the Judges in every State shall be bound thereby, any Thing in the Constitution or Laws of any State to the Contrary notwithstanding." The state constitutions, in turn, set out the authority and responsibility under which all state officials operate. Local governments, as creatures of the state constitution and laws, are also in that line of authority and responsibility.[19]

Contracts in the business world, by contrast, operate on a horizontal model, based not on authority but on a foundation of negotiations. The rules of the relationship are established by mutual consent and can be enforced by either of the parties to the agreement. It is true that there is a body of contract law and that a contract is a legal instrument. Even so, great latitude is left to the contracting parties to shape the agreement and decide how it will be operated. In that sense, contract law in its traditional private law form is facilitative, supporting the ability of parties to an agreement to have the tools to fashion and implement it. Negotiations resulting in a meeting of minds is the dominant dynamic in most contracting.

Given their position in government and as participants in contracting, then, public officers who manage public contracts from start to finish operate at the intersection of the vertical, authority-based model of government action and the horizontal model designed to function on the basis of negotiation in business dealings.[20] These officials necessarily find themselves dealing with the inevitable tensions between the two approaches and the obligations that both present. In fact, government often acts as both a market participant and as a market regulator.

This position at the intersection of the two models of action makes public contract operations different from their private sector counterparts. In addition, it places very different kinds of demands on those public officers from the demands that arise in the direct provision of services or performance of regulatory functions by government agencies.

CONCLUSION

It seems clear, then, that public officials are increasingly and necessarily involved in making a host of contractual deals for the delivery of services and purchases of materials. Government, at all levels, depends on such contracts to meet its public policy obligations. The size and scope of public contracts, in turn, have a broad and dramatic effect on the economy and on the private sector organizations, both for-profit and nonprofit, that operate within it.

It is clearly, however, a complex matter to determine just what constitutes a good deal for the public. Such a judgment necessarily goes beyond the lowest price or seemingly most efficient contract to a complex set of trade-offs involving economy, efficiency, effectiveness, responsiveness, responsibility, and equity. Any evaluation of a good deal using those criteria cannot be focused simply on the bid and award process but must contemplate the whole contract relationship. Just as clearly, then, public contract management, so essential to all aspects of modern public management, must consider the entire contract relationship.

Even as public contract managers work through this process, they are burdened by a history of suspicions about corruption. They also face tensions between the authority-driven model of constitutional governance and the horizontal, negotiation-centered business model that is at the heart of contract operations. The public contract manager must use the contract process as an essential tool of public policy implementation and yet be clear at all points that it is a means to an end and not an end in itself. The end is the achievement of the public interest, which is determined through the democratic processes of the constitutional Republic. These are political processes, but they are also processes shaped and constrained by public law.

These foundation principles that arise for public officers operating at the intersection of the two very different models are important to an understanding of the special challenges of public contract management. Chapter 2 focuses on life at the intersection of the vertical and horizontal models of action.

Notes

1. Dwight Waldo, *The Administrative State* (New York: Ronald Press, 1948), chap. 10. See also Fritz Morstein Marx, ed., *Elements of Public Administration* (New York: Prentice-Hall, 1946).

2. See Luther Gulick, "Science, Values, and Public Administration," in *The Papers on the Science of Administration,* ed. Luther Gulick and Lyndal Urwick (Fairfield, N.J.: Augustus M. Kelley, 1977; originally published by the Institute of Public Administration, New York, 1937), 189.

3. Donald F. Kettl, *Sharing Power: Public Governance and Private Markets* (Washington, D.C.: Brookings Institution, 1993), chap. 1.

4. Waldo, supra note 1.

5. See Kettl, supra note 3.

6. I have addressed the complex nature of equity in Phillip J. Cooper, *Public Law and Public Administration,* 3d ed. (Itasca, Ill.: F. E. Peacock, 2000), 621 et seq.

7. See, e.g., Executive Order 13166, 65 Fed. Reg. 50121 (2000).

8. See H. George Frederickson, ed., *Ideal and Practice in Council-Manager Government* (Washington, D.C.: International City/County Management Association, 1989). See also John Nalbandian, "Tenets of Contemporary Professionalism in Local Government," in *Ideal and Practice in Council-Manager Government,* 2d ed., ed. H. George Frederickson (Washington, D.C.: International City/County Management Association, 1994).

9. U.S. Office of Management and Budget, *Summary Report of the SWAT Team on Civilian Agency Contracting* (Washington, D.C.: Office of Management and Budget, 1992).

10. See John E. Chubb and Terry M. Moe, *Politics, Markets, and America's Schools* (Washington, D.C.: Brookings Institution, 1990).

11. David Osborne and Ted Gaebler, *Reinventing Government* (New York: Penguin, 1993).

12. Al Gore, *From Red Tape to Results: Creating a Government That Works Better and Costs Less,* report of the National Performance Review (Washington, D.C.: Government Printing Office, 1993).

13. See, for example, E. N. Savas, *Privatization* (Chatham, N.J.: Chatham House, 1987).

14. During the same period George W. Downs and Patrick D. Larkey, *The Search for Government Efficiency* (New York: Random House, 1986), argued that, apart from ideology, a good case could not be made that the private sector was more efficient than the public sector.

15. William O. Douglas, *Democracy and Finance* (Port Washington, N.Y.: Kennikat Press, 1969), 8.

16. Polly Ross Hughes, "Flap Threatens Lone Star Card: Operator Considers Suing State, Pulling Out of Welfare Contract," *Houston Chronicle,* November 21, 1997, A1.

17. Arthur S. Link, ed., *The Papers of Woodrow Wilson* (Princeton: Princeton University Press, 1968–1969), 5: 689–690.

18. Peter A. Harkness, "Dollars and Discipline," *Governing Magazine State and Local Sourcebook 1998,* 8.

19. *Reynolds v. Sims,* 377 U.S. 533 (1964).

20. These two models and the relationships between them make up a conceptualization that I have developed over an extended period. The earlier portions and versions of this evolving framework appeared in part in "Government Contracts in Public Administration: The Role and Environment of the Contracting Officer," 40 *Public Administration Review* 459 (1980); (in Spanish) "Beyond the Bidding Process: The Dynamics of Public Contract Management," in Ministerio de Planificación Nacional y Politica Económica (MIDEPLAN), *La contratación privada para la renovación del estado* (San José, Costa Rica: Ministry of National Planning and Political Economy, 1998); and *Public Law and Public Administration,* 3d ed. (Itasca, Ill.: F. E. Peacock, 2000).

2

From Power to Contract: Governance by Agreement versus Policy from Authority

If the key to understanding public contract management is the realization that contract officials operate at the intersection of the vertical and horizontal models, it is important to ask just what that intersection looks like, how it came to be that way, and what difference it makes for the contract managers involved and for the public interest. The answers to those questions, in turn, arise from a consideration of several important threads of practice, politics, and law that together provide the context of contemporary public contract management. After all, contemporary government contracting is more the result of practice and efforts at problem solving than of any overarching theory.

HOW DID WE GET INTO THIS SITUATION? EARLY FOUNDATIONS OF THE CONTRACT STATE

It is surprising how many contemporary critics and, for that matter, practitioners of public contract management know little or nothing about why the world of public contracts functions (or malfunctions) as it does. It sometimes seems as if the morass of statutes, regulations, court rulings, and political oversight devices were relatively recent creations invented to frustrate efficient and flexible working relationships. Not true. A brief reconsideration of the rise of the contract state tells us a good deal about why the current system looks and functions as it does. That history, like much of the evolution of modern public policy and management, is associated with particular eras marked by dominant political, social, and economic trends. At the same time, it becomes clear that clusters of issues

16

emerged over time that cut across those eras and shaped the evolution of public contract relationships.

From the Failures of the Revolution to New Constitutional Foundations

The Revolutionary War presented a wide range of problems well known to Americans today. Those challenges included the effort to feed, arm, and clothe the military. Under the best of circumstances it would have been hard to equip the many different groups of people who came to fight in the Revolution with what they needed to wage the battle against the well-organized and well-supplied British forces. And the American revolutionaries were in far from the best of circumstances. It quickly became clear that the leaders of the new nation could not expect suppliers to demonstrate any sense of concern for the public interest in their dealings with the government. In fact, American farmers and other suppliers were more than happy to do business with the British for gold rather than deal with the new revolutionary government. John Marshall, who later became chief justice of the United States, was then the provost marshal at Valley Forge. He witnessed the suffering of his own troops while farmers in the area provided the British with goods.

> The privations suffered by the army did not reflect any shortages in the land. Instead, they reflected the inefficiency of the Congress in arranging for adequate logistical support for its army. It also reflected the reluctance of farmers in the area to accept the atrociously inflated Continental currency. Washington, as a result, was forced to resort to somewhat unconventional methods that winter to provide food for his troops. He detached General Wayne and about three hundred of his men to rustle cattle. . . . And when spring came, Washington the fisherman ordered his cavalry into the Schuykill to stir up the shad run. His jubilant soldiers jumped into the shallows and caught the rich fish with their bare hands.[1]

Marshall would never forget his experiences with a weak, poorly organized, and economically dysfunctional government. Neither would George Washington. Writing to his brother in 1780, Washington "lamented, bitterly lamented" the fact that his troops went "five or six days together without bread, then as many without meat, two or three times without either."[2] His biographer noted: "The early summer harvests were plentiful but army commissaries were redirecting them along with herds of cattle paid for by Congress and destined for Washington's army to the French in Rhode Island, who paid in gold, not depreciated Continental paper money."[3] The situation led to mutinies and desertion.

Things were so bad that at one point the states were asked to provide support for the troops, an effort that failed miserably.[4] Looking back on the experience of the Revolution, the Federal Procurement Commission concluded: "Purchasing activity was characterized by sharp and primitive practices, untrained purchasing officials, profiteering, poor supplies, and deficient management."[5]

When he returned home to Virginia, John Marshall encountered further evidence of the need for a solid economic foundation for the new nation and of the dangers that could come from failure to address the importance of contracts. He served in the Virginia House of Burgesses, where he witnessed the move to repudiate debts and contracts that had existed before the Revolution, a clear violation of the peace treaty of 1783 ending the war.[6]

These issues of the integrity of contracts and protection of other financial obligations were important parts of the larger task of nation building. In a cynical age, it is sometimes difficult to remember that without some basic ability to believe that others will honor their promises, civil society—let alone a constitutional republic—becomes virtually impossible. Moreover, in those early days there was little in the way of physical or economic infrastructure to link the nation together: (1) the history of abusive taxation and other forms of discrimination by states against other states and their business is well known; (2) manifold currencies—often of highly doubtful value—were used in different states; and (3) the thirteen different legal systems in the thirteen states left most people in doubt about whether contracts entered into in one state would be honored in another. So debilitating was this situation that Alexander Hamilton could hardly contain himself in condemning it. "Thirteen independent courts of final jurisdiction over the same causes, arising upon the same laws, is a hydra in government from which nothing but contradiction and confusion can proceed."[7]

The Constitution: Critical Foundations for American Economic and Political Development

Given all that had come before, it is not surprising that the framers of the Constitution expended considerable effort attempting to provide a solid foundation for American economic as well as political development. Indeed, along with the broad designs for the institutions of government and the processes for choosing officials, the document contains a range of provisions intended to solve a host of very practical problems that had arisen during and after the Revolution. These provisions continue to be important today and create many of the characteristics that we find in contemporary public contract operations. They also establish boundaries for the use of contracts and shape many of the contours of the economy within which the government does business.

The very first of the enumerated powers of Congress listed in Article I, Section 8, is the "Power To lay and collect Taxes, Duties, Imposts and Excises, to pay the Debts and provide for the common Defence and general Welfare of the United States." And that provision is followed immediately by related critically important powers, including the power "To borrow money on the credit of the United States" and "To regulate Commerce with foreign Nations, and among the several States, and with the Indian Tribes." It was clear that the federal government would have important powers to build and regulate a national economy as well as the capacity to participate in it as a purchaser of goods and services.

In addition to these extremely broad foundations, the framers knew that many other problems had to be addressed. They were aware that issues of debt and bankruptcy are far more important and pervasive concerns than most people realize in regard to the maintenance of economic relationships among the members of society.[8] Therefore, the listed powers include the authority "To establish . . . uniform Laws on the subject of Bankruptcies throughout the United States."

Of course, one of the issues that had been at the heart of debates over debts and the contracts that produced them was the value of the currency with which obligations could be paid. For one thing, one of the problems that Washington encountered during the Revolution was that few colonists would accept Continental currency for anything. This was also a problem at the state level, not only among states but even within a single state. For example, in Rhode Island a butcher refused to accept the state's script despite the fact that the state legislature had authorized the currency. His action was later supported by the state court.[9] To address this and many similar situations, Article I, Section 8, granted Congress the power "To coin Money, regulate the Value thereof, and of foreign Coin, and fix the Standard of Weights and Measures." Of course, other forms of financial paper were used during this period, and there was concern about ensuring against counterfeiting. Thus, the same part of the Constitution gave Congress authority "To provide for the Punishment of counterfeiting the Securities and current Coin of the United States."

It is no small matter to provide incentives to develop useful contributions to economic development. That effort meant, among other things, providing incentives for innovation. Hence, Article I also provides the power "To promote the Progress of Science and useful Arts, by securing for limited Times to Authors and Inventors the exclusive Right to their respective Writings and Discoveries," matters we now understand as patent and copyright. A century and a half later, when the federal government was using contracts and grants to finance research and development in an increasingly significant way, these claims on innovation were both important and controversial. Whole industries, like commercial aviation and computers, owe their success and profits to both the financing and the incentives for innovation provided by government contracts. More recently, the question has arisen of the patenting of genes following years of public investment in the Human Genome Project. There is a continuing argument about whether taxpayers, who paid much of the cost of innovation, should enjoy some of the benefits or whether all copyright and patent rights should go to the private sector firms, universities, or think tanks that produced the innovations using those public funds.

Far more rudimentary and obvious from the lessons of the Revolutionary War years was the need for Congress to have the power "To raise and support Armies, but no Appropriation of Money to that Use shall be for a longer Term than two Years" and its authority "To provide and maintain a Navy." As basic as it may seem, these provisions of Article I continue to be the focus of much of the most vociferous criticism of government contracting. One of the great problems that has interfered with our ability to think creatively about government contracting is the fact that so much focus has been placed on the acquisition of weapons systems, a unique type of contract operation.

Although these items in the list of enumerated powers are obviously important to public contract management, other provisions are critical both to the contract process and also to the larger economic infrastructure. Of particular importance is the so-called necessary and proper clause, Article I, Section 8, Clause 18, that authorizes Congress: "To make all Laws which shall be necessary and proper for carrying into Execution the foregoing Powers, and all other Powers vested by this Constitution in the Government of the United States, or in any Department or Officer thereof." It was this provision that, for example, was cited in upholding the creation of a national banking system.[10] Today, this clause and some combination of the commerce clause and taxing and spending powers are at the heart of most federal programs.

The listing of legislative powers in Article I, Section 8, is not the only part of the Constitution that is important to the nation's economic infrastructure or its contracting activities. After listing the powers specifically granted to Congress, Article I includes Section 9, setting forth limitations on the Congress, and Section 10, placing constraints on the states. Like the powers that were granted, the limitations were the result of lessons learned not only from life under the Articles of Confederation but also from the behavior of the British monarchs and their ministers, issues that were among the causes of the Revolutionary War.

Even as they made the central government powerful so that it could be effective and remedy the problems of the past, the framers also constrained the authority of both Congress and the president. They remembered that the Crown had abused the power to create and staff offices so as to take care of friends and allies with the costs transferred to taxpayers. Similarly, the kings and queens had a history of foreign adventures that too often plunged the nation into costly wars and in other cases resulted in alliances that could only be termed bad deals for the public even if they were effective at protecting the royal family. Hence, the president was given the appointment power under Article II, but with the check of advice and consent of the Senate and the creation of offices left to Congress. The chief executive was to be commander in chief, but the war-making power was to be left to the legislature. The president was given the ability to check the Article I legislative power in the form of the presentation clause permitting a veto, but, unlike that of the king, the veto was not absolute and could be overridden. Today most Americans think of the initiative in fiscal matters as in the hands of the president, who offers the executive budget for approval by Congress. However, the current arrangements for the executive budget and other fiscal affairs have existed only since 1921. By the same token, there was concern about possible abuses of Congress's newly created fiscal powers. Hence, Article I, Section 9, was included among the limitations on the legislature. "No money shall be drawn from the Treasury, but in Consequence of Appropriations made by Law; and a regular Statement and Account of the Receipts and Expenditures of all public Money shall be published from time to time." This provision, generally referred to as the audits and accounts clause, is known by few people outside the system.

The list of problems created by state legislatures, was long, serious, and in fact one of the primary reasons that the new Constitution was written. Article I, Section 10, provides a litany of thou-shalt-nots that responded to those abuses of the states' own citizens, citizens of other states, other states as states, and even the nation as a whole in regard to international matters. Not surprisingly, many of the prohibitions concerned commercial, monetary, and fiscal affairs. It specifically prohibited states from passing laws impairing contractual obligations.[11] Finally, it prevented states from entering into compacts with other states or foreign nations without congressional approval.

It may seem that these are ideas and problems of an older day, not really relevant to modern public contract management. Not true. Competition among the states for economic development is an important, if often regrettable, fact of life. This practice, once known as smokestack chasing because it described efforts to attract large industrial plants and the jobs that came with them, is often referred to in today's parlance as chip chasing—battles among states and cities to attract environmentally clean, high-technology firms with high-paying jobs. And given globalization, these dynamics have also seen states and even individual cities sending missions abroad, seeking to establish their own trade agreements. In other instances, states or communities have sought to protect themselves and their citizens from troublesome politics and economics of globalization.[12] Domestically, taxation issues, necessary to generate the resources to provide community services and infrastructure support for local businesses, have become all the more complex in an era of toll-free catalog order and Internet businesses.[13]

Concern about problems in the states extended beyond the list of prohibitions on state legislatures cited above. If regional, state, and local economies were to be knitted together into a national commercial and economic fabric, more was needed. For this reason, Article IV provides that "Full Faith and Credit shall be given in each State to the public Acts, Records, and judicial Proceedings of every other State. . . . The Citizens of each State shall be entitled to all Privileges and Immunities of Citizens in the several States." To make sure that none of the specific provisions obscured the overall effort at nation building, including its economic infrastructure, Article VI made two more critical points. First, "All Debts contracted and Engagements entered into, before the Adoption of this Constitution shall be as valid against the United States under this Constitution, as under the Confederation." Second, it provided what is now known as the supremacy clause, which reads: "This Constitution, and Laws of the United States which shall be made in Pursuance thereof; and all Treaties made, or which shall be made, under the Authority of the United States, shall be the supreme Law of the Land; and the Judges in every State shall be bound thereby, any Thing in the Constitution or Laws of any State to the Contrary notwithstanding." This supremacy clause is the basis for the complex doctrine of federal preemption under which the federal government can permit some state involvement in particular fields or prohibit it altogether, including in such areas as deregulation of parts of the economy.[14]

Of course, one of the prices for ratification of the Constitution was an agreement to prepare a Bill of Rights to protect individuals against the powers of this newly created national government. Included among its provisions was the Fifth Amendment prohibition against the taking of private property for public use without just compensation. During periods of war and national emergencies and in demobilizations, this provision has required negotiated resolutions of economic problems that began as confiscations but ended with a kind of backward contractual agreement in which government and business firms resolved the government's obligations for its use of private property through settlements. These have been matters of great moment, for they have involved entire fleets of merchant vessels or whole industrial facilities.

The Tenth Amendment was particularly important, in part for what it said and in part for what it did not say. During the Convention, there was a discussion about whether to include the provision that had been part of the Articles of Confederation that limited the central government to those powers expressly delegated to it. Not only did the framers reject that language then, they did it a second time when the Tenth Amendment was debated and the same issue was raised. Thus, the federal government's authority was given great scope.

The Tenth Amendment reserve powers clause did, however, provide that "[t]he powers not delegated to the United States by the Constitution, nor prohibited by it to the States, are reserved to the States respectively, or to the people." Over time that provision has been read to mean that the power to regulate in matters of health, safety, and public welfare, commonly referred to as the police powers, are reserved to the states. Indeed, the Supreme Court has been increasingly willing in recent years to support that state authority and limit federal power.[15] For this reason the federal government has had to rely on a system of intergovernmental grants and contracts to make important policies in these fields. Today, it has become standard for the federal government to offer grants filled with conditions that are then provided with a proportional matching fund from the states. The states then contract out the delivery of services in a host of areas at the community level, often through local nonprofit organizations.

Of course, history demonstrated that there would likely continue to be difficulties with state governments and localities as the nation grew, and there were. The post–Civil War amendments, particularly the Fourteenth Amendment, addressed some of these. Unlike the Thirteenth and Fifteenth Amendments, which spoke specifically to race and previous condition of servitude, the Fourteenth spoke to the rights of persons without regard to race or gender. In particular, the amendment's requirement that no state shall "deprive any person of life, liberty, or property, without due process of law; nor deny to any person within its jurisdiction the equal protection of the laws" has been the focus of much of the law that affects contracting. In addition to the obvious issues of discrimination and questions of due process that often present themselves in contracting, this provision also has been used to apply almost all of the protections of the Bill of Rights to people dealing with state and local governments through what is known as the incorporation doctrine.

The Early National Period through the Civil War: Hard Lessons and Flawed Policies

It was one thing to write these provisions into the frame of government; but it was quite another to adopt and implement the policies necessary to create and build the new and expanding nation. To meet that challenge, government not only had to build and regulate the economy but had to participate in it as well, purchasing the goods and services it needed for everything from the postal system to the military. Indeed, problems quickly arose in both of those areas, leading to the first national legislation on government contracting. The effort to work through those difficulties raised a host of contracting issues that remain important today. In particular, challenges arose with respect to postal contracts, military logistics, support for emerging industries, the financing of internal improvements as the nation expanded westward, and the early judicial response to contract clause challenges.

The use of government contracts to create a postal system quickly became a focus of controversy. As early as 1785 the Continental Congress authorized contracts for carrying mail on stage coaches.

> That the postmaster general be, and he is hereby authorized and instructed, under the direction of the board of treasury to enter into contracts under good and sufficient security, for the conveyance of the different mails by the stage carriages, from Portsmouth, in the State of New Hampshire, to the town of Savannah, in the State of Georgia and from the city of New York, to the city of Albany in the State of New York, according to the accustomed route.[16]

However, no sooner had this system been developed than issues emerged. Among the first of these was the relationship between price and reliability. There was no law governing contracting or any requirement that the government advertise for bids. On the one hand, there was a concern to obtain a reasonable price, since it became clear that price gouging was likely to be a problem. At the same time, there was a fear that requirements that bids be advertised and that the government accept the lowest bid might lead to contracts with businesses that could not really provide the necessary service or at least not at the price quoted in their bid. Postmaster General Samuel Osgood put it this way: "The advertising for proposals for carrying the mail places the Postmaster General in a disagreeable predicament: for many poor people make proposals at so low a rate that it is obvious the business cannot be done as it ought to be, and consequently there cannot be a strict adherence to the lowest proposals. Discretion must be used, and the contract must be given to him who will most probably perform the duty with punctuality."[17] That is, the bid must be responsive to the service requested by the government (bid responsiveness), but the bidder must also be responsible in the sense of being actually able to provide the service at the price quoted (bidder responsibility). This concern led Postmaster Timothy Pickering to argue against a requirement for advertised bids and to prefer what today would be called a sole source contract. That is, Pickering suggested continuing to do business with the current contractor on the theory that the government could be assured of good service and the contractor would likely be willing to offer a favorable price.[18]

On the other hand, there was the question whether the government should be required to accept a bid, even from a responsible bidder, if the price was too high. Postmaster General Joseph Habersham went even further, suggesting that if the lowest responsible bid was too high, the bids should be rejected and the contract should be advertised again.[19]

It was becoming clear that contractors were quite willing to gouge the taxpayer and did not always live up to their promises about the level and quality of service. What we now call the problem of quality assurance, the need to guarantee, quite apart from price, that contractors deliver quality services and goods, was quickly becoming important. Stagecoach operators realized that they had a virtual monopoly once they had won the mail contracts and sometimes acted as if they could get away with poor service. This was such a problem that Habersham felt the need to develop a system of government stagecoaches to substitute for a poorly performing contractor on the Philadelphia-to-Baltimore postal route.[20] These difficulties led in 1792 to the enactment of the first federal contracting law as part of postal legislation that mandated publicly advertised bids.

The early years also saw challenges in the area of military procurement. President Washington needed to dispatch naval and land forces for a variety of purposes, both foreign and domestic. However, the ships, weapons, uniforms, food, and other supplies all had to be acquired. The contracts developed to meet those needs illustrated several critical issues that remain with us today. For one thing, there was, and is, the question of the degree to which control over contracting should be centralized in one agency or decentralized, with each major unit having its own contracting authority. Beyond that, should those agencies then be able to subdelegate the contracting authority to their field units? While the secretary of war wanted his department to control its contracting, the secretary of the Treasury, Alexander Hamilton, was committed not only to centralizing control but to placing that authority in his agency.[21] After some widely publicized military debacles in 1790 and 1791 (known as the Harmar and St. Clair campaigns against the Miami Indians) were blamed in part at least on a failure of military contracting, Hamilton got his wish.[22] Congress enacted a statute in May of 1792, placing authority in the Treasury.[23] In fact, he was able to obtain further legislation in 1795 creating a central purchasing office for the national government known as the Purveyor of Public Supplies.[24] Legislation adopted in 1798 required that all federal government contracts be filed in the Department of the Treasury, a role that was later given to the U.S. General Accounting Office.[25]

The War Department was able to win back control over its contracting later, in 1798, using an argument that continues to be an important counter to the potential efficiency and accountability reasons that support centralization. The argument is that central purchasers simply do not understand the special needs of the various line organizations and their field units. Hamilton did not agree with the action and told Secretary of War Henry Knox that his department was bungling contract operations after taking them back from the Treasury Department: "The management of your Agents, as to the affair of supplies, is ridiculously bad. Besides the extreme delay, which attends every operation, articles go forward in the most incomplete manner. Coats without a corresponding number of vests. . . . Tis the scene of the worst periods of our revolution war acted over again even with caricature."[26]

From the contractors' point of view, the way the government structured control over contracts was important then and remains so today because it affected the balance between the need for effective audit and control operations to ensure accountability and the need for those doing business with the government to receive reasonably prompt payment. James O'Hara spent five years trying to collect on a contract he had performed simply because the comptroller objected to the fact that the contractor had delivered the nonperishable rations to the troops at one time but delivered the perishable commodities in periodic shipments to ensure quality.[27]

Contractors began to realize early on that officials were placing significant burdens of effort and time on businesses without compensation. In fact, the contractors were coming to understand that efforts were being made to shift the balance of risks involved in contracting to the contractor. A business could find itself risking time, money, and effort, but receiving little in the end. Although any honest businessperson could understand the need for reasonable fiscal and quality controls, the firms had legitimate expectations as well, leading some to think twice before bidding on a government contract.

Of course, the government had reasons for caution. The public had been repeatedly victimized by profiteering contractors who provided shoddy goods at inflated prices and sometimes failed to provide what they promised at all. Defense officials also experienced in these early years what we have now come to call cost overruns. These are cases in which contractors bid one price at the time of the contract and then return to the government for far more money later as costs mount well beyond the original bid. The now-famous ship USS *Constitution,* better known as *Old Ironsides,* was one of the early exemplars. The government originally contracted for six ships in 1794, but the contractor used up all the funds and a great deal more and completed only three ships by 1798, one of which was the *Constitution.*[28] Still, the government got excellent ships for its money. It has often been the case over the years that some of those involved in contracting have focused most on obtaining the highest quality, or what we might today term the leading-edge equipment, for the public's dollar. Politicians often object, however, suggesting that these are "Cadillac contracts," which pay too much and obtain equipment built to standards far higher than are reasonably required for their assigned mission.

At the same time that the early national government was learning these lessons about contracting, it was also clear that the government would use contracts for purposes beyond simply obtaining goods and services that it needed immediately. The government began early in our national life to use contracts and methods of contract administration to help evolving industries and important individual businesses to survive and prosper. The government could then have confidence that there would be contractors available in the years to come to meet its needs and that those firms would even have incentives to innovate in order to respond to future contract opportunities. Federal contract historian John Nagle explained that Secretary Hamilton early on "began advancing money to contractors because contractors often could not perform without advance payment and, considering the snail's pace of late eighteenth century communications, could not wait for payment to be sanctioned after a Treasury audit."[29]

The famous inventor of the cotton gin, Eli Whitney, was one of the leading examples of this practice in the early years. Whitney's patent on the cotton gin was running out and he decided to get into the arms-manufacturing business, despite no experience in the field. Whitney obtained contracts that provided him with a foundation to learn and develop the arms business as well as advance payments that kept him afloat, even though he virtually defaulted on the contract in the early years. Whitney explained: "Bankruptcy and ruin were constantly staring me in the face. . . . Loaded with a Debt of 3 or 4000 Dollars, without resources, and without any business that would ever furnish me a support, I knew not which way to turn. . . . By this contract I obtained some thousands of Dollars in advance which saved me from ruin."[30] The government kept him going despite the fact that he produced only 12.5 percent of the number of weapons required in the first year and took eleven years to complete the contract.

Also in those early years, the federal government, as it has since, used military contracts to develop infrastructure for national development. There was great controversy over the degree to which the national government should be involved in building infrastructure as the country grew and expanded to the west. However, there was a clear need and authority for the federal government to expand the postal system and to do what was necessary to provide military support for the new territories. This is not to suggest that U.S. policy toward Native Americans or toward Mexico was appropriate but merely to recognize that, having undertaken the kinds of expansionist policies that it did, the government was bound to support them. These postal and military activities provided government with an excuse for contracts that built roads, expanded water transport, and developed postal, and later telegraph, communications throughout the nation. If this kind of strategy sounds familiar, it should. This same approach was used in the 1950s to justify federal financing of the interstate highway system, ostensibly constructed to enable the military to rapidly reposition troops and equipment.

Finally, the early national period saw the development of a significant body of case law that supported the federal government's efforts to build an economic infrastructure for national development and to participate in the marketplace as a contractor. Much of that effort was led by Chief Justice John Marshall, the very same veteran of the Revolutionary War and the Virginia House of Burgesses who had learned hard lessons about what happens in the absence of such authority.

Marshall and his colleagues promptly established the Supreme Court's co-equal stature in the new constitutional republic with its famous opinion in *Marbury v. Madison*,[31] asserting the Court's authority to strike down unconstitutional actions of the federal government. It was also critically important for the Court to establish the power of federal courts to review both the civil[32] and criminal[33] decisions of state courts where they present questions of federal law. The Court also provided expansive readings of the commerce clause and the necessary and proper clause that allowed Congress to adopt a host of federal statutes, affecting a wide range of economic activity in the nation.[34] What is often forgotten, however, is that the first case in which the Supreme Court declared an act of a state legislature unconstitutional had to do with the state's impairment of the obligations of contract.[35] The Georgia state legislature sought to overturn land grants that had been obtained by corrupt means from former legislators. However, sections of that land had long since been sold to innocent third parties in Georgia and elsewhere. The Court protected those innocent purchasers from the impairment of their contracts.

The Supreme Court was quickly called on to address a range of issues involving public obligations as well as state government attempts to interfere with private agreements. Even before Marshall became chief justice, the Court had insisted that states could be sued in federal court over their financial obligations.[36] But there were also questions about just what counted as a public contract. Thus, it was a matter of considerable importance when the Supreme Court ruled in the famous Dartmouth College case, that a state charter to the college was a contract protected from impairment by the state.[37]

Of course, one of the important questions was whether and to what extent government, including the federal government, had the authority to enter into contracts in any case. After all, the Constitution said nothing about the power of government to contract, nor was there any broad statutory authority to do so. It was not until the 1830s that the Supreme Court ruled that the government had inherent authority to contract.

> Upon full consideration of this subject, we are of opinion that the United States have such a capacity to enter into contracts. It is in our opinion an incident to the general right of sovereignty; and the United States being a body politic, may, within the sphere of the constitutional powers confided to it, and through the instrumentality of the proper department to which those powers are confided, enter into contracts not prohibited by law, and appropriate to the just exercise of those powers. . . . To adopt a different principle, would be to deny the ordinary rights of sovereignty, not merely to the general government, but even to the state governments within the proper sphere of their own powers, unless brought into operation by express legislation.[38]

The Court had implied as much in 1818 when it held that the federal government had the authority to sue or defend itself from suit in contract cases,[39] but it was 1831 before the Court directly authorized contracting by the federal government and states.[40] Still, the Court was already recognizing the need to lay down some important limitations. Thus, it held that public contracts are to be strictly construed in favor of the government.[41] The constitutional rule against impairment of contracts would be applied only retroactively to contracts that already existed so that government could establish controls for the future of government contracting.[42] It also ruled that government could not contract away certain basic governmental powers. Although we generally would include such matters as lawmaking within that restriction, the range of activities contracted out today makes the judgment about what is inherently or "inalienable" government activity a continuing subject of debate.

Notwithstanding all that had come before, the Civil War marked a new era in American governance, beginning with the fight for survival of the Republic. Whether it was the sheer scope and intensity of the war, the scale of the rapidly growing nation within which battle raged, or the changing technology of war, this was an era of challenge in government contracting. Three primary elements would affect the law and policy governing public contracts for decades thereafter. First, there was the outrageous corruption, primarily by those seeking to feed at the public trough, but there were also some widely publicized cases of official corruption. Second, there was the effort by Congress and the White House to develop laws governing public contracts to meet these problems, the beginning of an effort that has produced more than four thousand statutes since then just governing contracting by the federal government. Finally, there was the beginning of what is now sometimes known as spending in the black, referring to the use of contracts for covert operations and other classified activities.

For those who believe covert operations are recent phenomena, it might come as a surprise to learn that President Abraham Lincoln hired William A. Lloyd in July of 1861 to spy for the United States government in the South. The contract called for a salary of $200 per month. Lloyd fulfilled his obligations but was ultimately paid only for his expenses and not his salary. The administrator of Lloyd's estate sued to recover the salary in the Court of Claims but the suit was dismissed. The case, *Totten v. United States*,[43] ultimately found its way to the U.S. Supreme Court and raised two important and interesting questions. First, can the president, in the absence of statutory authority, enter into a contract for covert operations? Second, can a party to such an agreement sue to enforce a contract with the federal government concerned with covert operations?

Writing for the Court, Chief Justice Stephen J. Field had no difficulty finding that "[h]e was undoubtedly authorized during the war, as commander in chief of the armies of the United States, to employ secret agents . . . and contracts to compensate such agents are so far binding upon the government as to render it lawful for the President to direct payment of the amount stipulated out of the contingent fund under his control." However, the Court also found that if the government chose not to fulfill its part of the bargain, there was really nothing that the other party to a covert contract could do to collect.

> The service stipulated by the contract was a secret service; the information sought was to be obtained clandestinely, and was to be communicated privately; the employment and the service were to be equally concealed. Both employer and agent must have understood that the lips of the other were to be forever sealed respecting the relation of either to the matter. This condition of the engagement was implied from the nature of the employment, and is implied in all secret employments of the government in time of war, or upon matters affecting our foreign relations, where a disclosure of the service might compromise or embarrass our government in its public duties, or endanger the person or injure the character of the agent. If upon contracts of such a nature an action against the government could be maintained in the Court of Claims, whenever an agent should deem himself entitled to greater or different compensation than that awarded to him, the whole service in any case, and the manner of its discharge, with the details of dealings with individuals and officers, might be exposed, to the serious detriment of the public. A secret service,

with liability to publicity in this way, would be impossible; and, as such services are sometimes indispensable to the government, its agents in those services must look for their compensation to the contingent fund of the department employing them, and to such allowance from it as those who dispense that fund may award. The secrecy which such contracts impose precludes any action for their enforcement. The publicity produced by an action would itself be a breach of a contract of that kind, and thus defeat a recovery.[44]

This was but the beginning. As the United States assumed an active and important role in international affairs following World War II, it built a large, complex national security system that increasingly employed covert operations around the world. The *Totten* case has served as a precedent limiting the ability of courts to look into such contracts ever since.[45] This precedent controlled cases arising in connection with World War II, the war in Vietnam,[46] and CIA operations in locations as varied as Cuba[47] and Mauritius.[48]

Far more prosaic, but of much greater significance than the covert contracts, were the hundreds of routine contracts for all the goods and services needed to support the conduct of the Civil War. Swarms of would-be war profiteers converged on Washington for the feeding frenzy. One official described them as "a cloud of locusts alighting down upon the capital to devour the substance of the country."[49] It was so bad that offices had to limit their public hours of operation in order to have peace enough to perform their responsibilities. When the contracts were awarded, the businesses often produced shoddy goods. In fact, the term "shoddy" came out of contracting during the Civil War era and derived from the material that looked like cloth but was really a kind of pressed together collection of cloth scraps, thread, and whatever came off the factory floor. Not surprisingly blankets and uniforms fashioned from this material literally fell apart in no time. When the full picture of business abuse of contracting emerged in congressional investigations, Lincoln is reported to have said that these merchants "ought to have their devilish heads shot off."[50]

Although it is true that most of this corruption came from the private sector and that there were many dedicated public servants who fought against the efforts to rob the public treasury, it was sadly the case that there were some corrupt officials as well. The most often repeated story is about Maj. Justus McKinstry, assistant quartermaster in Maj. Gen. John C. Fremont's western command. Among other things, McKinstry was known to allow outrageous profits and to offer contracts to disreputable businesses. He also let it be known that these firms would be more likely to get paid in a timely fashion if they provided gifts to Fremont or Fremont's wife.[51] McKinstry was eventually court-martialed. Fremont was not punished. Quartermaster Robert Allen, who was transferred in to clean up the mess, warned that the reputation of the Quartermaster Corps as well as the effectiveness of the army's western command would be destroyed unless he got help from higher authorities to correct the "wanton, reckless expenditures in this command."[52] Even higher up was the well-known corruption of Secretary of War Simon Cameron, of whom President Lincoln said: "He was so corrupt, the only thing he wouldn't steal was a red hot stove."[53]

Congress and President Lincoln were determined to do something about the situation, and they did. Indeed, this period marked the enactment of statutes aimed at protecting the integrity of government contracting and making it more effective. That effort has continued and has today grown into a body of more than four thousand pieces of legislation just for federal government contracting. In fact, with the flurry of legislation at various points, it is not clear precisely how many such statutes exist. In the 1860s most of these statutes (1) sought to require open, advertised procurements; (2) separated the purchasing, accounting, and financial disbursement functions to ensure control and responsibility; and (3) attempted to erect protections against conflict of interest by elected officials, appointed executives, and other government employees.

The Era of Reform: Populists, Progressives, and the Rise of Modern Public Administration

Unfortunately, reform efforts of the Civil War era did not eliminate the difficulties. Indeed, the late nineteenth and early twentieth centuries marked a period in which money was king, and those who amassed the greatest amount of it by virtually any means were celebrated. Indeed, it was a period that gave rise to social Darwinism, a theory that held that those who had wealth and power were most worthy and those at the other end of the spectrum deserved their fate. Not surprisingly, the values of the larger society were reflected in the political arena as well.[54]

In an ironic twist, however, it was the pervasiveness of corruption and the damage that it produced that brought about an era of reform, which, in turn, fostered the development of modern public administration. The effort to stamp out corrupt contracting practices was one of the key motivators in that reform movement. Some of those efforts were directed at the federal government. Indeed, one of three papers that Woodrow Wilson put together to fashion his famous article that is now taken as the leading early work on public administration[55] was about corruption at the national level.[56] Also in the 1880s Congress adopted federal civil service law with an independent commission to regulate it. In 1893 the congressional Dockery Commission and in 1905 the presidentially created Keep Commission looked into ways to improvement management of federal contracts.[57] Presidents Theodore Roosevelt and William Howard Taft began to use executive orders to manage federal government contracting, a practice continued by later presidents.

However, much of the effort to eliminate corruption and improve the management of public contracting came at the state and municipal levels. The

Populists, a largely agrarian movement, battled corruption at the state level with the Grange as a central organization. Grange-sponsored candidates won control in some state legislatures in an effort to throw out what were commonly referred to as the finest legislatures money could buy. Influenced by these reform efforts, Illinois, as early as 1870, pioneered what we would now call public utilities regulation, using independent commissions to avoid interference by corrupt politicians.[58] The Progressive movement, a largely urban and generally upper-middle-class group of reformers, also attacked corruption at the state level in efforts to improve ballot access, to eliminate corrupt election practices, and generally to open the political process.

The Progressives, however, focused much of their attention on reform at the municipal level and were part of a major national effort at the local level, often known as the Good Government movement. As industrialism grew, the cities experienced burgeoning growth and with that came the rise of corrupt political machines. The Progressives attacked the machines both by seeking to improve the political process but also by efforts to support a professional approach to government, using the developing professions and evolving social sciences in the public interest. The other factor present in Progressive efforts was a social conscience, an effort to address the social effects of industrialization and the commercial market generally. The urban reform led to creation of the National Municipal League and the New York Bureau of Municipal Research.[59] The bureau's research into New York City contract corruption helped to bring down the political machine that had been in power and install a reform administration. The city management movement also grew out of these reform efforts, an initiative driven in significant part by an attempt to bring an end to corrupt contracting processes. The International City/County Management Association (ICMA) was founded in 1914 as the council/manager plan was taking root in such cities as Dayton, Ohio, and spreading around the nation. Under the classic plan (of which there are today many variations), the elected governing body (city council, municipal commission, or village trustees) possesses the responsibility for making the political decisions for the community. The city manager is a professional who is accountable to the governing body but has the authority to manage the municipal government's units free of political interference.[60] One of the manager's particularly important areas of responsibility is professional contracting.

Ironically, during much of this period, the U.S. Supreme Court was responding positively to efforts by business to constrain federal and state government regulatory authority based on freedom to contract and restrictive interpretations of the interstate commerce power. The Court issued numerous opinions striking down child labor laws, blocking wage and hour limitations on employment, and restricting the scope of antitrust enforcement.[61]

World War I and the New Deal: Reshaping Law and Practice

In the midst of the reform era came U.S. involvement in World War I. One of the leading historians of federal contracting, F. Trowbridge vom Bauer, saw World War I as a watershed for public contract law and administration—indeed, as the true beginning of modern government contracting.[62] He highlighted many factors that made World War I different from what had come before. But beyond that, he pointed to important factors that influenced what came after the so-called war to end all wars. Among the most important features were the nature of mobilization, the question of balance of risk, the increased use of negotiated contracting, the concept of termination of contracts for the convenience of the government, and dispute settlement issues. In addition to these items, the period was important because of the effects of demobilization, the "merchants of death" theory of foreign policy, and the creation of a new budget and finance regime for the federal government.

To vom Bauer, World War I presented two important facts that have been important in many emergencies since then: the nation had to mobilize rapidly in a world in which technology was increasingly complex, and the scale of that mobilization was far greater than anything seen before. Unfortunately, the pressures to mobilize under these conditions began a tradition of effectively suspending the law of government contracting at the outset of emergencies, on the theory that it could always be restored in calmer times. Unfortunately, the experience in World War I and in later emergencies showed that it is easier to suspend the rules than to recover from the chaos after the fact and to regularize contracting after the emergency has ended. The tendency in such periods is to allow the commander in chief to use executive orders to govern, and Woodrow Wilson certainly did so. During his tenure in office, Wilson issued more than 1,700 executive orders, many of which dealt in one way or another with the war. In virtually all such conflicts, Congress comes along with a war powers act authorizing such actions and ratifying those already taken.[63]

In addition to these relatively obvious issues, vom Bauer found other factors that arose during World War I that we have seen repeated. One of these is the problem of the balance of risk in government contracting. Often, government asks contractors to undertake and rapidly deliver technologically sophisticated work that requires research and development or to produce goods on a scale that necessitates large capital investments. In either case, the contractor is assuming a significant level of risk if he or she is held to a fixed-price contract. One of the responses to this problem adopted in World War I was to make purchases in the form of what came to be termed cost-plus contracts.

These cost-plus contracts were of two basic types. The first was a cost-plus-percentage-of-cost contract. That type provided the contractor with reimbursement for reasonable expenses required for executing the contract and a percentage of that cost as a profit. This type of contract obviously gave the contractor an incentive to increase costs and to write off as much overhead expense for the other operations of the firm as possible as an expense on the contract. For these reasons this type of contract was later outlawed. The other type of cost-plus contract, the cost-plus-fixed-fee, is still used in a variety of settings, but there is an ongoing debate about how to determine precisely which costs should be reimbursable. Although there are still dangers to the public treasury from the possibility of excessive costs, the alternative for a contractor facing high levels of risk and uncertainty is either to refuse to bid at all or to seek a premium price.

Another approach to the special problems of World War I contracting was to suspend normal advertised bidding and to make increased use of negotiated procurement. In this mode of contracting, the government would identify one or more possible contract partners and then begin negotiations with the most desirable firm until an agreement could be reached. Failing that, the government could move on to the next-best firm, and so on. This approach has obvious dangers, but it offered a degree of flexibility and speed, particularly where there were few likely bidders in any case. This approach is enjoying renewed popularity as policy makers since the 1990s have tried to find ways to avoid rigid bidding processes that prevented government from taking advantage of the dynamics of the marketplace.[64]

One of the other areas of risk for the government is that, under conditions of mobilization, it has to contract for large quantities of equipment even though situations and needs change rapidly and unexpectedly. Technology, too, often changes rapidly, and the government would not want to be held to buying outdated weapons or other equipment. During World War I the federal government increasingly sought to terminate contracts "for the convenience of the government." This practice was upheld by the Supreme Court, but such an action also meant that the contractor was due reasonable compensation.[65]

Many of the contracting techniques used in war conditions resulted in increased costs in addition to profiteering behavior by contracting firms of the sort seen in earlier conflicts. So expensive was the war effort that it became common for those opposed to the conflict to argue that the U.S. involvement in the war was not justified but came from the "merchants of death" who pressured the nation to enter the war.[66] Such accusations, which seem to surface in any military or foreign affairs emergency, add the weight of constant political baggage to an already difficult task.

After the war, in 1921, Congress adopted the Budget and Accounting Act. In addition to establishing the executive budget process that remains today, albeit in amended form, the legislation created the General Accounting Office (GAO) and the office of comptroller of the United States to head that agency. The GAO was made a congressional agency with a long-term appointment for the comptroller in order to provide independence from inappropriate political influence. The comptroller was given authority to determine claims against the government, including contracts.[67] The GAO was also given general audit and investigative authority. Today, the agency remains the leading government source of analysis and evaluation of government contracting.

After the war years came the roaring twenties, followed promptly by the Great Depression. When he took office, President Franklin D. Roosevelt, who had served as assistant secretary of the navy, determined to approach the economic crisis as if the nation were mobilizing for war.[68] In his inaugural address, FDR indicated that he hoped Congress would adopt the legislation to repel this economic invader. However, he was prepared to act if Congress did not. "But in the event that the Congress shall fail . . . , I shall not evade the clear course of duty that will then confront me. I shall ask the Congress for the one remaining instrument to meet the crisis—broad Executive power to wage a war against the emergency, as great as the power that would be given to me if we were in fact invaded by a foreign foe."[69] An emergency session of Congress the day after his speech enacted the equivalent of a war powers resolution, ratifying the president's initial actions, and supported broad executive power to address the economic emergency.

The use of government contracts to encourage industry and to provide public works jobs were part of the arsenal with which FDR's New Deal attacked the depression. Of course, government contracts had been used before to support nascent industries and keep important producers in business during difficult times. The federal government *Procurement Commission Report* later concluded that what was different about this period was that such contracts were used for social as well as economic purposes.[70] The commission also noted that one of the reasons for using government contracts to accomplish some of these purposes was that the kinds of judicial rulings discussed earlier had blocked efforts to sustain legislation that would have tackled issues more directly.[71] Some of these policies came in the form of legislation requiring that federal agencies place conditions on the contractors with which it chose to do business. Examples included requirements for wage and hour protections for workers and the Wagner-O'Day Act calling for a preference for purchasing from federal prison industry operations and from workshops for blind people.[72] Others were imposed by the president directly, using executive orders, such as the requirement that agencies not contract with firms engaging in racial discriminatory practices.[73]

In addition to public works contracts, the federal government undertook other contracts to support industry more generally. Some of these had begun before the Great Depression. Just as postal and military contracts had been used in the nation's early years to foster transportation and infrastructure construction, so the twentieth-century contracts to carry mail were used to help the emerging airline and merchant shipping industries. However, it was during the New Deal that scandals surrounding these contracts exploded onto the public stage. Hugo Black, then a senator from Alabama, took the lead on investigations of these two industries. Black found that the U.S. government had subsidized the building or refurbishing of ships that companies were then allowed to buy at bargain basement prices. Those companies later received lucrative postal contracts that Black concluded ended up costing the taxpayer some $66,000 per pound of international mail sent abroad.[74] To make matters worse, forty-seven out of the fifty-two marine postal contracts were awarded without competitive bidding.

In some ways even more dramatic was Black's investigation into air mail contracts awarded during the administration of President Herbert Hoover. Black's inquiry uncovered the fact that President Hoover's Postmaster General, Walter F. Brown, had decided that he was going to use the contracts to foster the airline industry and that he was going to do so by deciding which developing firms were worthy of investment while excluding the others. In fact, he held meetings in Washington in May and June of 1930 at which he laid out his plans with representatives of the favored airlines. After Black's investigation brought this to light, Roosevelt's postmaster, James Farley, did his own internal analysis and concluded that the sweetheart deals with the airlines had resulted in overpayments of some $47 million between 1930 and 1936.[75] Farley announced that he would immediately cancel the contracts, but there was no real fallback position for the government to ensure delivery of airmail. This was an early lesson, but not one that was well learned, about the danger of becoming dependent on contractors and having few or no effective alternatives in the event that the contract for services failed. U.S. Army Air Corps pilots were asked to carry the mail, but they did not have the right kinds of aircraft and were neither trained nor experienced for the type of flying necessary for airmail operations. Several died in crashes as a result. Eventually, the new airmail contracts were developed on a fair basis with virtually all airlines. The evidence is strong that these airmail contracts provided the subsidies that allowed almost all of today's major airlines to develop and grow.[76]

World War II and Postwar Transformations

Notwithstanding the support for aviation development, the United States was far from ready for a conflict as it became increasingly clear that another war was coming. By the time it arrived, the United States had already been providing equipment to England under the Lend/Lease program. As early as 1939, FDR issued a proclamation declaring a limited national emergency to begin mobilization. On May 27, 1941, the president proclaimed "that an unlimited national emergency confronts this country" and directed that priority be given to diversion of resources to preparation for war.[77] Field Marshall Hermann Göring counted on Germany's ability to outproduce the United States, particularly in the critical field of aircraft manufacturing,[78] but American firms turned out some

300,000 aircraft to meet that challenge. In the process, firms like Boeing, Douglas, Lockheed, and North American grew dramatically into leaders in the aviation industry for decades to come.[79]

Of course, in order to achieve that level of production, other values were sacrificed. In the First War Powers Act and in the implementing of executive orders, most restrictions on government contracting were waived. Two key exceptions were cost-plus-percentage-of-cost contracts and excess profits.[80] In fact, advertised procurements were barred on security grounds. Negotiated contracts were the order of the day.

Not surprisingly, it was not long before there was pressure to move against apparent cases of excess profits. However, in 1942, the Supreme Court served noticed that the existing tools for attacking such profiteers were inadequate. In *United States v. Bethlehem Steel*, Justice Black wrote:

> The problem of war profits is not new. In this country, every war we have engaged in has provided opportunities for profiteering and they have been too often scandalously seized. . . . To meet this recurrent evil, Congress has at times taken various measures. . . . It may be that one or some or all of these measures should be utilized more comprehensively, or that still other measures must be devised. But if the Executive is in need of additional laws by which to protect the nation against war profiteering, the Constitution has given to Congress, not to this Court, the power to make them.[81]

In response, Congress enacted the Renegotiation Act,[82] permitting the government to reopen contracts in the event that there appeared to be excess profits. This policy was upheld by the Supreme Court against constitutional challenge.[83] The legislature continued to wrestle with the problem, adding amendments along the way.[84] However, just how to determine what constitutes an excess profit in the kinds of contracts in which government becomes involved is an ongoing challenge.

There was a more general argument about disputes over government contracts. Going into the war, contracts made the contract officer's decisions on disputes authoritative but allowed an informal appeal to the head of the cabinet department involved.[85] However, the process, which provided no opportunity for a hearing or any other protections for the contractor, was rejected by the Court of Claims in 1942. The case was brought by an Ohio businessman who was treated in a grossly unfair manner. In fact, after his appeal was bucked around the War Department, the final ruling was drafted for the assistant secretary of war by a person who was a subordinate of the contracting officer whose decision the businessman was appealing. Judge Charles Whitaker put the matter bluntly.

> The plain truth is that the appeal was in reality denied, and it was denied, forsooth, because, said the Assistant Secretary of War, "he couldn't take the time to consider these matters because he had too many other weighty things to do."

Yet it was The Assistant Secretary of War who had required the plaintiff [as part of the contract] to surrender its right to appeal to the courts and who had insisted that he should be the final arbiter of plaintiff's rights. The procedure was a travesty of justice. It cannot be countenanced in an enlightened civilization. In such a case the courts must step in and protect plaintiff's rights.[86]

After a study of the situation, the War Department created a Board of Contract Appeals that provided for due process protections and ensured independence of board members from contracting officials.[87]

On Capitol Hill, then-senator Harry S. Truman chaired what became known as the Truman Committee, which studied contract difficulties after 1941. Among the issues raised by the committee was the fact that the overwhelming amount of federal contract dollars went to the nation's largest firms. Consideration for small businesses in government contracting was another issue that would continue to be a concern down to the present.

Another critical wartime contracting issue that the Truman administration tried to anticipate had been highlighted by the World War I experience. The end of World War I demonstrated the potential for economic chaos that could be brought on by rapid demobilization involving cancellations of huge numbers of federal contracts. Nagle reports that, in light of that experience, Roosevelt's people began work on demobilization processes in 1943, and Congress responded with a settlement act in 1944. Then the administration moved to establish implementing rules and procedures that were in place in 1945.

> The regulations' effectiveness was proven on V-J Day when, within five minutes of the announcement of Japan's surrender, previously prepared telegrams were dispatched directing the procurement districts to terminate war contracts. Within two days, 60,000 contracts, totaling $7.3 billion, had been cancelled. Similar actions, although not as large, had occurred three months earlier on V-E Day. In all, the government terminated $20 billion in contracts and minimized litigation. The orderly termination process helped avoid a general postwar depression.[88]

The fact that government cancelled some $15 billion in defense contracts in one month meant that more than 60,000 employees were laid off by just two firms. Jobs had to be found for millions of returning veterans.[89] The difficulty of demobilization is compounded by the fact that unions and others are often willing during emergencies to forgo significant wage increases. However, when the emergency ends, there is often legitimate concern about inflation and about lost ground during the time when patriotic sacrifice was the order of the day. For Truman, that meant major labor unrest, with more than a million and a quarter workers on strike at some point from the fall of 1945 through much of 1946. It was becoming increasingly clear that although government contracts were not the primary force in the economy, they were certainly a major factor in its viability.

The period immediately after the war produced a variety of wide-ranging policies in many fields. Some of these, such as the Administrative Procedure Act (APA),[90] were based on the experiences of the New Deal and the War Years. Others had to do with the changing nature of American society, economy, and business practice, such as the new federal codes of civil and criminal procedure. Still others came with the growing U.S. international role and the nuclear age, such as the National Security Act of 1947 and the other policies developing what has come to be known as the national security establishment. Government contracting was another focus for such broadly based policymaking.

Two major statutes on federal government contracting, which remain the foundation policies today, albeit with a variety of amendments and supplements added along the way, were adopted at that time. The first to be enacted was the Armed Services Procurement Act of 1947 (ASPA).[91] This legislation was the result of recommendations made by a Pentagon study group. Even though it recognized that peacetime rules had to be somewhat different from those appropriate to war, the group warned against the dangers of moving back to a time in which contracting officials had too little discretion to act. That necessary flexibility included the appropriate use of negotiated contracting, assuming of course that proper safeguards were in place to protect against excess profits. Congress accepted that approach and constructed the statute to require advertised contracting, but it then added seventeen categories of exceptions. The law also included encouragement for contracting with small businesses, allowed advance payments in some circumstances, set limits on profits in the case of cost-plus-fixed-fee contracts, and continued the prohibition against cost-plus-percentage-of-cost contracts.[92]

The second major piece of legislation targeted civilian contracting and was entitled the Federal Property and Administrative Services Act of 1949 (FPASA).[93] The basis for this legislation was a set of recommendations provided by the first Hoover Commission. The Hoover Commission's task force on contracting suggested (1) a statute for civilian contracting that would be a good match for the ASPA; (2) a coordinating body for both military and civilian contracting; and (3) a centralized contracting organization for purchasing standard items. That was the basis for what we have come to know as the General Services Administration (GSA). The idea for such an agency was also copied by many state governments. As the administrative services required across the federal government have changed over time, so has the nature of GSA operations.

There were two ironies in the fact that these two major policies were enacted at that moment in time. First, the Administrative Procedure Act governing general agency operations specifically exempted contracting.[94] The two contracting statutes were entirely separate from the APA. This separation was an attempt to compartmentalize important offices, functions, and processes of governance that were in reality not truly separate. That was enough of a problem at the time, but it has become less appropriate as agencies have increasingly used contracting to perform functions that many agencies formerly conducted directly with their own people. The second irony is related precisely to that new reality. These two main contracting policies were adopted based on the lessons of past and recent history just at a time when the context and character of governance and contracting were beginning to change significantly.

Two of the more important changes were the increasingly intergovernmental character of government operations and the shift from an emphasis on purchases of goods and systems and toward contracting for services at all levels of government. Despite the tendency to see the federal government as growing dramatically in the postwar decades to a point where it seemed the states and localities had lost their importance, the reverse has been true. The baby boom was, of course, the product of returning veterans and their partners forming families. Those families needed places to live, the infrastructure to support the burgeoning suburbs they inhabited, and services. It should come as no surprise that road construction and education were the leading features of many state budgets. Many of the services these communities required were labor intensive, and it should also have been obvious that the growth in state and local government employment would rapidly outpace that in the federal civil service.

Those states and localities needed to contract for a wide range of construction and goods to provide the foundation for the required services. As an increasingly mobile population demanded a minimum acceptable level of service across the nation, pressure grew for greater federal support to states and localities. In addition, the acute problems of the nation's cities and the increasingly apparent stresses in rural communities added to the calls for federal action. Many of these problems were in areas that the federal government could not constitutionally reach directly, such as education and health care. That fact, in addition to political reality, meant the creation of what Deil Wright called fiscal federalism.[95] Indeed, the term "intergovernmental relations" became a more common way to speak about federal, state, and local structures for service delivery than the more traditional term, "federalism." The full significance of this evolving intergovernmental reality would not become fully apparent until the late 1960s and early 1970s, but it was under way throughout the postwar decades.

FROM KENNEDY'S TECHNOCRATS TO REINVENTING GOVERNMENT: CONTRACTING IN A HIGH-TECH, MARKET-DRIVEN WORLD

The postwar period was also the era of the cold war, when fear generated by the nuclear arms race between the United States and the Soviet Union and the rise of the space race after *Sputnik* kept the attention of those concerned with contracting on what President Dwight D. Eisenhower termed the military-industrial complex. In fact, the formal declaration of what came to be known as the cold war came in National Security Council Memorandum 68 developed by the Truman administration. It meant a commitment to massive defense spending. The espionage operations that provided the Soviet Union with nuclear weaponry and the invasion of South Korea only served to support the growing cold war fever. Ironically, it was Gen. Dwight Eisenhower who quickly concluded upon entering the presidency that more than $5 billion needed to be cut from national security spending. To critics he replied: "Perhaps the [National Security] Council should have a report as to whether national bankruptcy or national destruction would get us first."[96]

These same forces meant that the federal government increasingly focused on research and development contracts.[97] Those contracts were to become an important source of income for major universities as well as fueling controversy on those campuses. The federal government was also letting contracts to encourage private firms to innovate in new fields like computers, just as it had let contracts to promote the aircraft industry in an earlier time.

The factors that were driving national security policy meant contracting for new nuclear weapons, new aircraft to deliver them, and generations of air-to-ground, surface-to-air missiles, and intercontinental and intermediate-range ballistic missiles. These forces also helped to speed the advent of the nuclear navy, led by the USS *Nautilus*, first of several classes of nuclear submarines capable of launching nuclear missiles from under the sea. When President John F. Kennedy added the goal of sending Americans to the moon and returning them safely by the end of the 1960s, the scale of aerospace and national security contracting was awe inspiring. To complicate matters, into all of this came the increasing U.S. involvement in the war in Vietnam.

White House efforts to deal with these challenges and the congressional concern with how well they were being met would lead to efforts to reexamine all federal contracting operations. President Kennedy's secretary of defense, Robert McNamara, sought to make contracting more rational and less risky for the public. He worked to limit the use of cost-plus-fixed-fee contracts and to shift the balance of risk more toward the contractor, leaving less risk on the government. One of the ways he sought to do that was to reduce the likelihood of what are termed "buy in" or "iceberg" contracts. These are situations in which contractors enter unrealistically low bids with the expectation that they could "get well" (meaning to more than make up for the low bid) by requesting increases once the contract was under way.[98] This practice is also known these days as "lowballing" a contract. Instead, he wanted fixed-price contracts that put the burden of cost overruns on the contractor rather than the public.

McNamara advocated something he called Total Package Procurement. The idea was that contractors should submit a bid that included all the costs associated with a contract, including the research and development, production, and maintenance, at the outset and then be held to that contract. Although such an approach sounded eminently reasonable, it turned out to be far more complex in practice than it seemed in theory. The classic example of the failure of that approach was the contracting for what became known as the C-5A Galaxy, then the world's largest cargo aircraft. It soon became clear that the innovations needed to build such a large aircraft were far more sophisticated than had been anticipated. Moreover, the bid had been submitted before the Vietnam War drove up the cost of materials and labor. Ultimately, the government was faced with demands by the manufacturer for increases of tens of millions of dollars.[99] Although the government could have pulled the contract, huge costs that had been sunk into the project would be lost. One of the nation's premier aircraft manufacturers was facing financial disaster, putting at risk an important supplier and thousands of jobs. That was a threat not lost on members of Congress whose constituents faced unemployment and whose communities confronted the possible loss of millions to the local economy. Then there was the question of who could be enticed to pick up a contract at that point to complete the work on a plane that the government had decided was necessary? Even if a manufacturer could be found, how long would it take to get the project on track and aircraft delivered?

Cost overruns were but one criticism confronting the federal government in its contract operations. By the late 1950s, the comptroller general had issued findings highly critical of public contract management processes on grounds that the federal government could not effectively assess contract costs or contractor profits, since it was not receiving adequate and accurate cost data from the companies. That led in 1962 to the passage of the Truth in Negotiation Act, requiring full disclosure.[100] In that same year, the Bell Report, a study of research and development contracting by a commission appointed by President Kennedy and chaired by David Bell, raised questions about the use of cost reimbursement contracts and other practices in the research and development field.

As early as the mid-1960s, a proposal was evolving for a major study of the federal contracting process. That project really began in March 1966, when Rep. Chet Holifield (D-Calif.) came to the conclusion, following a study of GAO auditing, that most attention was focused on a relatively limited set of issues and mostly concerned with the Department of Defense even though other agencies shared related problems.[101] It took Holifield and his colleagues until 1969 to pass the legislation authorizing the study. It would prove to be an important event in the history of government contracting.

From the Procurement Commission to the Reagan Revolution and Beyond

The bipartisan Federal Procurement Commission issued its report in late 1972.[102] The commission was supported by thirteen study groups with five hundred participants screening, analyzing, and preparing recommendations about 450 contracting problems.[103] The four-volume report advanced some 149 separate recommendations for change. At the heart of those recommendations was a call for the creation of an Office of Federal Procurement Policy within the Office of Management and Budget in the Executive Office of the President. This office would have overall responsibility for the supervision of federal contracting policy across the executive branch and would issue regulations to implement its policies. It was to be responsible for recruiting and training of personnel for contracting. These recommendations were implemented with the Office of Federal Procurement Policy Act in 1974.[104]

Other things worthy of note were happening at the time. For example, the intergovernmental fiscal situation had become even more complex. In an attempt to clarify the situation, federal contracting and grants were redesignated as acquisitions and assistance; and the OMB worked to develop guidance for both. In that regard, the OMB continued to work on the so-called A-76 process (named for the OMB Circular A-76), an effort to control the types of activities that would be appropriate to contract out and those that should be carried out by government directly. The political concern about competition with the private sector from public employees has been ongoing from the days nearly a century ago when efforts were made to block competition from convict labor.

In the formal policy arena, two other developments were of broad importance. The first was the creation by the Office of Federal Procurement Policy (OFPP) in 1980 of the Federal Acquisition Regulation (FAR), the basic regulations governing contracting by both the Department of Defense and civilian agencies. The supervision of the FAR was to be by the OFPP, but the basic responsibility was to be vested in a Federal Acquisition Regulatory Council (FARC).[105]

New Public Management and Reinventing Government Contracting

By the turn of the twenty-first century, however, government contracting was anything but coherent and clear. There were three broad competing tendencies, three very large challenges, and many complex contexts in which these tendencies and challenges had to be addressed.

For much of the period from 1981 on, all levels of government came under an ever stronger pressure to contract out more public activities. At the same time, highly visible public contracting failures and the sheer magnitude and importance of government contracting were leading to increased calls for greater accountability, with particular attention to traditional audit and control techniques, and to demands for performance-based operations that focused less on audit and control and more on outcomes.

Finally, there was, simultaneously, a growing stress from attitudes that seemed to be conveyed by the increasing controls and expectations on contracting officials. Almost two dozen contracting statutes were enacted in a five-year period in the 1980s.[106] Some of these carried criminal sanctions, and several high-level prosecutions caused already frustrated business executives to avoid government contracting. This situation was so bad that during Operation Desert Storm in 1992, the Department of Defense could not make an emergency purchase of off-the-shelf commercial radios even though the agency was prepared to waive most of the regulations. The Japanese bought the radios and donated them to the U.S. military.[107] As Steven Kelman, later director of the Office of Federal Procurement Policy, argued at length, the impression was that Americans thought all public servants involved in contracting were crooks who had to be constrained at every turn. Even so, there were repeated political demands that government should be more like private sector businesses that prize flexibility and should have the ability to move quickly to get the most for the taxpayer's dollar.[108]

Kelman was appointed to head the Clinton administration's OFPP operation and was able to see many of his suggestions presented in the agenda for contracting reform, a part of the National Performance Review (NPR), headed by Vice President Al Gore. Congress enacted critical portions of the agenda as the Federal Acquisition Streamlining Act[109] and the Federal Acquisition Reform Act,[110] which are general statutes on government contracting, and the so-called Clinger-Cohen Act,[111] which reformed the acquisition of information technology. To these statutes were added executive orders and presidential memoranda intended to implement the new statutes.[112]

While these obviously difficult tensions over flexibility and accountability played out, three serious challenges hovered in the background. The first, and most significant, was the growing lack of contract management capacity at virtually all levels of government. The federal government had experienced waves of retirements from the contract management workforce. First, the Carter and early Reagan years saw the departure of civil servants who had entered the field of government contracting in the period between the end of World War II and the Korean War. Then a drop of more than 20 percent occurred during the 1990s as the federal government moved to reduce positions.[113] There were problems at the top as well. Although the OFPP was created in 1974, it was not made a permanent agency for another fifteen years. It did not have a high priority in the Office of Management and Budget. In fact, during the Reagan years, when contracting was dramatically increasing, OFPP shrank from a staff of forty-one to a total, by 1986, of eight professionals and five support staff. There was not even an administrator from 1984 to 1986. Many states and localities were also trying to do more with less, which often meant more functions contracted out with little effort to ensure adequate people and resources to do the job. Moreover, those who did enter the public contract management workforce quickly became attractive to private sector employers, who could offer them a great deal more money and fewer controls than they faced in the public sector.

A second challenge was the general shift from contracting focused on the acquisition of goods or construction to a much heavier focus on service contracting. The GAO found in the case of the federal government that "between fiscal year 1990 and fiscal year 2000, purchases of supplies and equipment fell by about $25 billion, while purchases of services increased by $17 billion, or about 24 percent. Consequently, purchases for services now account for about 43 percent of federal contracting expenses—the largest single spending category."[114]

The use of service contracting was even greater at the state and local level. Although state and local governments had always done a good deal of contracting, the level of service contracting increased as governors and state legislatures rushed to downsize the public workforce. Of course, their federal and state legislative service mandates remained. That meant that these governments had to place greater reliance on contractors.

Then there was the "new public management" movement, a global phenomenon that emphasized deregulation, decentralization, downsizing, and outsourcing (as contracting came to be known) as key components. Popularized in the United States as the reinventing government movement (a label drawn from the title of a best-selling book), the new public management was an important theme for the Clinton administration. The administration's effort in this area was led by Vice President Al Gore through his National Performance Review (NPR). But the *Reinventing Government*[115] book drew most of its examples from state and local governments and advocated a wide range of market-oriented approaches to service delivery, with contracting out a key component. But it became increasingly clear that government at all levels was dependent on contractors to deliver services because the government units involved either never had or no longer had the capacity to deliver mandated services themselves.

Contracting for services is in many important respects different from purchasing goods or contracting for construction. That difference became particularly visible when government moved beyond activities like contracted janitorial services and started transferring the delivery of health care or mental health care services, school operations, or even program management to contractors. As will become clear later, this kind of contracting creates very different types of accountability challenges, management difficulties, and policy problems. Many of these contracts are, in their own way, every bit as complex as the purchase of a weapons system for the military, and their effects can be even greater, particularly when government and the citizens it serves become dependent on the contractor.

This level of complexity has in part to do with the third challenge: the growing dependence on a combination of government agencies, nonprofits, and for-profit firms for service delivery. Just as contracting for services is different from contracting for goods, contracting with nonprofit organizations is different from contracting with for-profit firms. For reasons that will become clear in the chapters to follow, nonprofit organizations have their own special characteristics, needs, and challenges. As governments have increasingly come to rely on networks of contractors to provide services, some of which are for-profit firms and some of which are nonprofits, the challenges of contract management have grown. The fact that the nonprofit organizations have come to rely less on philanthropic or membership support and much more on a combination of grants and contracts has only heightened that complexity and interdependency.

Finally, during the 1980s and 1990s government increasingly became both a market regulator and a market participant. As a market participant, many governments have become not merely purchasers of goods and services but also vendors. States and localities have sold not only to the private sector but also to each other. Thus, so-called intergovernmental agreements have become important contracts across the nation and range from police to fire protection to recreational programs to water and sewer operations.

The variety of contexts in which all these activities are taking place should be clear by now, but there is one other dimension to be added. These days government is buying and selling in a global marketplace. The guidance from the U.S. Supreme Court, limited though it is, suggests that, for some purposes, government will be treated less like a government and more like a private party in the marketplace.[116] In other instances, however, it will be watched to ensure that it does not do through contracting what it could not do directly through policy.[117] Insofar as state or local governments seek to use their leverage in the marketplace for various purposes, they can expect that federal foreign policy and treaties will constrain their choices in the marketplace.[118]

THE MOVEMENT FROM AUTHORITY TO CONTRACT

Beyond shaping the nature and operation of public contracting today, the forces described above, and the political, economic, and social context within which they have evolved, have created a new reality for governance in the early twenty-first century. It is a shift from governing through authority, that is, properly exercised power, to contract. This is not merely to say that there is more contracting for goods and services, although that is true. It is to point out that, increasingly, the move has been toward governing by agreements, often informal, rather than through direct legal and political action. That even includes such traditionally authority-based activities as regulatory enforcement. The Clinton administration, as part of its reinventing government strategy, deliberately emphasized negotiated settlements in most areas over authority-based enforcement. The discussion of public contract management to follow must be understood in light of that shift, for it affects not only normative judgments about what government should do, but also analytic concerns about what government actually does and how it does it.

The move to deregulate, the drive for privatization, the effort to contract out more for public service delivery, the increased use of contract-type service evaluation by public sector "customers," the effort to reduce the size of the government, the encouragement to let market forces loose on matters previously the province of direct government action, the reorientation of public agencies as brokers rather than direct service providers, the call for a move to public/private partnerships, the call for replacement of enforcement and adjudication by negotiation and alternative dispute resolution, are only some of the many changes in the way we govern and are governed that have emerged as driving forces since the late 1970s. We are advised to downsize, deregulate, decentralize, devolve, deinstitutionalize, reinvent, right-size, and reengineer. The advice is to move away from so-called command and control operations and move toward a focus on negotiation-driven, incentive-based processes and performance-evaluated operations, often with market-oriented values as key criteria of success or failure. Whatever we do, the point has increasingly been to move away from the use of mechanisms of authority and toward governance by agreement, whether that means negotiated arrangements with regulated enterprises, service contracts with profit-making or nonprofit nongovernmental organizations, interjurisdictional agreements with other agencies of government at any level, service agreements with citizen clients, or internal performance agreements with personnel within a government organization. These admonitions have intensified under both conservative and moderate governments of the 1990s around the world, in both industrial and developing nations. What all these trends and forces have in common is a move away from action based on the exercise of government power through government institutions and toward government by contract. That is a singularly important shift in the basis for ordering the public aspects of society.

Despite the debates of the 1970s, 1980s, and 1990s over privatization, public choice, the role of macroeconomic policy, and managerial reforms, this move from authority to contract has not attracted the attention it deserves. Just as Sir Henry Maine tried a long time ago to explain what it meant that society had moved from status to contract,[119] the shift from authority to contract matters. The implications of that change will be discussed throughout the book.

That does not mean that there are no circumstances in which authority, or even raw political power, will be the basis for action. It does mean that, by degrees and on a continuum at one end of which is raw power and the other end of which is contract, we have moved the center of gravity of governance a significant way toward contract. A move from authority to contract does not mean an end to public institutions but, rather, a need to develop the institutional and management capacity necessary to meet the many new challenges before us. That will, in turn, require hybrid institutions that can both carry out a variety of what might be regarded as traditional responsibilities of governance and, simultaneously, emphasize various kinds of contractual agreements, both formal and informal, as a critically important mode of operation.

These changes matter for many reasons, but, for purposes of this book, it is important to understand that the model of the contract process—even informal contracting—is quite different from the traditional authority-driven model of governing. In its traditional form, authority-based governance is a vertical model based upon a hierarchy of law, institutions, and politics that dictates action and provides for special kinds of sanctions and processes for violators of law. It imposes specialized forms of responsibility to restrain those who govern and to control the institutions they head.

Thus, both for public contract management in particular and for contemporary governance more generally, it is important to understand that two quite different models of behavior are in operation at the same time. The challenge for the public manager is that he or she operates at the intersection of the two models, which is precisely the cause of many of the challenges that the manager faces. Many of the difficulties inherent in making decisions with respect to the short case study provided at the beginning of Chapter 1 have to do with the tensions between traditional issues of business practice, such as the efficiency, effectiveness, and responsiveness criteria for action, and the traditional governmental concerns of economy, responsibility, and equity.

THE INTEGRATION-OPERATION-SEPARATION MODEL

Thus, public contract management must be viewed from the perspective of both models. The vertical model is about authority relationships: the way that decisions get from the democratically elected political process through appointed executives and down through agencies to the contracting officer who is ultimately authorized to negotiate for the needs of the community and then to commit its resources in a legally binding relationship. This set of expectations about authority, transparency, and accountability drive what is authorized in public contracts and sets the ethical as well as the legal judgments that must be made once a contractual relationship is formed.

The second model comes into play once the decision to contract for goods or services has been made[120] and operates in tandem with the vertical model. While basic governance relationships are about authority and are in their nature vertical, contractual relationships are horizontal in character and operate from a base of mutual commitment in which, theoretically at least, the parties are equals. In the vertical model—for example, in a regulatory relationship—government establishes the rules and determines when and how they are to be enforced. In the contractual context, both parties set the rules and either can trigger enforcement of the contract's requirements. This tension between the vertical and horizontal models provides the essential tension in public contract administration. It is precisely at this nexus that contract administrators must balance economy, efficiency, effectiveness, equity, responsiveness, and responsibility.

The horizontal model is based on the three core aspects of the contract relationship. They are (1) integration of a nonprofit, a firm, or another agency with the primary government unit; (2) operation of the joint endeavor; and (3) separation or transformation of the relationship when a contract ends or undergoes major revision. These phases roughly correspond to the private sector contract phases of agreement, performance, and termination.

Each of the chapters that follow addresses one of these major portions of the model. Each of the chapters also considers the significance of the presence of the vertical, authority-driven model on the contract managers who must live and work in public contract relationships.

CONCLUSION

The effort to ensure a good deal for the public is one of the most important tasks for the public contract manager. Beyond the sometimes competing criteria for determining what constitutes a good deal, there is a broad group of factors that sets the context and constraints within which public contracts are managed. These factors have evolved over the nation's history from the Revolutionary War to the present. They have become more important as government, at all levels, has become more dependent on contractors to provide goods and services. These services operate in a complex intergovernmental web in which federal funds go to states and local governments that in turn contract with for-profit and nonprofit organizations to provide the actual services needed by citizens.

The increasingly important role of contracting, the changing context in which it is done, the increasing interdependency of the people, their governments, and their contract providers have altered much about the way we govern ourselves. We have seen a move from authority to contract in which the emphasis has more and more been placed on negotiated operations that are formally or informally in the nature of contracts. This is a quite different way of operating from the more authority-based approach to governance of an earlier time. The vertical, authority-driven model still operates, but it functions along with a horizontal, business-oriented, and negotiation-driven model of contracting. The public contract manager operates at the intersection of the two modes of governance. The following chapters work through the integration, operation, and separation/transformation portions of the contracting model.

Notes

1. Willard Sterne Randall, *George Washington: A Life* (New York: Henry Holt, 1997), 351.

2. Id., at 371.

3. Id.

4. U.S. Commission on Government Procurement, *Report of the Commission on Government Procurement* (Washington, D.C.: Government Printing Office, 1972), 1: 163. (Hereafter, *Procurement Commission.*)

5. Id.

6. Albert J. Beveridge, *The Life of John Marshall* (New York: Houghton Mifflin, 1916), 1: 224.

7. Alexander Hamilton, James Madison, and John Jay, *The Federalist Papers* (New York: Mentor Books, 1961), 476.

8. One need not accept the controversial Beard thesis, alleging that the framers were overwhelmingly motivated by concern with the economic well-being of the well-to-do, to understand that mechanisms to deal with economic default are important to support a structure of economic relationships. Charles A. Beard, *An Economic Interpretation of the Constitution* (New York: Macmillan, 1935).

9. *Trevett v. Weeden* (R.I. 1786). "James Mitchell Varnum, *The Case, Trevett Against Weeden: On Information and Complaint, for refusing Paper Bills in Payment for Butcher's Meat, in Market, at Par with Specie* (1787). 'The case—decided by the Superior Court of Judicature of the City of Newport in 1786—is unreported, but the case and its aftermath are meticulously detailed by James Mitchell Varnum, counsel for defendant Weeden, in Varnum. . . . It is noteworthy that Varnum's pamphlet was available for sale in Philadelphia during the Constitutional Convention.'" Suzanna Sherry, "The Founders' Unwritten Constitution," 54 *University of Chicago Law Review* 1127, 1138 (1987).

10. *McCulloch v. Maryland,* 17 U.S. 316 (1819).

11. A similar provision was enacted during that same summer of 1787 by the Continental Congress as part of Title II of the Northwest Ordinance, which provided for governance of territories.

12. See *Crosby v. National Foreign Trade Council,* 530 U.S. 363 (2000), and *United States v. Locke,* 529 U.S. 89 (2000).

13. See, for example, *Quill Corp. v. North Dakota,* 504 U.S. 298 (1992).

14. *Morales v. TWA,* 504 U.S. 374 (1992).

15. *United States v. Morrison,* 529 U.S. 598 (2000); *Printz v. United States,* 521 U.S. 898 (1997); *United States v. Lopez,* 514 U.S. 549 (1995).

16. Quoted in John F. Nagle, *A History of Government Contracting,* 2d ed. (Washington, D.C.: George Washington University School of Law, Government Contracts Program, 1999), 57.

17. Leonard D. White, *The Federalists* (New York: Macmillan, 1956), 183.

18. Id.

19. Id.

20. Id., at 184.

21. See White, supra note 17, at 360–361.

22. Nagle, supra note 16, at 63–65.

23. 1 Stat. 279 (1792).

24. 1 Stat. 419 (1795).

25. *Procurement Commission,* supra note 4, 1: 164.

26. White, supra note 17, at 363.

27. Id., at 344–345.

28. Nagle, supra note 16, at 67–68.

29. Id., at 61.

30. James Joy, "Eli Whitney's Contracts for Muskets," *8 Public Contract Law Journal* 140, 142 (1976) quoted in Nagle, supra note 16, at 77.

31. 5 U.S. (1 Cranch) 137 (1803).

32. *Martin v. Hunter's Lessee,* 14 U.S. (1 Wheat.) 304 (1816).

33 *Cohens v. Virginia,* 19 U.S. (6 Wheat.) 264 (1821).

34. See, for example, *McCulloch v. Maryland,* supra note 10; *Gibbons v. Ogden,* 22 U.S. (9 Wheat.) 1 (1824).

35. *Fletcher v. Peck,* 10 U.S. (6 Cranch) 87 (1810).

36. *Chisholm v. Georgia,* 2 U.S. (2 Dall.) 419 (1793). That ruling was so controversial that it led to the adoption of the Eleventh Amendment to the Constitution.

37. *Dartmouth College v. Woodward,* 17 U.S. (4 Wheat.) 518 (1819).

38. *United States v. Tingey,* 30 U.S. (5 Pet.) 115, 128 (1831). See also *United States v. Bradley,* 35 U.S. (10 Pet.) 343 (1836).

39. *Dugan v. U.S.,* 16 U.S. (3 Wheat.) 172 (1818).

40. *United States v. Tingey,* supra note 38.

41. *Charles River Bridge v. Warren Bridge,* 36 U.S. 420 (1837).

42. *Ogden v. Sanders,* 25 U.S. (12 Wheat.) 213 (1827).

43. 92 U.S. 105 (1875).

44. Id., at 106–107.

45. See Kelly D. Wheaton, "Spycraft and Government Contracts: A Defense of *Totten v. United States,*" 1997 *Army Law* 9 (1997).

46. *Vu Doc Guong v. United States,* 860 F.2d 1063, 1065–66 (Fed. Cir. 1988), cert. denied, 490 U.S. 1023 (1989).

47. *Mackowski v. United States,* 228 Ct. Cl. 717, 718 (1981).

48. *A. H. Simrick v. United States,* 224 Ct. Cl. 724 (1980).

49. Quoted in Nagle, supra note 16, at 177.

50. Quoted in id., at 192.

51. Lt. Col. Douglas P. DeMoss, Assistant to the General Counsel, Headquarters, Department of the Army, "Procurement during the Civil War and Its Legacy for the Modern Commander," 1997 *Army Lawyer* 9, 12 (1997).

52. Quoted in Nagle, supra note 16, at 194.

53. Quoted in id., at 184.

54. See *Lochner v. New York,* 198 U.S. 45 (1905), Justice Holmes, dissenting.

55. Woodrow Wilson, "The Study of Administration," 2 *Political Science Quarterly* 209 (1887).

56. See Phillip J. Cooper, "The Wilsonian Dichotomy in Administrative Law," in *Politics and Administration,* ed. J. Rabin and J. Bowman (New York: Marcel Dekker, 1984).

57. *Procurement Commission,* at 164–165.

58. *Munn v. Illinois,* 94 U.S. 113 (1876).

59. Dwight Waldo, *The Administrative State* (New York: Ronald Press, 1948), 31–33. See also Fritz Morstein Marx, ed., *Elements of Public Administration* (New York: Prentice-Hall, 1946), 24.

60. See John Nalbandian, "Tenets of Contemporary Professionalism in Local Government," in *Ideal and Practice in Council-Manager Government,* 2d ed., ed. H. George Frederickson (Washington, D.C.: International City/County Management Association, 1994).

61. *E. C. Knight v. United States,* 156 U.S. 1 (1895); *Lochner v. New York,* 198 U.S. 45 (1905); *Hammer v. Dagenhart,* 247 U.S. 251 (1918); *Bailey v. Drexel,* 259 U.S. 20 (1922); *Adkins v. Children's Hospital,* 261 U.S. 525 (1923).

62. F. Trowbridge vom Bauer, "Fifty Years of Government Contract Law," 29 *Federal Bar Journal* 305 (1970).

63. These issues and examples are developed fully in Phillip J. Cooper, *By Order of the President: The Use and Abuse of Presidential Direct Action* (Lawrence: University Press of Kansas, 2002).

64. See, for example, Steven Kelman, *Procurement and Public Management: The Fear of Discretion and the Quality of Government Performance* (Washington, D.C.: AEI Press, 1990).

65. See id., 313, citing *Russell Motor Car Company v. United States,* 261 U.S. 514 (1923); *United States v. Corliss Steam-Engine Company,* 91 U.S. 321 (1875).

66. Nagle, supra note 16, at 191–192.

67. 42 Stat. 23, 31 U.S.C. §41 et seq.

68. Frank Freidel, *Franklin D. Roosevelt: A Rendezvous with Destiny* (Boston: Little, Brown, 1990), 93.

69. Franklin D. Roosevelt, *The Public Papers and Addresses of Franklin D. Roosevelt* (New York: Random House, 1938), 2:15.

70. *Procurement Commission,* 1:167.

71. Id.

72. See Nagle, supra note 16, at 361–362.

73. Ruth Morgan, *The President and Civil Rights: Policy-Making by Executive Order* (New York: St. Martin's, 1970).

74. This investigation is discussed in greater detail in Howard Ball and Phillip J. Cooper, *Of Power and Right* (New York: Oxford University Press, 1992), 58–59.

75. Id., at 59–60.

76. See Nagle, supra note 16, at 312–333.

77. Proclamation of May 27, 1941, 55 Stat. 1647.

78. William L. Shirer, *Berlin Diary* (New York: Popular Library, 1941), 183.

79. Nagle, supra note 16, at 435.

80. *Procurement Commission,* 1:170–171.

81. 315 U.S. 289, 309 (1942).

82. 56 Stat. 245 (1942).

83. *Lichter v. United States,* 334 U.S. 742 (1948).

84. *Procurement Commission,* 1:171.

85. vom Bauer, supra note 62, at 324.

86. *Penker Construction Company v. United States,* 96 Ct. Cl. 1 (1942).

87. vom Bauer, supra note 62, at 321–322.

88. Nagle, supra note 16, at 442.

89. David McCullough, *Truman* (New York: Simon and Schuster, 1992), 469.

90. 5 U.S.C. §551 et seq.

91. 62 Stat. 21, 10 U.S.C. §2303 et seq.

92. vom Bauer, supra note 62, at 328–332.

93. 63 Stat. 393.

94. 5 U.S.C. §553(a)(2).

95. Deil S. Wright, *Understanding Intergovernmental Relations,* 3d ed. (Pacific Grove, Calif.: Brooks/Cole, 1988).

96. Chester J. Pach Jr. and Elmo Richardson, *The Presidency of Dwight D. Eisenhower* (Lawrence: University Press of Kansas, 1991), 76–77.

97. See, for example, Don K. Price, *The Scientific Estate* (Cambridge: Belknap Press, Harvard University Press, 1965); Vannevar Bush, *Science—The Endless Frontier* (Washington, D.C.: Government Printing Office, 1945); Daniel S. Greenberg, *The Politics of Pure Science* (New York: American Library, 1967).

98. Nagle, supra note 16, at 472.

99. A. Ernest Fitzgerald, *The High Priests of Waste* (New York: Norton, 1972).

100. 76 Stat. 528, 10 U.S.C. §2306(f).

101. Chet Holifield, "Federal Procurement and Contracting Reform," 41 *Brooklyn Law Review* 479, 489–491 (1975).

102. *Procurement Commission,* supra note 4.

103. Holifield, supra note 101, at 492.

104. P.L. 93-400, 88 Stat. 796, 41 U.S.C. §401 et seq.

105. P.L. 100-679.

106. John W. Whelan, "Reflections on Government Contracts and Government Policy on the Occasion of the Twenty Fifth Anniversary of the Public Contract Law Section," 20 *Public Contract Law Journal* 6 (1990).

107. Department of Defense, *Streamlining Defense Acquisition Laws: Report of the Law Advisory Panel to the United States Congress* (Washington, D.C.: Department of Defense, 1993), 1–6.

108. Kelman, supra note 64.

109. P.L. 103-355, 108 Stat. 3243 (1994).

110. P.L. 104-106, 110 Stat. 186 (1996).

111. P.L. 104-208, 110 Stat. 3009 (1996).

112. See, for example, Executive Order 12931, 59 FR 52387 (1994).

113. U.S. General Accounting Office, *Small Business: Trends in Federal Procurement in the 1990s* (Washington, D.C.: GAO, 2001), 10.

114. U.S. General Accounting Office, *Contract Management: Trends and Challenges in Acquiring Services* (Washington, D.C.: GAO, 2001), 2.

115. David Osborne and Ted Gaebler, *Reinventing Government* (New York: Penguin, 1993).

116. *White v. Massachusetts Council of Construction Workers,* 460 U.S. 204 (1983); *Reeves v. Stake,* 447 U.S. 429 (1980).

117. *South Central Timber Development v. Wunnicke,* 467 U.S. 82 (1984); *United Building Trades Council v. Camden,* 465 U.S. 208 (1984).

118. *Crosby v. National Foreign Trade Council,* 530 U.S. 363 (2000).

119. *Ancient Law* (London: Dent, 1972).

120. Ruth Hoogland DeHoog, *Contracting Out for Human Services* (Albany: State University of New York Press, 1984), chap. 5.

Integration: Forming the Relationship and Setting the Rules

The first portion of the public contract model is the integration stage, which includes the processes and challenges involved in forming the contract relationship and setting the rules by which that relationship will operate. The fact that we begin by referring to a relationship rather than a purchase matters. It is important to begin the discussion of the integration process with an exploration of how we have moved from perceptions of contracting based in models of purchasing to those grounded in public/private partnerships to the recognition that many of the most important relationships are more like alliances between government and the for-profits and nonprofits. This is increasingly true in a context in which government no longer possesses the ability to deliver the services directly. In such a setting, it is necessary to understand the interdependencies created when a relationship is formed. The chapter then turns to the important realities that the beginning of contracting is not advertising for bids and that the process of forming the relationship is multifaceted. It then moves to the discussion of whether and when to contract and the constraints that shape the process from the outset, such as national or state goals clauses. From there we go on to more specifics about the initial steps in the contract process leading to the selection of a contractor.

FROM PURCHASING TO PARTNERSHIPS TO ALLIANCES

When an individual goes to a store and makes a one-time purchase, it is a simple act that ends when the customer leaves with the merchandise and the store deposits the money. But when an organization buys a large quantity of items, a relationship may be formed in which there are negotiations about the terms of sale, efforts to judge the reliability of the supplier in regard to its record of performance, and resources invested to ensure the financial soundness of a supplier. If one of those parties is the government, that relationship becomes more complex still because the public purchaser acts in the name of the people to advance policy decisions reached through a political process and must respond to mechanisms of accountability far more intricate than those faced by a private sector organization. And when government enters into a relationship not just for simple purchases of goods but to acquire services, where the expectation is for an ongoing partnership, then that relationship takes a quantum leap in complexity. That is particularly true if government no longer possesses the internal capacity to step in when there is a problem or if the number of ready suppliers in a given sector is limited. It is at this point that the many generally unseen but critically significant decisions about the management of public contracts become central to achievement of large public purposes. That challenge is even greater in a nation that has traditionally relied on government as a direct service provider and in which there has been a broad conception of the role of the public sector.

Purchases, Partnerships, or Alliances?

In the contemporary world of public management, the use of contracts to carry out governmental responsibilities is commonly referred to as a move to public/private partnerships. That pleasant-sounding phrase hides a host of complexities that quickly become apparent when public managers begin to implement policies that require them to work with and through for-profit or nonprofit organizations.

One of the greatest barriers to improving the administration of public programs in an era of extensive contracted operations is the failure to understand the nature of the relationships that emerge in that process. Is contracting about making purchases, forming partnerships, or building and maintaining alliances? What are the differences in these relationships and why do they matter?

Purchasing, Procurement, and Acquisitions

Of course, as explained in Chapter 2, there is nothing new about the government issuing a host of contracts to obtain what it needs. It is not surprising that the metaphor that most quickly comes to mind in such discussions is that of a consumer making a purchase in a store. Indeed, the language that has been used to describe government contracting and the officers responsible for its administration over the years has emphasized purchasing, procurement, or, more recently, acquisitions. Even today, commentaries on government contracting tend to compare the amounts of time and human resources required to make a purchase in the public sector with those required in the private sector, whether the subject is office supplies or computers.[1]

To be sure, governments do purchase a wide range of goods and commodities that are the same type as those bought regularly by virtually any business. It is therefore no surprise to find that such initiatives to improve acquisitions practices as simplified credit card–type procedures for small and routine purchases, innovations led by Australia and Canada, have been widely praised and copied as ways to make government purchases more businesslike.[2] Still, dramatic negative publicity attracted by scandals in the purchasing of goods has motivated many governments to spend considerable time and effort contemplating the purchase of almost any big-ticket item.

From Purchases to Partnerships

For many years now, government contracting has been about far more than just the purchasing of goods. As explained in Chapter 2, in the second half of the twentieth century, governments expended significant amounts of money in research and development (R and D) contracts. Many large private firms were developed and grew largely on the basis of government R and D support. The importance of R and D dollars poured into military aviation over the years and then into companies that used the technology and manufacturing techniques developed under defense-related contracts to produce commercial aircraft was discussed in Chapter 2. The development of those airlines was then, and continues to be, subsidized in many countries with postal contracts and other government service agreements. Universities around the globe have increasingly come to rely on research grants and contracts from their home governments or international organizations to offset limited public appropriations and tuition income.

As the range of labor intensive social service programs increased, requiring larger and more sophisticated public workforces, personnel contracts in various forms grew in number and complexity. In more recent years, following the global trend toward privatization, the number of service contracts given to NGOs has grown dramatically in many sectors, from health care to education.[3] In the same period, calls for greater decentralization have led to creative interjurisdictional agreements (also sometimes known as interagency agreements) among local governments that range from joint projects for the construction and management of youth soccer fields to agreements about control of water use and solid waste disposal. Demands to take more comprehensive approaches to policy solutions for problems on the public agenda at the national level have led to increased use of interagency agreements, a practice that is sometimes referred to as government by memorandum of understanding.

More recently, contracting has involved activities that were traditionally regarded as "work of an inherently Governmental nature, such as negotiating leases, writing statements of work, and managing contracts with other contractors."[4] These are not mere consulting contracts but long-term operating agreements. One of the more controversial examples has been the commercial operation of prisons.[5] In addition, contractors have been brought in to pre-draft regulations and facilitate negotiated rulemaking proceedings, to facilitate dispute resolution procedures, and even to adjudicate some types of social service claims.[6]

In the international arena, donor organizations like the World Bank and the International Monetary Fund have consistently encouraged not merely contracting for services but a wide range of what are commonly called public/private partnerships. Even the international agreements for human-centered sustainable development—from Agenda 21 through the Copenhagen Social Summit Commitments and Programme of Action to the Habitat II Agenda—commit the signatory states to partnerships as a mode of action, a recognition that government could not implement programs needed for sustainable development without such partnerships. Thus, the Istanbul Declaration from the 1996 Habitat II conference asserts:

> We adopt the enabling strategy and the principles of partnership and participation as the most democratic and effective approach for the realization of our commitments.
>
> The sooner communities, local governments, partnerships among the public, and private and community sectors join efforts to create comprehensive, bold and innovative strategies for shelter and human settlements, the better the prospects will be for the safety, health and well-being of people and the brighter the outlook for solutions to global environment and social problems. . . .
>
> Enabling structures that facilitate independent initiative and creativity, and that encourage a wide range of partnerships, including partnership with the private sector, and within and between countries, should be promoted.[7]

Clearly, the use of the term "partnership" here is intended to mean more than just cooperation. Even so, relatively little consideration has been given to precisely what is needed to accept the challenge to govern through partnerships, perhaps because the discussion has been dominated by advocates who have little interest in considering the possible difficulties that can result during implementation. This is not to suggest that it is a bad idea to build more and stronger partnerships, only a recognition that public managers cannot afford the luxury of the politicians' simplistic rhetoric. We must come to understand these relationships better and build the capacity to manage them effectively.

If we take the partnership concept seriously, we find that partnerships in the private sector are used, but they are not always the most attractive form of enterprise. If they work well, they suggest a joining of resources for a common endeavor based on mutual commitment and mutual risk. However, not all business relationships are true partnerships, and relatively few of what are called public/private partnerships involve equivalent levels of either commitment or risk.[8] Moreover, the state is not the same kind of partner as the normal entrepreneur. That is even more the case when contractors are performing functions that are traditionally governmental and not generally found in the private sector.

Further, no partnership is any stronger than its weakest member; thus, governments must take great care in deciding with whom to form partnerships. This is one reason that many private sector entrepreneurs in the traditional business community prefer other forms of business relationships to partnerships.

Besides, operating dozens or even hundreds of public/private limited partnerships amid market failures—for example, the presence of conglomerates, mobile capital markets, and resource mismatches—is a difficult challenge. The fact that such partnerships tend to be ad hoc renders the task of coordination more daunting.[9] The management of numerous and often quite different partnerships is no less complex than the operation of large public institutions.

The common myth that contractually arranged partnerships are based in the "hidden hand" dynamics of the marketplace, which will provide the directing force needed to maintain those relationships, as opposed to more traditional, hands-on management, is both misleading and a dangerous oversimplification. Political rhetoric is no substitute for sound management in contemplating governance through partnerships.

Two other concerns are worthy of note with respect to partnerships. First, there is complexity and risk in assuming partnerships to be a set of standardized practices in a multicultural world. Working relationships, both personal and institutional, are particularly subject to cultural variations.[10] Culture, in this sense, refers to standard anthropological notions of national, regional, and local social, political, and economic patterns that are maintained through received traditions. However, it also relates to organizational culture.[11] Thus, it is one thing for two private firms that provide business training to form a working partnership in that field. It is quite another for those same firms to form a contractual partnership with a department of labor or commerce or with local schools to operate job-training programs in the public school facilities during or after normal school hours. Each of these partners brings a different set of values and perspectives to the common enterprise that will affect all aspects of the program's management as well as critical issues of transparency and accountability. That is not to argue that such arrangements are bad or unproductive, but merely that it is not enough simply to label such an arrangement a public/private partnership without a careful understanding of what such a partnership entails at the very fundamental level of culture, in both the anthropological and organizational senses.

Second, partnerships can be a kind of no-man's-land, a realm between political power and economic markets in which neither set of rules applies precisely or consistently. The important differences among legal, political, and market accountability will be addressed in depth later. For the present discussion about entering into new contractual relationships, it becomes extremely important to know what the basis for and guiding values of any particular partnership will be.

From Partnerships to Alliances

In short, conceptualizing government by contract in terms of public/private partnerships is a complex enterprise and one fraught with a range of significant risks. And if individual partnerships are intricate arrangements to create and manage, these complexities only multiply when governance is based on a large number of such partnerships.

One of the reasons why the calls for public/private partnerships have grown relates to the effort to reduce the size and cost of government and, for some, to reduce the number of fields in which government is directly involved. Indeed, the most commonly employed measures of success in these endeavors have been reductions in costs and numbers of government employees. Some have argued that it is perfectly appropriate to hollow out government and transform its role into that of a broker that gets resources to those organizations that can deliver goods and services efficiently and effectively without maintaining that capacity within government itself.[12] Whether one agrees or disagrees with these assumptions, motives, or measures of success, the result is clear. At some point, government becomes dependent on contractors for operational support and service delivery. If agencies or cities divest themselves of the capacity to step in to perform services themselves, and particularly if the activity is in a sector or a location in which alternative contract partners are not readily available, the dependence can become so significant that it is really not appropriate to think of the relationship as just a partnership.

When that point of dependency is reached, the relationship between government and its for-profit or nonprofit service providers becomes more like a set of alliances in which government needs its contractors as much as they need the state. In certain fields that has been true for some time. Indeed, that is why contracts often appear to be more like treaties than purchasing agreements. In such situations, the process has moved a long way from the notion of purchases. In these alliances, the expectation is developed early on that the contract is the beginning of a long-term working relationship. Often, there is no expectation that the contract will terminate, since partnerships are not purchasing arrangements but long-term enterprises. Thus, consider the experience of one federal cabinet department.

> DOE [the Department of Energy] continues to award most of its contracts noncompetitively. Of the 24 decisions made from July 5, 1994, to the end of August 1996, DOE decided to extend 16 contracts on a noncompetitive basis and to competitively award the other eight. DOE has had long-term relation-

ships with many of the contractors whose contracts it decided not to compete. The average age of the 16 contracts was about 35 years, and 12 of them had never been competitively awarded.[13]

Indeed, if it appears likely that a contract will end, that possibility is often understood to be a threat or an indication of failure rather than an expected conclusion to a contract. That is particularly true where, as is often the case, there comes to be a strong political interest in maintaining partnerships. "Contracts and subcontracts combine the interests of regional economies, unions, industry and legislators with those of the program. The award of contracts makes for political support through economic dependency."[14]

Contract Partners and Their Diverse Perspectives

For all the reasons mentioned above, it is important to understand something about the kinds of contractors with which public managers work. Each comes to the relationship with its own set of issues that will help to shape the nature of the working relationship and its ultimate success. Where service contracts are involved, the public administrator can expect to develop relationships with for-profit firms, nonprofit organizations, and other government units.

For-Profit Firms. Although discussions of public contracting often focus on the largest corporations, there are in truth many sizes and types of for-profits firms that do business with the government. Many contracts go to local law firms, tradespeople, and transportation companies. Something that often surprises a newcomer to a particular state or community is that there may be only a handful of, perhaps only one or two, companies able to bid on, for example, significant road or bridge construction.

Whatever the type of firm, it is important to be alert to the reality within which the contractor operates. For one thing, the goal of such organizations is, by definition, to produce a profit, which makes it fundamentally different from the public agencies with which they are contracting. Firms are responsible not to the taxpayer but to their stockholders, if they are publicly traded businesses. They do not survive by focusing on the public interest; and survival is a critically important fact of life for many firms. Market analysts expect managers to ensure as great a return on investment as possible each quarter. That means that businesses must sometimes behave in the short term in ways that may or may not be in their long-term best interest. It also means that business executives are often focused far more in the short term than in the kind of strategic thinking that business schools advocate. That is a reality despite the amount of discussion in private sector management about business strategy and strategic planning. Failing to keep those realities in mind can mean that a firm will become a target for a takeover. Such forces as globalization and deregulation have meant a dramatic rise during the past two decades in mergers and acquisitions. Smaller businesses, in turn, must be concerned about meeting the needs of their employees and remaining viable as larger corporations use their size to drive the smaller firms out of the marketplace.

That is not to say that these forces or tendencies are positive, but they are facts of life. Many of those who pressed their retirement planners to put them in rapid growth stocks in the 1990s found that the accounts went down just as fast when the economy stalled. By the middle of 2001, for example, the previous high-flying dot-com companies were failing at a rate of sixty businesses per month.

These market pressures have often meant fewer large firms in various sectors, leaving governments with fewer potential vendors for the services they require. Thus, the firm mentioned in Chapter 1 that ran into trouble in its contract with Texas on the welfare assistance cards left the business and was replaced by a large firm that operates similar programs in some two dozen states.

Business executives bring these factors with them to the table. Wise public managers pay attention to the trends in the marketplace and the forces driving them. For one thing, governments in a particular location are likely to be working with the same firms in one way or another over time. Clashes between firms and governments can lead to contract failures that can rapidly become very intense and politically charged. Controversies associated with a failure to consider these realities also mean that working relationships in the future may be difficult, if not impossible.

In the end, the realities of modern business affect the behavior of a firm's representatives at the negotiating table. As Lloyd Burton points out, the very real and important differences in the values, priorities, and responsibilities between private sector negotiators and public administrators mean there are different negotiating cultures operating on the two sides of the table.[15]

Sometimes, these differences are so great that they produce what Burton calls "ethical discontinuities" that can interfere with communication, negotiation, and, ultimately, resolution of important issues. Consider the example of the community that finds a significant environment pollution problem that must be cleaned up. Suppose the major potentially responsible party comes to the table to discuss the cleanup with the city manager, who is working in cooperation with the state environmental agency. The company might say to the community that the firm wants to keep its business there, seeks to be a good corporate citizen, wants the problem to be fixed, and does not want to spend years in court fighting about how much it should have to pay. At the same time, the firm clearly does not agree with the estimated cost of remediation or the amount it has been asked to pay. The firm's representative says that he is prepared to cut a check immediately for 80 percent of the cost presently estimated by the government for the cleanup. That, he says, is far more than the company is convinced its liability should be, but this is an opportunity for everyone to come out better in the long run than they would if the matter were to be thrown into litigation for years. Besides, energy can then be devoted to accomplishing the cleanup rather than fighting about it. And, the company says, that resolution will allow it to stay in town.

The city manager looks at her team's faces and responds that she appreciates the offer, but she doubts the government could settle for that amount. The business representative replies that he understands the hesitancy, but the city and state must realize that the firm has to make a decision now about whether it can resolve the matter quickly or simply accept that the situation will go to litigation and get on with other business. In an effort to avoid that situation, the firm will offer an immediate 85 percent cash settlement as its best and final offer. At this point, the manager recognizes that by most reasonable assessments, this represents a realistic and positive opportunity even if it is not the optimal solution. She might agree, only to find that the newspaper headlines the next day read, "A City Manager Sells Out Community Environment!" On top of that, the state environmental agency might then block the agreement. Thus, it is important to understand the kinds of constraints posed by the bargaining culture each side brings to the table.

In some instances the issue is neither quite so dramatic nor focused on ethical issues as such but on differences in the basic responsibilities of public and private organizations. Consider the following real-life situation examined by Craig E. Richards, Rima Shore, and Max B. Sawicky.[16] A firm went to a troubled school district offering a contract to take over the management of the district's schools. For the same amount of money that the district was then spending, the firm promised to improve significantly—even dramatically—the quality of the school environment and student performance. This sounds like a deal too good to be true. The important question is how would a firm make money on such a deal, since, after all, it is a for-profit firm, especially in light of the promise by the firm to invest a significant amount of its own capital in improving the physical conditions of the schools and on high-technology teaching tools, including computers. Certainly, the firm promised that it would be able to accomplish these dramatic improvements through efficiencies resulting from better management. Every good manager, to be sure, seeks to "do more with less" as the saying goes, precisely in this way. Any experienced manager, however, also knows that the savings produced by more efficient operations would not be enough to make a significant profit for the firm and accomplish all the substantive improvements the firm was promising.

In reality there were five aspects to what the firm had in mind in addition to the catchall claim of better management. First, the argument was that the private firm would have less overhead associated with the red tape that public sector organizations must address. Put slightly differently, the argument is that private firms are less bureaucratic and more results oriented. Second, the firm wanted to be able to promote its success in this district in its efforts to build business with future prospects. Third, its success in winning the contract would rapidly increase its market value and attract capital. Fourth, the firm wanted the per-student funds from the state and district up front so that it could manage these funds as operating capital, freeing up some of its own resources. Finally, and very much at the heart of the profitability of the contract, it would cut personnel costs through increased use of technology. The firm's efforts were largely built around a set of computer-based learning tools that it claimed would enhance individualized instruction and reduce the standard teaching costs at the same time.

As it turned out, the costs of bringing the school facilities up to the promised level and installing the technology were substantial. The question of reducing bureaucracy, which sounds so attractive, ultimately came down to the question of how accountability was to be maintained, since, after all, one person's red tape is another's accountability. Later, there were significant debates about how the firm wanted to measure student accomplishment, how costs were being addressed, and how public money was being managed.[17] Questions were also raised about how the firm was using its present contract to represent itself to the financial markets and potential future customers.

Then there was the question of personnel. Whatever else is promised, the most common way in which for-profit firms seek to make money on government contracts for the same amount of money government is spending now to do the job itself is to reduce personnel costs. That goal is accomplished in two ways. First, the private firm expects to increase productivity. Second, firms find savings simply by hiring people for lower pay or reduced fringe benefits. In the end, the object is often to reduce the number of people and to replace some of them with technology. For instance, in the school case, the expectation was that some of the local people hired part time as instructional assistants could be eliminated along with teacher's aides because the teachers would do less standard teaching and could provide the one-on-one assistance themselves. In truth, the community had a very positive feeling about having local residents working in the schools, and eliminating those jobs could mean reducing the sense of ownership by the community. Not only that, but when reducing personnel costs means reducing jobs, that can increase the demand for government services for the unemployed. In the contemporary environment, it also means that some of the money that would be paid to local employees who would spend it in the local economy with the attendant rollover effects would now go to corporate headquarters to be invested elsewhere. These were only some of the issues. The moral of the story is that how government contractors expect to operate, how they expect to make money, and what they intend to do with the money matters in the public context in ways that would not be considered anyone else's business in the private sector.

Although these differences cannot be eliminated, awareness of these factors can help to reduce misunderstandings and produce a better working relationship. In particular, Lloyd Burton suggests that public managers should come to the table with a concern for the identity of the parties to the relationship and an awareness of everyone's negotiating goals. He distinguishes between the substantive resolution, which is the basic bottom line that each side hopes for in the relationship, and negotiation goals, which are the several other objectives that people bring to the table. These goals include personal and institutional reputation, precedent, future working relationships with the parties, transaction and opportunity costs, and self-regard.[18] To deal with potential tensions in the relationship, including possible ethical problems, Burton advocates defining early on in the process the rules of fair dealing for those who will represent the government in the relationship; avoiding professional mismatches in interactions, such as situations in which lawyers are asked to negotiate with engineers; providing early training for contract managers; and giving consideration to alternatives in the event that the working relationship becomes unacceptably difficult.[19] Burton focused his concerns and recommendations primarily on the ethical dimension, but they are useful advice for any public manager who is forming a working relationship with a for-profit firm. In any case, it is important when entering the marketplace to buy, or for that matter to sell or trade, services to be alert to the dynamics of that marketplace and its trends.

Nonprofit Organizations. In some respects contractual dealings with non-profits are even more complex than with for-profit firms. These organizations, so essential to the delivery of services at all levels, are formed for different purposes by a broad array of people and institutions. Thus, they have widely varied organizational cultures and capabilities. However, like for-profit firms, NGOs have much in common.

First, it is difficult to overstate the importance of NGOs to service delivery, not only in the United States but in many other countries as well. Burton Weisbrod made the point that the trend toward increased reliance on nonprofits was well established by the 1990s.

> In health care, in 1990, 67 percent of all patient days of hospitalization in the United States were provided by nonprofit hospitals. In education, nonprofits enrolled 11 percent of all primary and secondary school students in the United States and 22 percent in the United Kingdom. In the child day-care industry, nonprofits cared for over 35 percent of the children in France, Germany, and Japan; 56 percent in the United States; and 82 percent in the United Kingdom. . . . In the service sector as a whole, where most nonprofits operate, they account for 9 to 10 percent of total employment in Japan, the United Kingdom, France, and Germany and more than 15 percent of total employment in the United States . . . in Israel nonprofit organizations employ over 13 percent of the entire Israeli labor force. . . .

> What is really dramatic is the rapid growth of the nonprofit sector. In the United States, the last 30 years have seen a tripling of the number of nonprofits, from 309,000 in 1967 to nearly 1 million today. Their total revenues,

less than 6 percent of GNP in 1975, exceeded 10 percent in 1990. In the decade from 1980 to 1990, nonprofits' paid employment grew by 41 percent in the United States and 36 percent in Germany—more than double the overall growth of national employment.[20]

In a more recent study focusing on the United States, Paul Light noted that "[f]rom 1972 to 1982, the sector grew roughly 200,000 jobs per year, increasing from 4.6 million full- and part-time jobs to 6.5 million. . . . But from 1982 to 1996, the sector jumped by almost 300,000 a year to 10.2 million, a net increase of almost 4 million jobs. . . ."[21] He added that by 1998, nonprofits were receiving record high revenues from various sources, reaching $625 billion.

These numbers provide some sense of how much we depend on NGOs for the services we need. However, perhaps as important, the result of reductions in government employees is insufficient internal capacity in most agencies at all levels to step in and substitute for contract providers in the event of a service breakdown. That means that the relative importance of NGOs has increased far beyond what the numbers might suggest.

Contracting with NGOs is attractive for many reasons. One is the nature of many nonprofits. They often began with a fervent commitment by a relatively cohesive group of people to solving a problem or providing assistance to people in need. The dedication and selflessness that characterize many of these groups mean that they will often push to get the maximum service for any support dollars they receive. Indeed, it is an unspoken fact of life that some of the institutions and agencies that provide grants and contracts to NGOs do so in order to leverage more action and impact than could be purchased outright from a private firm for the same amount of money.

Another important characteristic of NGOs is that they are often effective players in policy communities at the state and federal level. They can and do press their elected officials for continuation and enhancement of program funds. They are also often effective at heading off policy changes that they perceive might limit flexibility. On the one hand, such political behavior can take NGOs close to the edge, since most are tax-exempt organizations under section 501(c)(3) of the IRS code and therefore not supposed to be engaged in traditional lobbying activities. On the other hand, policymakers often appreciate the expertise, experience, and service to constituents that these groups provide and at least tacitly approve their involvement in the policy process with a wink at the tax-exempt restrictions.

Part of the generally positive attitude toward nonprofits comes from the fact that they are nonprofits, from their generally beneficent character, and from the fact that they often provide volunteers in support of public causes. Weisbrod noted that "[i]n the United States, the 89 million volunteers in 1993 donated the equivalent of 11 million full-time workers' time—more than 9 percent of the entire paid labor force. In Israel, the amount of labor volunteered to nonprofits is less dramatic, but still sizable; in 1991 it was the full-time equivalent of 7 percent of the paid labor in the nonprofit sector but only 1 percent of the entire Israeli labor force."[22]

In part because they involve so many people through volunteerism and reach so many people in the community through their service, NGOs provide useful vehicles for information and feedback on public programs. Since they are perceived as giving organizations, they may also receive information that would not be readily provided to a for-profit firm or government agency.

Finally, these organizations range from formal, highly professional operations to small groups with cultures that stress informality and flexibility above professional managerial values. The federal government recognizes differences between the circumstances and capabilities of nonprofits and those of for-profit firms.[23]

The same qualities that make these groups popular contract partners, however, can present special difficulties. Although NGOs can be effective allies, they are often single-interest advocates. Public managers, by contrast, must be concerned about many issues and constituencies. The same political abilities that allow NGOs to be supportive also allow them to resist change and to fend off accountability efforts.

Another accountability challenge can come from the very informality and flexibility that many like in NGOs. Thus, it is common to find smaller nonprofits that use part-time bookkeepers, do not have the regular services of a certified public accountant, and may never have developed a fully audited financial statement. They often operate in fields that involve many legal complexities and yet the organizations may have little or no professional legal assistance. They may not have carefully developed personnel policies. Because the NGOs are so committed to the people they serve, they may have leveraged themselves far beyond a reasonable level such that they are seriously undercapitalized.

The managers of nonprofits may or may not have training in administration and may not enjoy managing an organization. The special nonprofit challenges involved with managing volunteers, fund-raising, and working with boards of directors call for more and better management rather than less. However, the kinds of people who are prime movers in NGOs are often committed and creative program people rather than managers. They may be effective because of particular personality characteristics. Unfortunately, that kind of leadership may mean that little attention is given to management issues and that the organization becomes heavily, if not predominantly, identified with the personality of the executive director.

Many of these difficulties result not from any intentions on the part of those involved but from the way in which some nonprofits evolve and the ways in which governments work with them. Nonprofit service organizations begin in many ways and each is as unique as the people, problems, and communities that spawned them. However, NGOs do have some common characteristics to which contract managers in any agency or community may want to pay attention.

Groups are formed by citizens in response to a community problem, by existing church or civic organizations to meet special needs, by advocates seeking to support a particular group of people, or by people wishing to create local units of national service organizations. These new groups may grow or languish. Their boards of directors may be small, their staff may be limited, and their director may even be a volunteer. In many instances, leadership changes bring to the fore someone with a strong commitment to the organization's mission who has a drive to build the group. That person injects new energy into the group and others respond to that leadership. The group begins to grow and seeks new resources to support its activities. If its program efforts are successful, it may very well attract grants, donations, and contracts.

Often these grants or contracts will add sufficient administrative obligations that the group faces a need to expand or in some cases even to acquire a paid administrative staff. This is an appealing step, since the group may feel the need to have more in-house capacity to serve its constituents and support its executive director and board. Unfortunately, the grants or contracts usually do not pay the full cost of these additions. Indeed, it is not uncommon for groups to take on contractual obligations that actually cost more in real terms and over the life of the project than they actually provide in revenue. Still, the contracts do provide cash flow, and some executive directors see this as an essential step toward acquiring more resources.

Of course, new staff also means new and continuing obligations. Thus, there is more pressure for more resources. Sometimes these pressures can come from philanthropic grants. Institutions or firms making substantial grants to NGOs may condition the money on the nonprofit's ability to demonstrate that it has the management infrastructure to manage properly and provide accountability for the funds. This can mean still further expansion on staff and even the need to hire management consultants to assist in building the systems needed.

The more the NGO feels the need to compete for dollars and the more pressure on it to expand resources, the more executive directors find themselves boundary spanning and, particularly, operating in the political arena.[24] The original volunteers and board members who had a very different view of the organization can begin to feel that the executive director is building an empire rather than paying attention to the core mission of the group and its people. This creates a tension that is exacerbated when the executive director hires others to do the internal management and gives the impression that he or she is interested only in making new deals and not in tackling the challenges such deals can produce. The director can feel torn between the need to manage and the desire and felt need to operate outside the organization. The departure of the executive director can be a critical point for the organization, and the process of replacing the director can be traumatic.

If the group acquires a large contract, it may have to staff up rapidly, including both service delivery personnel and managers. It may also have to open additional offices and replace face-to-face interaction with electronic communications. Such changes can increase internal stress, particularly if the existing staff begins to feel that the new people are "taking over" or changing the organization in dramatic ways.[25]

Externally, nonprofits are increasingly in competition with one another and with for-profit firms.[26] As competition increases, and especially during periods of declining resources, the groups can come to behave more like feuding barons, and the effort to support cooperation can be a challenge. Government agencies may come to have significant expectations of the relationship that they have with the nonprofits they deal with on a regular basis even beyond the formal terms of the contract. There can be mismatches between sets of expectations and, hence, tensions between the agencies and the groups.

Nothing that has been said to this point is meant to be a criticism of nonprofits as contract partners. They are absolutely indispensable players in the service delivery system. Rather, this discussion is meant to indicate that nonprofits are different from for-profit firms. Developing and managing contractual relationships with them requires an awareness of their special strengths and challenges. For example, an agency may wish to look carefully at the group's infrastructure if a program is of significant size. The contract agency may still find the group has unique capabilities appropriate to the contract but may want to shape the relationship with requirements for ensuring sufficient management capacity as well as providing supports to build that capacity if necessary. Also, if entering into a contract means a significant need to expand the organization's operations, it may be useful to phase in the contract to avoid adding undue pressures in addition to avoiding breakdowns in service delivery. In the end, just as with for-profit firms, it is essential to understand the primary goals and character of nonprofits when entering into a relationship with them.

Other Government Units. It has become increasingly common over time for governments to be sellers as well as purchasers and for them to enter into agreements with other governments in addition to contracting with nonprofits and for-profit firms. Although much of this book is about the special challenges faced by governments in contracting with those outside, there are issues worthy of note with respect to government-to-government agreements.

First, treaties entered into by the federal government supersede state or local policies. Treaties are agreements in the nature of contracts—intergovernmental agreements at the international level. Under the Constitution's supremacy clause discussed in Chapter 2, they apply notwithstanding anything in the constitution or laws of the states, and state courts are bound to respect them.

When, as is increasingly the case, state or local governments enter the market-place as purchasers or sellers of goods or services in the international arena, their actions are preempted not only by formal treaties but also by the general foreign affairs powers of the federal government. Even actions that the state might consider domestic, such as refusing to do business with certain firms or placing local regulations on shipping in local waters, are under the control of Washington, D.C., and may be contested by other countries. Thus, Washington State's efforts to enhance safety regulations for oil tankers in the Puget Sound and Massachusetts' restrictions on trading with firms doing business with Myanmar (Burma) were met with opposition from oil-producing nations and the European Union in addition to the U.S. federal government. Both state efforts were struck down.[27] In some cases, as in situations in which other countries object to state or local contracting restrictions before the World Trade Organization (WTO) panels, it is the government of the United States and not the states that decides on whether and how to mount a defense.

Traditionally, government-to-government agreements in this country are thought of as interstate compacts or interjurisdictional agreements. As explained in Chapter 2, interstate compacts require congressional approval under the Constitution. In some instances, only a limited number of states are involved, as in the case of the Tahoe regional planning agreement between California and Nevada (controlling development in the Lake Tahoe basin) or the now-defunct New England Dairy Compact (created to maintain floors under dairy product prices). In other cases, many parties are included, such as the compact on sales taxes for mail-order commerce. This agreement was reached after the U.S. Supreme Court struck down efforts by states to tax mail-order businesses in their states if the mail-order firms did not actually have people or a facility in that state.[28]

Congressional approval for such agreements is required by the Constitution for basically two reasons. The first is that there was a desire to prevent efforts by some states to join together in ways that created conflict with other states. Disagreements about the validity of a compact can be addressed in Congress rather than in legal actions between states. The second reason is that once the compact is approved, the states are bound by it, and the governing body of the compact comes to have significant legislative and administrative authority.[29]

Of course, local governments are creatures of the state,[30] and the degree of latitude that they enjoy to enter into agreements with each other is controlled by the law and politics of that state. That said, there are many reasons that local governments have chosen to enter into such agreements and that states—at least tacitly, if not actively—support them. These agreements are clearly appropriate to deal with interjurisdictional problems, such as metropolitan public transit needs. Another example comes from Flagstaff, Arizona, where the city entered into an agreement with the U.S. Army Corps of Engineers, the U.S. Forest Service, the National Park Service, the state Game and Fish Department, the state Lands Department, and the county to develop and execute its community development plans. The cooperation was necessary because the plan involved flood plain issues, parks, trails, and other elements that fell under the purview of one or more of these agencies.

Another driving factor is simple cost reduction, such as in agreements for unified 911 call centers and emergency services dispatch rather than multiple communications centers in several communities in the same general area. Other examples include the purchase by one jurisdiction of police, fire, or ambulance services from another community or agreements among neighboring communities for the operation of youth programs or more generally for the use of parks and recreation facilities and programs. These relationships are often designed to save both operating budgets and capital funds. Thus, some cities have eliminated their water departments and contracted with the water district to provide not only water but also construction and maintenance, saving the community the significant capital expenses involved in purchasing and maintaining heavy equipment used only infrequently and also permitting better utilization of public works employees.

Yet a third reason involves that dreaded term in contemporary parlance, the achievement of synergies. Some agreements permit communities to do together what no one of them could do alone. Two brief examples make the point. The Chittenden Unit for Special Investigations was established to allow several Vermont communities with small police departments to create a special unit for the investigation of sex crimes, including child sexual abuse. The member communities contribute either cash or officers or both. Only the largest city in the agreement could possibly have supported a specialized unit, but together they have developed a unit that has generally received positive community support.

A very different example is provided by the city of Yankton, South Dakota, and the Yankton School District. The school district needed significant new school construction that it could not afford, at least with the right kinds of facilities and amenities. The community required a multipurpose community center with facilities for physical fitness programs, library, and fine arts activities. The school district and the community discovered that state law permitted them to enter into an agreement and fund such a project. Each achieved its goals and in the process built an effective working relationship for the physical operation and maintenance of an excellent new facility as well as for the recreational and arts programming in that facility.[31] Such agreements are increasingly common.

A fairly prosaic but nevertheless effective example of synergistic effects from intergovernmental cooperation is what is sometimes called cooperative purchasing. At the national level, the idea behind having a federal supply schedule goes back to the historical discussion in Chapter 2 about achieving economies of scale and volume discounts by unified contracting government-wide. In other situations, two or more agencies might cooperate for items or services that were of common concern but not broadly enough used to warrant centralized acquisition. In 1994, as a result of the National Performance Review analysis of contracting, Congress adopted provisions in the Acquisition Streamlining Act that allowed state, local, the Commonwealth of Puerto Rico, and Indian tribal governments to buy through the federal supply schedule to obtain some of the advantages of scale. The GAO found that, given special requirements in particular states' contracting laws, the usefulness of this type of cooperative contracting varied across the country.[32] Still, cooperative purchasing is commonly used at the state or local levels. A simple but common case in point is cooperative purchasing of road chemicals and materials for winter plowing.

There is no uniform format for interjurisdictional agreements in many areas, although some states do have templates. The general tendency is to want to keep them as clean and uncomplicated as possible. Even so, it is important to consider the needs, capabilities, and political posture of the other participants when entering into such agreements. Although they may be challenging to create, they can be even more challenging to terminate later. For obvious reasons, government units are contract participants different from either for-profit firms or nonprofits.

FORMING THE RELATIONSHIP: THE DECISION TO CONTRACT

The process of forming a contractual working relationship begins when a decision is made to meet a need through a means other than direct government service. The decision to contract, particularly in large-scale policy decisions, is often made by elected officials rather than professional public managers. However, professionals are often asked to advise governing bodies on the question and in other circumstances have the authority to choose contracting as a mode of service delivery themselves. So it is useful to consider a few basic guidelines about whether and when to contract.

First, it is important to recall the earlier discussion of the difference between contracting out and privatization. Real privatization involves taking the government completely out of a particular area of service delivery, whereas contracting continues the government's responsibility for a service but uses another organization to perform the service delivery. Despite a great deal of rhetoric to the contrary, there has been relatively little true privatization of what had been government functions in most jurisdictions. Recent examples of the real thing include the sales during the 1990s of community hospitals and clinics to for-profit firms and the sale of utilities owned by local governments. One reason there has not been more divestiture is that many government functions are mandated by statutes or federal or state regulations, or are a condition of the receipt of federal grants. In the end, true privatization decisions are political decisions made by elected officials.

Second, apart from actual privatization, there are some settings in which it is not appropriate to contract out. In the 1960s the Bell Report provided some guiding questions with a particular focus on federal contracts.

> Will increased reliance on third parties pose the danger of contracting for those crucial powers to manage and control government activities which must be retained in the hands of public officials directly answerable to the president and Congress?
>
> Which kinds of non-Federal institutions are best suited for which purposes?
>
> How can contractors' private interest be prevented from conflicting with public purposes?
>
> If more government work is given to the non-federal workforce, and restrictions on civil service employment such as pay caps are retained, will the government retain the official talent needed to make "policy decisions concerning the types of work to be undertaken . . . to supervise the execution of the work . . . and to evaluate the results"? [33]

There is also federal government policy indicating that inherently government functions should not be contracted out.[34] In fact, the Office of Management and Budget Circular A-76, which in most instances encourages contracting out, contains a list of traditional government functions. Of course in an era in which functions such as the operation of prisons and the management of government contracts have been contracted out, it is becoming increasingly unclear just where the line can be drawn as to what is an inherently governmental function such that the government could not hire a contractor to deliver a particular service. The irreducible minimum seems to involve what is known as the nondelegation doctrine. Although it is rarely invoked, the nondelegation doctrine holds that some kinds of authority cannot be delegated to others. Thus, during the 1930s the Supreme Court struck down provisions of the National Industrial Recovery Act that allowed private sector trade groups to establish codes of fair competition that had the force of law once signed by the president. This, the Court said, was delegation run riot, permitting unaccountable private individuals to make rules having the force of law.[35] Even so, the Environmental Protection Agency and other federal agencies contract with consulting firms to recommend standards and draft language for regulations. They also contract with facilitators to operate what are termed "negotiated rulemaking" proceedings that generate draft regulations.

Third, it is not appropriate to contract when what is really intended is the use of a grant rather than a contract. Grants often seem like contracts in the sense that they provide funds for which the recipient agrees to carry out certain kinds of research or service activity. To those receiving the grants, any differences between grants and contracts seem illusory. However, the Supreme Court has ruled that "[a]lthough we agree with the State that Title I grant agreements had a contractual aspect . . . , the program cannot be viewed in the same manner as a bilateral contract governing a discrete transaction. . . . Unlike normal contractual undertakings, federal grant programs originate in and remain governed by statutory provisions expressing the judgment of Congress concerning desirable public policy."[36] That is, the grant is an exercise of the government's taxing and spending power in the public interest that prescribes activities that will be supported and not a contractual meeting of the minds between two discrete parties to deliver services for a fee. Or as a federal district court put it: "While no one denies that grant programs have certain contractual aspects, they differ significantly from traditional contracts, and classic contractual analysis is typically not applied to the federal-state relationships arising under grant programs."[37]

In fact, the federal government has guidance governing grants and cooperative agreements different from the Federal Acquisition Regulations (FAR) and Office of Management and Budget Circulars that apply to contracts.[38] The OMB Circular A-102 provides that

> [a] grant or cooperative agreement shall be used only when the principal purpose of a transaction is to accomplish a public purpose of support or stimulation authorized by Federal statute. Contracts shall be used when the principal purpose is acquisition of property or services for the direct benefit or use of the Federal Government. The statutory criterion for choosing between grants and cooperative agreements is that for the latter, "substantial involvement is expected between the executive agency and the State, local government, or other recipient when carrying out the activity contemplated in the agreement."[39]

Of course, each federal agency issues regulations governing the operation of grant programs that it is charged by statute to administer. Another way to think of the difference is to view these tools operationally in terms of who is served and what level of supervision is provided. As one state government put it:

> Broadly speaking, grants are appropriate when an agency retains very little control over the grantee's performance. At the other extreme, close or frequent supervision indicates that employment (temporary or permanent) should be utilized, particularly if the worker is expected to work regular hours. Contracts are generally appropriate when the agency's supervisory control falls between these two extreme.

> A grant, not a contract, should be used when:

> 1. Appropriated funds are characterized in the law as "grants";

> 2. The principal purpose is to support or stimulate a quasi-public activity, the primary benefit of which is to a client or customer group rather than the agency itself or wards of state government; and

3. There will not be substantial state oversight of the funded activity, other than providing guidance upon request and accumulating information on the progress achieved and financial status at the close of the program or activity.[40]

State laws sometimes mandate that contract personnel should not be used to perform the same task as a regular civil servant.[41] Where what were civil service positions were converted to contract jobs, some states have found that the administrative burdens of contracts constituted a heavy cost just to allow politicians to claim that civil service jobs had been cut. There has been considerable public embarrassment in recent years when employers, public or private, tried to use personal services contracts instead of hiring people and thus avoid tax withholding and Social Security obligations. If the agency provides close and regular supervision over the person involved, if the service is a standard agency activity, and if the person is not normally involved as a contractor in the field in which he or she is working and available to other clients, the federal government may determine that the person is not a contractor but an employee.[42]

John Rehfuss points out that it is also a bad idea to contract out if the purpose is to disguise service cuts as cost savings.[43] The reason publicly given for contracting is almost always a promise to save money. However, if saving money is really done by purchasing a lower level of services, then the savings may often be illusory. In such circumstances, the costs of negative response to the decline in level of service and the public reaction once people sense they have been misled far outweigh the possible financial gains.

Difficulties also often arise where there is a limited market or essentially no market choice available. Competition is one, although not the only, force involved in contracting intended to achieve better service and lower prices. When competition is lacking, that force is missing. Under such circumstances governments may attempt to stimulate the market into providing some competition or even provide that competition itself, by having public agencies bid against the private contractor. That has been done in several cities (Phoenix, Arizona, was a pioneer in this regard) and is also done by the federal government.[44]

In some situations, the public manager has no choice but to contract in a weak market, as in road building and bridge repair. Communities may not be in a position to do the work themselves. Unfortunately, it is common that in any particular area only a handful of contractors do that kind of work. The public manager must be particularly alert in the absence of the kind of market competition that could provide help in obtaining top-quality services at appropriate prices.

The reasons that argue for contracting are relatively obvious. Two students of government contracting have provided sets of criteria. Ruth DeHoog, focusing on state governments, summarized the reasons provided by advocates for contracting but added others that came from respondents in her survey. Most advised that contracting is best used to obtain better service, to lower costs, or to obtain greater flexibility. She gives the following brief checklist.

- Where demonstration, experimental programs, services, or methods can be tried with no long-term commitment to continuing the programs;
- When there is a genuine common need and desire to cut costs and maintain good quality service;
- Where government does not have the requisite experience, equipment, or expertise to supply the service;
- When government needs certain services occasionally or seasonally;
- Where economies of scale can be realized;
- Where government officials can set priorities, service levels, and outcome goals, with the opportunity to reward and punish if these are not met by contractors;
- Where there is adequate competition in the environment to ensure government choice;
- Where fair competitive procedures can be adopted and enforced;
- Where politically motivated awards can be minimized; and
- Where government agencies have the resources and desire to implement effective oversight methods.[45]

However, DeHoog noted, contracting is appropriate for those purposes only if there is real competition in the market and in the way the government unit involved actually conducts its contracting. She added that, to be effective, it is also important for government decision making to be truly intended to attain the goals of cost reduction and service quality. That situation exists where there is a "common goal of cost minimization with adequate service provision"; where there is "sufficient information to consider the major alternatives and to judge accurately the anticipated performance and consequences of each alternative in terms of this goal"; and when the government involved has an "effective watchdog capability."[46] Too often, she found, the real reasons for contracting were political (in the traditional sense of that term) and did not focus on the critical issues.

Rehfuss, who focused on local governments, echoed most of DeHoog's findings but offered some of his own.[47] Like DeHoog, Rehfuss noted that the obvious reason for contracting is to reduce costs or to increase management or policy flexibility. At the same time, he cautioned that it is essential to ensure that the services and the contracts to provide them can be monitored.[48] He added that it is useful to contract when complex or highly technical work is required. On a related point, contracting can be useful if there is a need for one-time help in adapting to new technologies. Finally, Rehfuss added that there may very well be appropriate political reasons, that is to say, policy choices by the elected officials that move the community toward more or different contracting.

In some instances, he noted, contracting can be used to establish benchmark costs.[49] The community that does not consider what the marketplace might offer in costs and service levels may not have a clear sense whether it is paying the right amount for its services. Still, using this technique for establishing benchmarks may not be as simple as it appears.

"First, true benchmark costs are not the costs of one bid on a contract; they are the actual costs revealed through subsequent bids after some years of experience. Second, true comparisons involve comprehensive government agency costs, including any costs of letting, awarding, and monitoring the contract. Until government accounting systems can provide these internal costs, there can be no real comparison."[50]

As strange as it may seem, these cautions are often overlooked. Such careful reviews and the kind of cost accounting recommended are not often done. Indeed, the General Accounting Office, responding to a congressional request to assess early state experiments with contracting out prison operations, concluded that it could not really make a determination as to either cost or quality of services because the data were inadequate to assess government costs either for providing the services itself or for managing the contracts.[51]

The GAO did conduct a study of a variety of jurisdictions in which efforts to contract out were said to have been successful. It found six requirements for success shared by these jurisdictions:

A political champion is required to lead and support the effort.
An adequate implementation structure is needed.
Legislative and resource changes may be needed to support the changed approach to services.
Reliable cost data are required to really understand cost savings or the lack of them.
There must be strategies for workforce transition in place or significant opposition can be anticipated.
Last but not least, monitoring and oversight capabilities must be in place.[52]

THE PROCESSES OF CONTRACT FORMATION

Once the decision is made to contract, authorization to contract is formally delegated to a contracting officer, and funds are made available for the purpose, the process can move forward. Although it is important to consider contract management in regard to the whole process, it is also essential to understand just how much of the nature of the relationship among the participants in a contract throughout its life is shaped by what happens in the integration phase. In addition to the standard elements of making the decision to contract and determining whether to submit the contract to competitive bidding or proceed by a sole source process, key dynamics shape what will follow in contract administration. Some of the parts of that process are standard and are dictated by statutes, regulations, or executive department directives. Others are management decisions and provide options that can be employed to develop an effective working relationship with the contractor.

Formal Elements of the Process

Traditionally, the steps taken to enter into a contractual relationship are known as the presolicitation and the solicitations award phases. Some practices central to these phases of contract should be ongoing in a city, a state agency, or even some federal government departments, but they often take place contract by contract. These are contract planning and market analysis and forecasting.

Many of the purchases of goods and services that governments make are predictable. Some items are large capital purchases, like vehicles, that can be anticipated and may be included, particularly at the local government level, in capital budget plans. Other contracts involve a significant number of small or low-cost items that are anticipated in annual budgets and can be acquired with few administrative burdens. Agencies at all levels now use purchase cards to acquire such materials as office supplies. Another way that this type of purchase is made is in what are termed task order or delivery order contracts. A task or delivery order contract might set a minimum and a maximum level for the purchase of particular services or goods in a year with a set price per service or per item. When the service is needed, the agency simply calls for the service visit and reimburses according to a preset schedule of prices. This eliminates the need for a separate contracting process every time a plumber or painter is needed or office equipment or furniture is required. If managers monitor these contracts carefully over time, the levels of need can be anticipated with reasonable accuracy.

The need for other kinds of goods or services are not quite so regular and involve far more expensive contracts. It is important for public managers to try to anticipate as many of these as possible. The more effort put into forecasting needs and planning for the contracts to meet them, the more the governments involved can ensure that the funds are available for the purpose, and the more effective they can be at doing the market analysis needed to get the best deal for the public. Unfortunately, many units of government, particularly the smaller ones, tend not to invest in acquisition planning or market analysis. This comes as a surprise to many private sector executives for whom forecasting and market analysis are critically important operations to which people are assigned and for which resources are invested.

By contrast many public agencies are expected to handle contracting as a normal part of their operations without special staffing or budgets for the task. To the degree that contracting is one more responsibility piled onto the already full agenda of a public manager, contract management may not get the kind of attention needed to ensure a good deal for the public, not only when the contract is awarded but over the life of the relationship. That is not to say that small cities, counties, or even state agencies must hire more people or appropriate more money. It is intended to point out that effective contracting requires person power and information resources. To the degree that a jurisdiction seeks to do more contracting or is not satisfied with its current contract operations, those needs must be considered. On the positive side of the ledger, contemporary computer software and a host of Web sites operated by public agencies, nonprofits, and even for-profit firms can assist in providing a good deal of contract effectiveness for the contract management dollar.

Market analysis does not have to be a purely passive activity. Public agencies can even work to stimulate the market and generate new options. For one thing, cities or state agencies can send signals that they want a vigorous, competitive market, and they can just as easily discourage potential bidders by conveying the opposite impression. Those signals can begin with the first effort to contract in a given area. If there is a sense of open and fair competition such that everyone involved feels that there was an honest attempt to get the best deal for the public, unsuccessful bidders are more likely to consider reentering the competition when the time comes to rebid the contract. Similarly, competence counts. It is true that some business people are happy to deal with a gullible or vulnerable public agency. However, just as wise public managers want to do business with a capable and responsible firm or NGO even if it is not the lowest bidder, so wise executives prefer to do business with competent, professional, and responsible cities or agencies. Providing evidence of competence and professionalism at every stage of the contract process is a way to ensure that more firms will want to bid in the future. Potential bidders expect their public sector colleagues to behave as professionally as possible consistent with the fact that democratic institutions must serve a multiplicity of goals and not simply a bottom line.

Agencies can use Internet listings of contract opportunities and contract awards to identify which service providers are bidding on particular types of contracts in other communities, states, or even nations. Busy administrators do not always have to do this kind of research alone. Many city/county or state libraries operate business support units that provide information to small businesses and nonprofits and can be of invaluable assistance to public managers as well.

Several other things can be done to enhance market options. For example, the government unit involved can use multiaward contracting, deliberately awarding contracts to more than one service provider. This practice encourages potential bidders to feel that the competition is open and that it is not a winner-take-all situation. It also allows bidders to demonstrate how well they perform on the same kind of work, and permits agencies to compare one provider against another.

Multiaward contracts are one type of tool that can be used either to support firms that are currently in business in a given market or to encourage developing groups to continue their efforts and compete in that market. As explained in Chapter 2, there is nothing new about governments using contracts to assist emerging businesses. This has often been true in federal government contracting where there are only a few providers in a given market and the government is the primary customer. Multiaward contracts can offer other benefits. For example, some state institutions have contracted with a travel agency to take care of its needs and seek savings at the same time. Others have used a multiaward contract to hire two or three travel firms at the same time in order to provide an incentive for the firms to compete with each other to attract more of the agency's business both as to price and service.

Related to this multiaward approach is partial contracting and public-private competition. The idea in this case is for government to retain some direct service capability and service delivery. Thus, the Swedish child care agencies have retained a limited in-house service capability while relying on contract providers for most of the critically important child care services. The limited government operation provides a training ground for contract administrators and also ensures a fall-back capacity in the event that a contractor defaults or fails to provide high-quality care.

One part of the presolicitation phase is done one contract at a time. That is the preparation of the specifications and statement of work. This is one of the areas in which public managers often feel cross-pressured. The history of selling shoddy goods to public agencies and the "good enough for government work" attitude has prompted many agencies to seek stringent specifications. Demanding specifications far beyond what is normally available commercially may limit the number of bidders willing and able to respond and is virtually guaranteed to drive up prices. Hence, some of the infamous public stories about very expensive screws that could be bought much cheaper in a hardware store or outrageously costly aircraft coffee pots involved hardware with exceptionally high tensile strength and a coffee pot that was supposed to withstand an aircraft accident. In some cases, high-stress hardware is necessary, but often it is not. And no reasonable argument can be made for requiring a coffee pot for a cargo aircraft to be more durable than that available in any airliner. This is one of the reasons that the Packard Commission, the Reagan administration's Blue Ribbon Commission on Defense Spending, and several other contract study groups have encouraged the use of off-the-shelf technology as long as it is adequate to the mission of the agency.

Of course, an agency that undershoots with its specifications for equipment or in its statement of services in the hope of obtaining lower bids often finds out that it would have saved money in the long run if it had moved up a notch in the capability of equipment or type of services in the first place. This is a common problem with regard to purchases of information technology.

One approach to developing specifications and statements of work is to hire a consultant. The agency must take care, however, not to hire a consultant that might have a conflict of interest. It has happened that an agency's consultant produced specifications that created a strong bias in favor of a bidder with whom he or she had a clear business relationship. This problem can be addressed in the consulting contract, which should require disclosure of business relationships and should include a no-bid clause that prohibits the consultants or their firm from bidding on the contract or related contracts for a specified period of time. Of course it is also essential to ensure that the consultant's fee does not provide perverse incentives, such as basing fees on a percentage of purchase price.

The other side of these efforts to provide safeguards is that they can discourage consultants from entering the relationship. There are methods for providing incentives for specialty firms to provide such consulting advice, even though they face disqualification from other agreements. The first is that the government may normally be expected to pay a premium for such a consultant to offset some of the potential losses that the consulting firm incurs, since it cannot bid on the contract. Another approach is to pay for the specific services associated with the request for proposal (RFP) or IFB but also use the consultant's services at other points during the contract to advise the organization on performance, accountability, or efficiency issues. It is also possible to provide an incentive in the form of a broader contract to consult over a period of time or for a collection of related contracts in the area of, say, communications rather than for one contract.

Yet another option is to invite potential bidders to participate in open conversations about specifications. For example, one smaller community that was seeking new radio equipment for its city vehicles chose this kind of open consultation. There was a particular challenge in that the town is located in a mountainous rural area that has severe winter weather conditions. The manager convened a public meeting after notice to potential bidders and facilitated discussions with the potential providers about what was available and the range of performance that could be specified. The manager then wrote the IFB specifications based on that input and his own research. The bidders were on notice as to the city's needs, and no bidder had an advantage over any other firm.

In addition to these more or less traditional ideas about specifications, often referred to as engineering standards, that spell out what must be done and how, there is an increasing tendency to use what is called performance contracting. Performance contracting is intended to focus not so much on the physical details but on the actual outcomes that are produced, allowing flexibility as to the means by which those goals are met.[53]

However stated, the efforts to this point come together in the solicitation and awards phase. This is when the IFBs or RFPs are issued, bids received, and a contractor is selected. In some situations, though, these steps are circumvented by a decision to contract on a sole source or single selected source basis without standard bidding.

A common example of the sole source contract is the personal services contract, in which a particular person is retained because of unique skills or experience or a firm is engaged because it is the only provider of a particular product or service. In most jurisdictions, some justification for sole source contracting is required, since taking such an approach is by definition a decision to forgo the benefits of market competition. This happens in some areas fairly frequently. The GAO study of the Department of Energy cited earlier in this chapter indicated, for instance, that in one study sixteen of twenty-four contracts examined were extended without competition and twelve of the sixteen had never involved competition.[54] Still, a former director of the Office of Federal Procurement Policy, Steven Kelman, points out that there is as much or more of what would be called noncompetitive contracting among private sector firms. Since they value a well-performing business relationship, many firms are loath to change suppliers.[55] Assessments of past performance are, he argues, central to business decision making. However, federal and state statutes such as the Competition in Contracting Act of 1984 attempt to push agencies to avoid sole source contracting.

Shirley Hansen and Jeannie Weisman present four simple recommendations for the preparation of solicitations.

Rule #1 Determine the results you want first.

Rule #2 Decide the criteria the organization will use to determine the [bidder] that can best deliver the results it wants.

Rule #3 The valuation procedures, which incorporate those criteria, should be well thought out before the customer issues an RFP.

Rule #4 In soliciting proposals: Keep it short! Keep it open! Keep it simple! and Get only the information you truly need to make an evaluation.[56]

In addition to price, the evaluation of bids considers bidder responsiveness, that is, whether all required elements of the solicitation have been addressed, and bidder responsibility, whether the bidder appears capable of meeting the commitments set forth in the bid. Some bidders who have been disciplined because of previous misconduct may be debarred, that is, prohibited from bidding on new contracts. In some instances, the qualifications of bidders are precleared. This is a process that was launched in Canada and elsewhere some time ago in an attempt to cut the time and cost associated with individual assessments at the time of each bid. Of course, there is a considerable range between the general prequalification of firms to bid on government contracts and debarment (a sanction disqualifying a bidder). Kelman argued at length that the most glaring gap in these assessments was the inability of government to evaluate and use past performance by contractors in evaluating their bids.[57] When he became OFPP administrator, Kelman focused on moving key changes through the political process, one of which was the amendment to the Federal Acquisition Regulations in 1995 to provide guidance on the use of past performance in evaluating contract proposals. In 1997 Kelman issued a memorandum to department heads reporting results from initial experiments with past performance assessments. He concluded that a study of forty contracts indicated significantly improved agency satisfaction with performance using the new approach.[58] However, state and local governments vary significantly in the degree to which their statutes and regulations permit consideration of past performance. It is critical for the public manager to be fully informed about the law in his or her jurisdiction.

Another of the interesting challenges government units face in evaluating potential contractors arises when a for-profit firm bids against a nonprofit organization or vice versa. As Weisbrod points out, this is an increasingly common situation.[59] On the one hand, it is almost always the case that established for-profit firms can demonstrate a stronger financial posture than nonprofits. On the other hand, the nonprofit may be a far more committed bidder in the sense that the service in question, say, the provision of specialized care services like home health assistance, alcohol abuse counseling, or assistance for women who have experienced domestic violence, is the very core of its mission. The for-profit may be larger, and contracting with the nonprofits may mean more individual contracts with smaller organizations scattered throughout the state or even the nation. Still, the locally based NGOs often have a solid sense of the community and can provide sensitive client contact as opposed to a more impersonal but perhaps more efficient process provided by a larger firm. It is not enough, then, merely to determine that the bidder is financially strong if the goal is to assess what the organization will be like as a partner later in the program administration stage of the contract.

In addition to the normal bid process, there is a process often referred to as two-step contracting. This is a kind of negotiated process but not a sole source situation. The two-step process is often preferred in complex service agreements or large systems purchases. The agency invites bids, from which it chooses a short list of desirable contractors. It begins negotiation with the highest-rated bidder until agreement is reached or discussions break down. The agency then moves to the second-ranking bidder and so on.

Conditions on Decision Making

In addition to these standard factors in the process, a variety of other conditions are placed on the public manager. Often referred to as national goals clauses or social goals clauses, these matters reflect the long-standing use by the government of contracts as vehicles to make public policy and to leverage change in the private sector as well (see Chapter 2).

These policies are often presented in the bid process in two ways. It is standard to require bidders to offer a list of certifications that they will comply with civil rights requirements, wage rate requirements, and other federally imposed conditions. The other way this is addressed, and the one that has drawn considerable controversy, is by awarding a bidder extra points in the evaluation process for meeting policy goals such as the use of environmentally friendly materials or hiring subcontractors that are minority or women's business enterprises.

The environmental example is widely used. A U.S. Environmental Protection Agency (EPA) study examined different types of incentive programs, such as the 5 percent price preference offered by San Diego County for recycled paper and the 10 percent preference for recycled oil and 15 percent edge for recycled paper given by King County, Washington (Seattle).[60] It is an indication of the thoroughgoing nature of contracting these days that the EPA study itself was prepared by a contractor.

In 1965 President Lyndon Johnson issued Executive Order 11246, which provided the basis for affirmative action contracting programs in the federal government.[61] There was nothing new about presidents using federal contracting to press for change in hiring and business practices. Indeed, every president since Franklin Roosevelt has issued such orders. However, as vice president, Johnson had chaired President Kennedy's committee on equal employment opportunity and was increasingly aware of the limitations of existing civil rights policy. When he came to the White House after the assassination of President Kennedy, he made civil rights a focus of his administration, successfully shepherding the Civil Rights Act of 1964 and the Voting Rights Act of 1965 through Congress. Even so, Johnson became convinced that ending segregation would not address the barriers that blocked employment and business opportunities for racial minorities, whether they were workers or entrepreneurs. In June 1965 Johnson committed the administration to an affirmative and active approach to civil rights.[62] Johnson said, in part: "You do not take a person who, for years, has been hobbled by chains and liberate him, bring him up to the starting line of a race and then say, 'you are free to compete with all the others,' and still justly believe that you have been completely fair. Thus it is not enough just to open the gates of opportunity. All our citizens must have the ability to walk through those gates."[63]

After Vice President Hubert Humphrey submitted a memorandum for the president laying out difficulties in the civil rights operations, Johnson issued Executive Order 11246.[64] The specific affirmative action policies did not come about until the Labor Department issued orders in 1969 in a controversy in Philadelphia that required minority hiring goals. Although what became known as the Philadelphia Plan was immediately challenged, the United States Court of Appeals for the Third Circuit upheld it.[65]

The court battles continued, with affirmative action opponents seeking a Supreme Court ruling against these programs. Nevertheless, in an opinion issued by Chief Justice Warren Burger, the Court upheld a federal contract set-aside program for minority business enterprises.[66] Later, however, the administrations of Ronald Reagan and George H. W. Bush, opposed affirmative action of that sort and appointed justices to the Court with similar views. In 1989 the Court struck down a contract set-aside program for the city of Richmond, Virginia, modeled on the federal program that had been upheld in the earlier case. Justice Sandra Day O'Connor wrote for the majority, arguing that the state was in a different position from Congress under the Constitution. In 1990, however, a sharply divided Court upheld a Federal Communications Commission program, providing affirmative action considerations in the granting of broadcast licenses.

Affirmative action contracting came back to the Supreme Court again in 1995. This time Justice O'Connor drew back from her earlier ruling and concluded that the federal government really was not in a different position from the states. Preference that was based on race would be treated as suspect, and a heavy burden would be placed on the government, state or federal, to justify the program. The *Adarand Construction Assn. v. Peña*[67] case involved a federal program providing incentives for prime contractors in the hiring of minority businesses as subcontractors. The Court issued a stringent standard for evaluating such programs, but the case was returned to the lower courts to determine the precise operation of the federal program in this situation. Justices Antonin Scalia and Clarence Thomas concurred in the decision in *Adarand,* but made clear that they would seek a broad prohibition on affirmative action programs. The *Adarand* case came back before the Supreme Court again, with affirmative action opponents hoping for a major ruling outlawing such programs. However, the Court sent it back to the lower courts without a ruling on the merits on grounds that the programs and therefore the case had changed.[68]

Of course, as the environmental examples discussed earlier indicated, race is only one of the bases for consideration. There are also programs to support women's businesses. Local purchase programs and state purchase programs, although raising serious interstate commerce clause questions, remain in operation in many parts of the country and give preference to local bidders.

CONTRACT OFFICERS AND PROJECT TEAMS

In addition to the formal processes that develop the contract, another factor can very much affect the long-term success of a contract relationship. It is the formation and operation of project teams. Although a single person designated as the contract officer is the only one legally authorized to commit the government to a contract, contractual relationships often, particularly in larger contracts, involve a government team. That team may involve a project director, technical experts, cost accounting and auditing specialists, on-site or field inspectors, and liaison officers, who ensure effective communications and prompt reporting. From the beginning of the relationship the project team can be fragmented, particularly when some members of the team operate from central offices and others are in the field or, worse, housed with the contractor, as is true in some defense contracts. One of the important challenges facing a project manager is to be alert to these potential tensions and manage them. It is too easy in the rush to start implementation of a contract-based project to overlook this team-building requirement, and it is just as easy later on, when operations have settled into a routine, to ignore danger signals that the team may be coming apart.

Some governments or agencies employ different contracting officers at different stages of a contract process. Thus, they may use a procurement contracting officer (PCO) in the integration phase, an administrative contracting officer in the operation phase (ACO), and a termination contracting officer (TCO) in the separation or transformation stage. The theory behind the distinction is functional specialization based on the assumption that PCOs have particular strengths in handling bid processes and contract negotiations, ACOs are people with special skills in management control and audit activities, and TCOs have particular knowledge and aptitudes for dispute resolution and potential enforcement activities. Originally developed in connection with large-scale systems purchases, often with research and development components, this seemingly attractive idea may present risks in the management of service delivery contracts. For one thing, the arrival and departure of three different types of contract officers can be damaging to the cohesion and culture of the project team.

In addition to the contracting team's need for management, it also needs protection from external pressures. It has sometimes been said that the reason there are so many burdensome restrictions on public contract managers is the need to protect against corruption by those career civil servants.[69] In truth, however, history suggests that the more difficult, and generally more pervasive, problem to address is political pressure from elected officials seeking to assist their constituents who either are doing business with the government or would like to do so. The normally complex interpersonal dynamics of a project team are difficult enough, but the management task becomes even more challenging if political pressures are brought to bear on members of the team. It is important for the project manager to be alert to the first indications of this problem. Indeed, team members may feel intimidated and thus might not be willing to come forward to report the problem when it arises, often in the early stages of the contract process. It is essential for the manager to develop a strong group culture from the beginning that encourages that kind of reporting and provides assurances to team members that they will be supported and protected if they are forthcoming.

TRADE-OFFS AND CONSEQUENCES

The process of planning for and shaping a contract relationship involves a series of trade-offs. The choices made at this stage affect the structure and character of the relationship in ways that may be difficult to change later in the process. And choices must indeed be made. The key choices are commonly discussed in federal government contracting materials and by authors who have considered the subject. They flow not only from those sources but also from the history discussed in Chapter 2.

One of the most commonly considered trade-offs is that between cost and quality. Although performance contracts (see Chapter 4) and other devices seek to provide incentives for contractors to exceed required standards at the same price or less, the most common reality is that the more stringent the standards and the more custom designed and built the product or service, the more expensive it will be.

Second, there is usually a trade-off between cost and speed. If a contractor must be ready to respond to a service demand or for materials on a moment's notice, they must maintain the people and materials necessary to do that. Moreover, expediting action often means using more expensive services, paying more overtime, and putting aside other pending actions. As these factors suggest, bidding on such a contract entails risks.

Another of the commonly understood trade-offs is between risk and cost. The history of contracting shows a continuing effort by government to avoid having the taxpayers accept more risk than is necessary. During several periods (see Chapter 2) the government has made concerted efforts to transfer more of the risk to the private sector contractor. In most instances, those who are asked to accept greater risks will be willing to take them if and only if the potential rewards make the gamble worthwhile. That translates into increased costs. The government's unwillingness to recognize this reality sometimes leads potential bidders to stay on the sidelines. It also can create the false economy of appearing to protect the public while in reality reducing competitive options and driving up costs.

Another trade-off relates to this problem of appearance and reality. There can be a trade-off between apparent contract savings and increased internal costs. Since there is often little effort to budget for contract management, the seeming ability of the contract to save money may be real or illusory, depending in part on how much it costs the agency or city involved to build and operate the systems needed to manage the contract in a competent manner. The failure to create and support that capability can cost the public a great deal in the long run, but this trade-off is often ignored. At that point, the agency must not only pay for whatever problems emerge in the contract, but often it must stop in midstream and spend the time and money to build the management capability that should have been built in the first place.

As social overhead (the costs incurred from national goals clauses) is added, costs tend to increase. At the same time, the failure to take account of social impacts can increase the costs of the contract to the government. When government adds preferences such as environmentally friendly products, preferences for local purchasers, and requirements for minimum wage levels and working conditions, the normal result is an increase in costs. That is not to suggest that the choice is inappropriate. There are costs associated with environmentally damaging business practices or abusive labor practices, and, in addition to the moral appropriateness of public policy efforts to prevent these problems, government will often feel the effects of irresponsible business practices. Indeed, the evidence indicates that the effort to fix problems after they occur, as in the case of environmental damage, is almost always more costly than preventing it in the first place. It is important to understand that these kinds of social overhead costs are present and should not be ignored. One reason is that the process can work the other way around. Consider cases in which contracting results in jobs losses, which can in turn lead to reduced spending in the local economy, increased demand for unemployment benefits and other social services, and reduced social cohesion.

Finally, as ironic as it may seem, there may be a trade-off between the effort to maximize competition and costs in contracting. Efforts to do more market research and to take steps to increase the number of bidders available in order to take advantage of the power of competition should reduce costs. However, there may come a point of diminishing returns at which the costs required to identify, notify, and encourage possible bidders along with the costs of evaluating the bids can consume more resources than the competition itself may save. This is one of the trade-offs affected, as Kelman points out, by the dread fear that some group or news media outlet will accuse the public manager of making sweetheart deals.

These trade-offs are not good or bad in themselves. They simply exist and should be consciously considered as decisions are made about forming contracting relationships. In an infelicitous phrase popularized by economist Milton Freedman, there ain't no such thing as a free lunch. Without some consideration of these trade-offs, it becomes virtually impossible to know whether the relationship that is being constructed will, in the end, be a good deal for the public or not.

CONCLUSION

In the end, then, the discussion about undertaking contract operations may be relatively simple and largely technical when routine purchases are at issue, but it is a different matter when government moves to enter into what are often termed public/private partnerships for major acquisitions or for the delivery of public services. Indeed, the very term "partnership" turns out, when carefully considered, to raise some cautions about the care required for good contractual working relationships. In truth, when government comes to rely on contracting to the point that it cannot deliver services itself, the situation is more like a set of alliances in which both the public sector and the contractors operate under conditions of mutual interdependence. It is far more than a simple business relationship as that concept is often understood by the public.

For one thing, it matters who government's partners are. Private for-profit firms are very different from government agencies, and the kinds of pressures they face in the marketplace along with the internal values on which they operate mean that they behave differently as well. Those differences must be understood if there is to be a good deal for the public. Nonprofit organizations, on which government has come to rely for so many of its human service programs, have their own unique characteristics and challenges. Simplistic images of small charitable or civic groups operating in purely local contexts are often misleading. Nonprofits have much to offer, but they also present their own sorts of challenges that must be recognized to protect the public interest as well as to avoid overloading organizations that are important in their communities. Finally, it is increasingly the case that governments operate a panoply of interjurisdictional agreements under which they buy, sell, and trade services. Obviously, these are different from other types of contracting, and their special challenges are also important in determining whether the public gets a good deal.

A mixture of decisions arise as public managers decide whether to contract and then seek to build working relationships with contract partners. Some of those decisions make up part of the formal processes, and others are more diffuse but still important. Even within the formal steps involved in the presolicitation and solicitation-award phases, options are available to make these processes more effective. Government is not just a passive acceptor of bids but an active participant in the marketplace whose decisions affect the amount of competition and the behavior of the organizations in a sector.

Effective public managers, as they come to integrate their operations with a contract partner, recognize that certain special conditions, sometimes referred as social goals requirements, are attached to their decisions. These are legitimate political requirements that governing bodies can and do impose on government in regard to the way it does business and with whom it may form such working relationships. In addition to looking outward at potential partners, public managers at the same time need to build effective teams internally who will develop and operate the programs and the contract relationships needed to make them work.

Finally, and indeed throughout this process of integration, public managers must be mindful of the inevitable set of trade-offs that exist in the contracting process. Each of the sets of trade-offs discussed in this chapter is not about binary choices as to which goal is to be valued. Rather, each set of value trade-offs is more of a spectrum, posing a challenge to the parties to arrive at optimal balances of costs and benefits. And it is crucial for both sides to see the needs of the other contract party in making such choices.

Still, however sensitive and skillful the parties may be in creating and building a contract relationship, the true test of its effectiveness in getting a good deal for the public comes after the integration stage. It is during contract administration, the actual operation of the relationship, that strengths and challenges emerge. Chapter 4 focuses on that critical dimension.

Notes

1. Al Gore, *Reinventing Federal Procurement: Accompanying Report of the National Performance Review* (Washington, D.C.: Government Printing Office, 1993), 1.

2. For a discussion of the results of implementation of the Federal Acquisition Streamlining Act of 1994 and Executive Order 12931, see U.S. General Accounting Office, *Acquisition Reform: Purchase Card Use Cuts Procurement Costs, Improves Efficiency* (Washington, D.C.: GAO, 1996). For earlier innovations on the simplification of such procurements, see Government of Australia, Department of Administrative Services, Financial Reform Group, *Purchasing Reform Group Guidelines* (Canberra: Government of Australia, n.d.).

3. Burton A. Weisbrod, "The Future of the Nonprofit Sector: Its Entwining with Private Enterprise and Government," 16 *Journal of Policy Analysis and Management* 541, 541–542 (1997).

4. U.S. Office of Management and Budget, *Summary Report of the SWAT Team on Civilian Agency Contracting* (Washington, D.C.: Office of Management and Budget, 1992), 23. (Hereafter *SWAT Team Report.*)

5. U.S. General Accounting Office, *Private and Public Prisons: Studies Comparing Operational Costs and/or Quality of Service* (Washington, D.C.: GAO, 1996).

6. See, for example, *Schweiker v. McClure*, 456 U.S. 188 (1982).

7. United Nations, *The Istanbul Declaration on Human Settlements* (New York: United Nations, 1996), Principles 1–10.

8. I've addressed this issue in greater detail in "Canadian Refugee Services: The Challenges of Network Operations," 18 *Refuge* 14 (2000).

9. I have addressed this in "Ejecución de la política social en tiempos de crisis de coordinacion," 7 *Reforma y Democracia* 99 (1997), and "Crise de Coordenação e Governance No Século 21: Compreendo as Tendências Centrais, in Fundação do Desenvolvimento Administrativo (FUNDAP)," *Sociedade e Estado: Superando Fronteiras* (São Paulo: FUNDAP, 1998).

10. Claudia Maria Vargas, "Bridging Solitudes: Partnership Challenges in Canadian Refugee Service Delivery—Symposium Introduction," 8 *Refuge* 1 (2000). See also Lucila Spigelblatt, "Creating a Partnership Conducive Environment: A Collaborative Approach to Service Delivery," 18 *Refuge* 8 (2000).

11. Edgar H. Schein, *Organizational Culture and Leadership,* 2d ed. (San Francisco: Jossey-Bass, 1992).

12. For a discussion of this concept and its complexities, see H. Brinton Milward, "Implication of Contracting Out: New Roles for the Hollow State," in *New Paradigms for Government,* ed. Patricia W. Ingraham and Barbara S. Romzek (San Francisco: Jossey-Bass, 1994).

13. U.S. General Accounting Office, *Department of Energy Contract Management* (Washington, D.C.: Government Printing Office, 1997), 17–18.

14. W. Henry Lambright, *Governing Science and Technology* (New York: Oxford University Press, 1976), 48.

15. Lloyd Burton, "Ethical Discontinuities in Public/Private Sector Negotiation," 9 *Journal of Policy Analysis and Management* 23 (1990).

16. This story is laid out in detail in Craig E. Richards, Rima Shore, and Max B. Sawicky, *Risky Business: Private Management of Public Schools* (Washington, D.C.: Economic Policy Institute, 1996).

17. Id., chap. 2.

18. Id., at 26–28.

19. Id., at 38.

20. Weisbrod, supra note 3, at 541–542.

21. Paul C. Light, *Making Nonprofits Work* (Washington, D.C.: Brookings Institution Press, 2000), 8.

22. Weisbrod, supra note 3, at 542.

23. See, for example, U.S. Office of Management and Budget, "Cost Principles for Non-Profit Organizations," Circular A-122, revised June 1, 1998; Circular A-133, "Audits of States, Local Governments, and Non-Profit Organizations," revised June 24, 1997.

24. See Judith R. Saidel and Sharon Harlan, "Contracting and Patterns of Nonprofit Governance," 8 *Nonprofit Management and Leadership* 243 (1998); Judith R. Saidel, "Resource Interdependence: The Relationship between State Agencies and Nonprofit Organizations," 51 *Public Administration Review* 543 (1991); and Saidel, "The Dynamics of Interdependence between Public Agencies and Nonprofit Organizations," 3 *Research in Public Administration* 201 (1994).

25. Barbara S. Romzek and Jocelyn M. Johnston, "Reforming and Privatizing Medicaid: The Nexus of Policy Implementation and Organizational Culture" (paper presented at the Fourth National Public Management Research Conference, University of Georgia, Athens, October 1997). Later published in revised form as "Reforming Medicaid through Contracting: The Nexus of Implementation and Organizational Culture," 9 *Journal of Public Administration Research and Theory* 107 (1999).

26. See Weisbrod, supra note 3; Light, supra note 21.

27. *Crosby v. National Foreign Trade Council,* 530 U.S. 363 (2000), and *United States v. Locke,* 529 U.S. 89 (2000).

28. *Quill Corp. v. North Dakota,* 504 U.S. 298 (1992).

29. See, for example, *Lake Country Estates v. Tahoe Regional Planning Agency,* 440 U.S. 391 (1979).

30. *Reynolds v. Sims,* 377 U.S. 533, 575 (1964).

31. Joseph J. Getsema and William R. Ross, "A Creative Approach to Financing Facility Construction" (paper presented at the International City/County Management Association, Yankton, South Dakota, 1996).

32. U.S. General Accounting Office, *Cooperative Purchasing: Effects Are Likely to Vary among Governments and Businesses* (Washington, D.C.: GAO, 1997), 5–6.

33. Quoted in Dan Guttman, *Making Reform Work: Contracting for Government* (Washington, D.C.: National Academy of Public Administration, 1997), 3.

34. OFPP Policy Letter 92-1, September 23, 1992.

35. *Carter v. Carter Coal Co.,* 298 U.S. 238 (1936); *Panama Refining Co. v. Ryan,* 293 U.S. 388, 415 (1935); *A. L. A. Schechter Poultry Corp. v. United States,* 295 U.S. 495, 537–538 (1935).

36. *Bennett v. Kentucky Department of Education,* 470 U.S. 656, 669 (1985).

37. *United States v. Kensington,* 760 F. Supp. 1120, 1136 (EDPA 1991).

38. U.S. Office of Management and Budget, "Grants and Cooperative Agreements with State and Local Governments," Circular A-102 (revised October 7, 1994, further amended August 29, 1997); online: http://www.whitehouse.gov/omb/circulars/a102/a102.html, September 11, 2001.

39. Id., paragraph 1a.

40. State of Vermont, Agency of Administration, "Contracting Procedures," Bulletin No. 3.5, August 10, 1995, 2.

41. Id., at 2–3.

42. Id.

43. John A. Rehfuss, *Contracting Out in Government* (San Francisco: Jossey-Bass, 1989).

44. See, for example, U.S. General Accounting Office, *Public-Private Competitions* (Washington, D.C.: GAO, 1998).

45. Ruth Hoogland DeHoog, *Contracting Out for Human Services* (Albany: State University of New York Press, 1984), 141.

46. Id., at 20.

47. Rehfuss, supra note 43, chap. 3.

48. Id., at 46–49.

49. Id., at 53–54.

50. Id., at 54.

51. U.S. General Accounting Office, *Private and Public Prisons: Studies Comparing Operational Costs and/or Quality of Service* (Washington, D.C.: GAO, 1996).

52. U.S. General Accounting Office, *Privatization: Lessons Learned by State and Local Governments* (Washington, D.C.: GAO, 1997).

53. See Shirley J. Hansen and Jeannie C. Weisman, *Performance Contracting: Expanding Horizons* (Lilburn, Ga.: Fairmont Press, 1998).

54. U.S. General Accounting Office, *Department of Energy Contract Management,* supra note 13, at 17–18.

55. Steven Kelman, *Procurement and Public Management: The Fear of Discretion and the Quality of Government Performance* (Washington, D.C.: AEI Press, 1990), 62–63.

56. Hansen and Weisman, supra note 53, at 27–30.

57. Id.

58. Steven Kelman, Administrator, Office of Federal Procurement Policy, "Final Report on Past Performance Pledge Program," memorandum for senior agency procurement executives and the acting deputy under secretary of defense (acquisition reform), January 27, 1997.

59. Weisbrod, supra note 3.

60. U.S. Environmental Protection Agency, "A Study of State and Local Government Procurement Practices that Consider Environmental Performance of Goods and Services," report prepared by ABT Associates, Cambridge, Mass., September 30, 1996, 11, 45.

61. 30 Fed. Reg. 12319 (1965).

62. Vaughn Davis Bornet, *The Presidency of Lyndon B. Johnson* (Lawrence: University Press of Kansas, 1983), 53–54. See also Bruce J. Schulman, *Lyndon B. Johnson and American Liberalism* (Boston: Bedford Books, 1995), 106–117.

63. *Public Papers of the Presidents of the United States, Lyndon B. Johnson,* 1965 (Washington, D.C.: Government Printing Office, 1966), 2: 636.

64. He also issued Executive Order 11247 at the same time, 30 Fed. Reg. 12327 (1965). This order assigned responsibilities for action under Title VI of the 1964 act to the attorney general.

65. *Contractors Association of Eastern Pennsylvania v. Secretary of Labor,* 442 F.2d 159 (3d Cir. 1971).

66. *Fullilove v. Klutznick,* 448 U.S. 448 (1980).

67. 515 U.S. 200 (1995).

68. *Adarand Constructors, Inc. v. Mineta,* 534 U.S. 103 (2001).

69. See Gore, *Reinventing Federal Procurement,* supra note 1.

4

Operations: The Management of Contract Relationships

It is ironic that policymakers and academic commentators continue to spend so much energy and time on the integration stage of the contracting process when many of the most important aspects of the contract relationship take place later, in the operation stage. The Clinton administration's National Performance Review (NPR) report on contracting is an example. Most of its recommendations focused on getting a contract in place faster, more flexibly, less expensively with respect to transaction costs, with fewer conditions and controls. Where possible, it advocated avoiding regular contracting processes altogether by using techniques such as purchase cards, and simplifying and clarifying bid protest processes where full-blown acquisitions processes are used.[1] These were, to be sure, not the only recommendations, but the primary thrust of the report was obvious. Just as clearly, the primary focus of the statutes and executive orders adopted during the 1990s, such as the Acquisitions Streamlining Act, was on recommendations of those types. To the degree that simple purchases, or in some cases, even complex items such as computers, are involved, emphasis on the front end of the contracting process may seem appropriate. However, it should be clear by this point that a growing percentage of public contracts involve continuing working relationships, such as service delivery agreements. These can be, for example, contracts by local governments for emergency services, state contracts under federal grants with nonprofits for social services, or federal contracts with organizations that manage national laboratories. It has become increasingly clear to investigators that serious and continuing emphasis on the operations stage of the contract is also necessary.

The Office of Management and Budget created a study commission with the slightly over-the-top but effective name of the SWAT Team on Civilian Agency Contracting. The SWAT Team (as in the police term for special weapons and tactics units) concluded: "The civilian agencies by and large have not given sufficient management attention (e.g., guidance, training, resources) to contract administration. Emphasis is placed on the award of contracts, not on assuring that the terms of the contract are met or that the procurement regulations are followed after contract awards."[2] That lack of attention applies not only to the federal government as a whole but also to individual agencies.

> While there is little disagreement on the importance of contract administration, many of the problems identified decades ago still exist, as reflected in several of the agency SWAT Team reports. Twenty-nine findings identified the lack of attention, by management, to contract administration. More than one agency reported that because bureau management concentrates on attainment of mission goals, the primary focus is on contract award and obligation of dollars in order to attain those goals. Monitoring contractor performance and costs is not emphasized.[3]

Unfortunately, having identified this weakness, the SWAT Team report proceeded to focus most of its attention on a traditional and relatively narrow audit and control view of the management of contract operations. It targeted, particularly, cost accounting, payment processes, and audit operations. It is certainly true that these technical functions are important, but they represent only a part—and not necessarily the most important part—of the operation phase of public contract management. This chapter takes a wider approach, including contract negotiation, contract drafting, managing the alliance, network management, and contractual relationships as agents of organizational change.

CONTRACT NEGOTIATION: THE SUBTLE MOVEMENT FROM INTEGRATION TO OPERATION

It is tempting to think of processes as linear and progressive, and contracting is no exception. To the degree that we envision contracting as a simple purchase, the process would seem to move from identification of a need, to locating a source, to making the purchase, with little more to be explained. Since much of public contracting is about far more than that, however, such a simplistic perspective would be deceptive. Although the most likely contractor may have been selected in the integration stage, much remains to be done at the beginning of contract administration, a term often used as the shorthand expression for the operation phase. That is especially true in complex service contracts.

The National Performance Review recommended moving away from the traditional sealed bid system, which focused primarily on lowest price, in favor of the two-step process, which allows selection of a short list of competitors from bids and then negotiations to select the final choice. This process, it was believed, would encourage best-value decisions and provide increased flexibility for public officials to work with contractors, thereby establishing a better all-around working relationship in the public interest. Of course, this two-step approach has been used at all levels of government for many years.

Even when a relationship has begun to form between the government and the preferred contracting organization, a host of issues often remains to be negotiated before a contract is finalized. Negotiations must take place within the original contracting authority, funding, and description of need. The contracting officials cannot simply toss out all that has come before and start over, although there is often still considerable latitude in the two-step process for negotiation. Several factors complicate those discussions, however.

First, by the time the stage of final contract negotiations is reached substantial sunk costs have already been incurred by all parties (investments of time, money, and effort that cannot be recovered if the relationship is terminated). The longer the negotiations continue, the more difficult it becomes to break them off and re-open the contracting process to other parties. Moreover, a working relationship is already developing among the members of the government's team and that of the contractor. Even so, both sides know that they will have to live with the details that they negotiate, possibly for a long time to come, and what was generally understood to be acceptable in early discussions must be firmly established at this stage. For these and other reasons, the negotiations can become challenging as each side seeks to get the most out of the agreement and to ensure to the greatest extent possible that it has the kinds of working conditions that will result in effective contract operations.

The differences in negotiating cultures discussed in Chapter 3 are an important reality of the negotiating process. Differences between for-profit negotiators and their government counterparts are certainly a factor, for, as Woodrow Wilson pointed out many years ago, "business-like government may and should be, but it is not business: it is organic social life."[4] Differences are also manifest between government negotiators and nonprofit representatives. Although nonprofits share many characteristics, each has its own organizational culture as well. Some are membership organizations with established boards of directors and see their role in ways that are not all that different from for-profit firms except that they may not be seeking a profit in the traditional sense. Others are volunteer-based organizations that are driven by strongly held religious, political, or social commitments. They often come to the table with strong advocacy tendencies, seeking to get the most for their cause and to win more than just money. Still others may represent coalitions of NGOs, an increasingly popular arrangement. They must be concerned both about the causes their coalition champions, the needs of the coalition leadership, and the problems of holding the coalition together. It is not at all unusual to have coalition representatives negotiate with government, only to have members of the coalition later challenge the agreement on grounds that the coalition officers misrepresented the commitments of the groups to the government or the government's position to the groups.[5]

Negotiations in interjurisdictional agreements have some unique characteristics, since all parties are negotiating in the shadow of politics. In many instances, interjurisdictional agreements are multiparty compacts, involving the federal government, states, counties, and cities. None of these participants operates solely in the horizontal negotiation-driven model. All operate within a vertical, authority-driven model and must obtain permission not only to enter into negotiations but in most instances also to validate whatever emerges from those discussions.

Whatever the dynamics of the different types of parties, there are really three sets of concerns at issue as these negotiations move along. First is the problem of reaching agreements that will ensure that the services are delivered. Second is the need of the government to guarantee its ability to maintain transparency and accountability throughout the contract's life. Finally, there is the process of building an effective working relationship that is both strong enough and yet sufficiently flexible to meet changing circumstances and unforeseen problems. The way a government unit handles itself in the present negotiation could affect the willingness of contractors to bid on future contracts and how others might approach negotiating with that government unit.

CONTRACT DRAFTING: LAYING DOWN THE LAW WHILE PRESERVING THE RELATIONSHIP

Whatever the character of the negotiation and recognizing the importance of the informal and relationship-based factors that are central to success or failure, the contract itself matters. It is another of the ironies of modern public management that little attention is paid to the contract itself despite the fact that it is the core of the relationship and is legally enforceable against both parties. Indeed, unlike the vertical, authority-based model of regulation, the horizontal model assumes a meeting of the minds between parties as the central feature of the operation, and either side may trigger its enforcement. The contract relationship is, after all, a legal relationship.

The Movement toward Real Contracts: The Good News and the Challenge

Government contracts used to be referred to as contracts of adhesion. That term means that government may impose a host of requirements, and the would-be contractor, with few exceptions, is required either to accept them or refuse to contract. The problem is that when a public contract is little more than an agreement by a group or a firm to submit to government regulation for a price in order to deliver products or services, the arrangement has relatively few of the characteristics of contracting that most advocates sought when they argued for expanded use of contracts in the first place. These advocates really wanted to take advantage of the horizontal, negotiated process that is characteristic of business relationships to obtain the flexibility, effectiveness, and efficiencies that can be obtained by that process. They particularly wanted to move away from a top-down regulatory approach. A continuing tension is at play here. Although most observers agree with the effort to move toward the horizontal approach, the vertical, authority-based and accountability-driven portion of the model still operates as the context for the government contract. Congress, state legislatures, and the courts have not suspended existing statutes and case law because there is a desire for more innovative business practices. Even so, there have indeed been many policy changes in recent years to move in the direction of greater flexibility, particularly at the federal level. States and localities have long had more flexible schemes than their colleagues in Washington, except of course for those situations in which state and local administrators contract under federal grants. In those cases, all the government levels involved impose their own requirements on each agreement.

The effort to move more toward a businesslike horizontal process means that public officials must take the contract itself seriously. The people on the other side of the table will take it seriously, and they are used to working with contracts as the constitution of a business relationship.

At the same time, it is important to remember that the contract is not an end in itself and it is not self-implementing. It is critical to negotiate and draft the contract with the implementation and management of that agreement as a primary focus. All the emphasis on price and performance in the end depend on the ability of the parties to make the agreement work in the process of delivering the goods and services. That means, in part at least, that one of the important goals of contract policy reform must be to move away from a primary focus on risk avoidance and, as Kelman has argued, toward the more affirmative goal of a positive and effective working relationship.

At the same time, the effort to negotiate more, better, and more workable contracts requires a recognition of the reality of risk. It is useful to add to the list of reasons discussed in Chapter 3 that a government unit should not enter into contractual relationships if its most important concern is risk avoidance. That is not to say that public managers should be free of the requirement to spend public funds prudently or that basic protections against corruption should be set aside. Still, the marketplace offers no guarantees, and when government becomes a market participant it must accept a degree of risk like any other market player. It is important for public managers to help their political supervisors face that fact when they decide to contract in new areas.

It is also critical for political decision makers to understand that paralysis based on fear of scapegoating or the concern that superiors will allow media attacks without support for line managers can devastate a government's ability to function effectively in a contract relationship. For one thing, even if policies are changed to allow more flexibility in contracting, public managers will not make use of that discretion if signals are sent that any losses or problems in market operations will be interpreted as incompetence or even corruption. Few, if any, effective market participants, however skillful and principled, can claim that they have never made a bad deal or entered into a problematic contract. It is necessary to focus on negotiating the best contracts possible and then administering them effectively. If contract or performance weaknesses are encountered, the incentives for public managers must be to get the difficulties out into the open, fix them, and learn the lessons that can be gleaned from the experience. The alternative is that, just as many private firms have come to avoid public contracting, so public managers can be expected to use the tools as narrowly and restrictively as possible if they fear scapegoating. Perhaps even more dangerous is the fact that such fear can breed a tendency to be secretive, and nothing fuels attacks from critics more than the charge that public managers are engaged in backroom deal making.

It is in part because of such fears, as well as statutory requirements, that many government contracts contain a great deal of what are called boilerplate provisions. These are standard clauses that have come to be inserted into the basic contract over the years, either to satisfy policy requirements or reduce risks. The amount of boilerplate in many public agreements seems to have grown in some jurisdictions as word processors make the reproduction of such clauses and form contracts as easy as the push of the button.

At the state and local level, many of the boilerplate clauses have come about because of requirements a state attorney general or a city attorney demands. Just as it is important to work with political officials about the effort to change their approach to contracting, the same is true with regard to the working relationship with legal counsel. If the relevant attorneys see their primary role as risk avoidance and protection against corruption, they will be reticent to allow more creativity or flexibility in the drafting of contracts.

By contrast, one area that has been characterized by flexibility and informality could benefit from slightly more care and attention. The number of interjurisdictional agreements has been proliferating in recent years, with many positive and creative results. Such agreements are often intended to remain in force for extended periods or provide for periodic renewal procedures. In such situations, or where there are several parties to the agreement, it is useful to include at least enough information so that the purposes of the agreement, the general implementation responsibilities of the participants, and the criteria for renewal, if any, are clear. It is common for there to be turnover in the offices of political figures and sometimes also in those of professional managers. Without seeking to inhibit the flexibility of contract negotiators, it is useful to ensure that there is enough information in the agreement so that officials who come into the operation later in the process can have some clarity on their obligations and options.

Performance Contracts: Incentives, Disincentives, and Keeping Focused on the Purpose

Even with all these boilerplate provisions, however, there is often much to be negotiated. In addition to the general statements of work and overall price agreements, governments these days seek to include incentive and penalty clauses that provide benchmarks to assess performance as well as mechanisms to encourage contractors to exceed those minimum levels and to do so at a lower cost than that absolutely required under the contract. Today, these are generally referred to as performance contracts. In an earlier time, they were simply called incentive contracts.

The most often repeated success story for performance contracts was the result of a disaster, the Northridge, California, earthquake. At 4:30 in the morning of January 17, 1994, a quake registering 6.6 on the Richter Scale struck, leaving more than sixty dead and major destruction to both private property and public infrastructure. In the heart of America's most famous automobile-dominated community, freeways became impassable. In particular, the vital Santa Monica Freeway, a road that at some points carried more than 340,000 vehicles per day, was shut down by several collapsed bridges. It was clear that the transportation crunch would be an ongoing nightmare.[6] The state transportation agency, Cal-Trans, broke its own speed records and almost immediately entered into contracts that called for completion of the road repairs by June 24. However, the contracts also offered contractors an additional $200,000 per day for each day that the contract was completed before the normal deadline and charged a penalty of that amount for each day that the work was late:

> Instead of giving bidders up to four months to bid a large job, Caltrans gave them only a few days.
>
> Instead of waiting as long as a month between bid openings and the execution of a contract, state officials are opening bids and approving contracts on the same day.
>
> Instead of allowing up to 15 days for contractors to start the job after the bid is awarded, they are expected to begin within 24 hours.
>
> All the major contracts require the bid winners to have crews working around the clock, seven days a week.[7]

On top of all that, the contract made no allowances for weather-related delays. The freeway actually reopened on April 12, some seventy-four days early, which meant a bonus of more than $14 million for C. C. Myers Construction Inc. on a contract originally bid at slightly less than $15 million. Ever since then, public officials and private contractors alike have pointed to this feat as an example of what can be done with performance contracts.

As explained in Chapter 2, governments over time have used incentives and also created disincentives to get a contract job done. Of course, in negotiations over such contracts, the would-be contractor will seek to protect itself from penalties and to maximize its own incentives without undermining its basic expectations as to the general character of the agreement. In an earlier time, governments made the mistake of entering into what are termed cost-plus-percentage-of-cost contracts. These are no longer lawful. The other variety, known as cost-plus-fixed-fee, is still used when government seeks to attract bidders in a situation that might be considered too risky for most potential contractors and in some other situations.

The challenge here is to be clear about the principles to be used in deciding which costs are to be paid by the government and which are not. From the government side, the debate is often about what kinds of operating costs, if any, the contractor will be allowed to include as reimbursable. At times government auditors have been concerned that companies were seeking to make the taxpayer carry too much of a load for the basic operating expenses of the company not really attributable to the costs of fulfilling the contract in question. Then there have been other issues about entertainment expenses or gifts that have sometimes found their way into cost calculations.[8] The federal government has also tried to avoid situations in which its provision of payments or other kinds of support amount to an operating subsidy to the company. From the contractor's side of the ledger, the desire is to ensure prompt cost recovery from the government and to have a set of cost calculation rules that are not so burdensome that they drive up accounting expenses.

Performance contracts with clearly stated incentives and disincentives are intended to avoid as many of these supervisory details and audit burdens as possible. Beyond that, the challenge is to build in incentives and penalties that will call forth the innovative energies of the contractor to produce the best service at the best price for the public. The intention is to be more positive and active in approach, aimed at what is often called gain sharing. In this setting, the government offers options such that if a contractor finds ways to carry out the contract that save money, then the contractor shares in those savings. The use of gain sharing is an effort to counter the tendency for contractors and governments to stop seeking improvements once the initial terms of the contract have been settled. Of course, such clauses must ensure that any gain sharing is based on actual savings and not estimates.

These sorts of efforts to engage the creative energies of the contractor are particularly important in service contracts that are likely to be of long duration. The engine of competition is not readily available over the life of the contract to stimulate high levels of productivity and quality assurance and there may be few, if any, other bidders when it comes time for contract renewal.

As in any other effort at innovation, there are caveats. It is not enough to provide rewards for a contractor to come in under estimated costs. Without enhanced quality control requirements such cost incentives become perverse and can encourage poor performance, since the fastest way to cut costs is to reduce service or product quality. The challenge is to structure incentives both to improve quality and save money.

The other challenge in setting performance standards in the contemporary world of the new public management is how to integrate what are often called customer satisfaction standards with internally generated goals and government-selected benchmarks. One method for doing this is to combine performance measures by, for example, setting a benchmark based on performance in a comparable program, allowing personnel with the contracting organization to participate by proposing their own measures within acceptable limits, and using client surveys to elicit external input. Thus, for example, the government benchmark may provide the standard for the first year, with incentives for the contractor's employees to set and meet higher standards in succeeding years of the contract. Similarly, some cities use improvement in responses from citizen surveys from one year to the next as one of the measures used to assess overall performance. Thus, for example, if the users of recreational facilities rate the facilities as 3.2 on a 5-point scale one year, the measurement in the next year may be based on whether a new survey yields improved results by a certain minimum level, say a change to 3.4 on the same scale.[9]

Contracting organizations may appreciate a performance-oriented approach, particularly if it offers attractive incentives. It is even more attractive if it limits detailed reporting obligations during contract administration, simplifies audit requirements, or loosens other requirements to allow more flexibility and reduce costs. Executives of nonprofit organizations often find that reporting and contract administration burdens tend to take them away from the focus on social services that brought them to the organization in the first instance.

The challenge is to provide a basis for contract administrators to have criteria that can be applied effectively and in a nonarbitrary manner without either destroying initiative or excluding citizen input. A variety of interesting studies have been made on performance management, but there is still a great deal of room for innovation. This is an area very much in need of new ideas and management skill.

MANAGING THE ALLIANCE

All these elements of negotiation and contract drafting are critical to contract administration, but they are only the beginning of the process of managing the working relationship between government and its contractors. Certain realities exist in the operation phase. One of the problems is that to some, contract management is about audit and control. Although that is an important part of contract administration, it is only one part.

A second problem is that contract management is often regarded as automatic. As the quote from the SWAT Team report at the beginning of this chapter pointed out, contract administration is often given little priority and limited resources as compared with the attention given to the bid processes. Many small agencies and jurisdictions may in fact give little or no attention to contract administration unless a problem arises. In some instances, these contracts in operation may look more like grants than contracts. The money is awarded to a recipient organization that goes away and carries out a task with little supervision and reports when the work is complete, providing financial accounting as part of close out when the work is done or when it is time for contract renewal.

A third difficulty in contract administration is a factor that operates in the background most of the time and yet is critical in contemporary public management. This is how the management of current contracts will affect future opportunities for good deals for the public. Good contract administration is about building and maintaining a positive and effective working relationship that ensures a good deal for the public in the operation of the contract and not just in the selection of a bidder or the drafting of the contract. In fact, some agencies that are involved in important service or design-and-build contracts have even begun the operation stage of the contract with retreats to support team building. The point of the contract is not to create a cops and robbers mentality in which the relationship between the government and contracting organizations is adversarial and based on negative assumptions. Rather, the point is to build and maintain an effective service delivery operation that is focused on good service to the people intended to benefit by the contract.

While they are making efforts to focus on the positive, public managers must also maintain oversight of the contract operations. And even as the agency involved tries to maintain a close working relationship with the contractor, it must protect itself and the public against a relationship that is—or is perceived to be—so cozy that it compromises the public interest. For example, sometimes it is a question whether to have staff onsite with the contractor so that they can monitor activities or to keep them offsite so as to avoid the danger of overidentification with the contractor.

Properly done contract administration is a challenge and an increasingly important aspect of public management, in part because government is now contracting in new ways for new services. For example, it comes as a surprise to most people to learn that the National Parks Service entered into a contract with a research and development firm for bioprospecting in Yellowstone National Park. Under this contract, the Diversa Corporation promised to pay the government approximately $20,000 per year and 5 to 10 percent royalties on products that result from the company's exploration for microbial organisms in the park, and particularly in its hot springs, geysers, and mud pots.[10] Although the company did not get exclusive rights to the organisms, it did obtain the right to patent or copyright any discoveries that it could qualify for that protection. Washington, D.C., is now contracting with the Lockheed-Martin Corporation to equip some of its police cruisers with cameras that automatically take pictures of speeding cars; the pictures are then processed into traffic tickets sent for collection. A firm located in Utah has contracted with the California State University system to take over the information technology operations for the huge system's management. Under the agreement, student records, financial documents, and other key management information would actually reside in computers in Utah to be accessed by the campus officials as needed. Another firm has contracted for the personnel management functions of entire state civil service systems. Pennsylvania contracted with a firm that evaluates unemployment compensation claims; this firm, in turn, contracts with other firms to do various reviews on those claims. Many jurisdictions have contracted with private firms or with other states or counties to provide their corrections facilities and programs.

The Government's Capacity to Manage Its Contracts

These challenges and tensions mean, among other things, that in order for cities or agencies to carry out their responsibilities in the operations stage, they must have the capacity to manage their contracts. That may seem obvious, but in reality few if any government units can truly claim that they have adequate, and well-trained, contract management capacity, particularly if that term is used in anything but the narrowest sense.

There are at least four areas of concern with respect to capacity building. The first is the need to budget for contract management. It is rare to find agencies consciously and adequately budgeting to provide resources for contract management. In fact, it is unusual in all but the largest contract operations to find any budgeting for contract management at all. It is appropriate as a city or an agency considers entering into new or expanded contract operations to examine existing budget practices to determine whether they adequately address the special needs of contract administration.

Contract administration can be a labor-, information-, and technology-intensive activity. At a minimum, there needs to be a clear sense of the degree to which contract administration needs are being placed in competition with substantive program needs. The process of costing and budgeting for contract management operations makes it possible to know what the net savings of contracting are as compared with providing the service directly. Indeed, the GAO has concluded that it can be virtually impossible to know whether a given contract saves money without knowing government's true cost as well as the actual cost of direct service delivery. If management costs and payments to contractors are higher than direct provision of the services by government, answers will be needed to very thorny questions about just what is gained in some contract arrangements. Certainly, there will be efficiency and economy questions to address. One of the difficulties is that a failure to fund and maintain an adequate contract management infrastructure may not produce serious consequences in the early stages but may become apparent and serious during the later life of the contract.

Second, there is the problematic assumption that many or even most of the costs of contract operations can be transferred to the contractor. In some cases efforts have been made to avoid building more infrastructure within the agencies or local governments by expanding reporting requirements for contractors in a variation on the theme of self-regulation. Of course, increased reporting means increased costs, which, in turn, means that contractors will join the move away from bidding or increase their prices to cover their costs. Increased reporting also tends to drive smaller, not-for-profit contractors out of the process, since they may lack the capacity to prepare numerous complex compliance reports and will be concerned about the size and burdens of audits that may follow to cross-check those reports.

The self-regulation idea that quality control personnel employed by the contractor can handle contract administration tasks assumes that all that is involved is a kind of regulatory activity when what is really needed is careful, but not excessively intrusive, management. Even in the regulatory side of the process, there can be difficulties, particularly if it is perceived that public managers are not adequately monitoring the contractors.

Third, there are issues of education for public managers. The National Performance Review study of contracting recognized a need for training, as have most of the earlier studies on the subject. However, the need is not just for training for specialized contracting officers, people who are identified as part of the contract workforce. Given the amount and scope of government contracting as compared with direct services, it is scandalous that few master of public administration programs and virtually no master of public policy programs teach students anything about the subject beyond debates over whether or not to privatize. Not only is education on how to manage the contracts themselves needed but also education on managing the public sector people who handle the contracts.

Another area of education needed for contract management is interjurisdictional agreements. It is common for a new public manager to enter a position and not be informed of all such agreements that may exist in his or her organization. Consent decrees may have been entered in cases brought concerning matters as diverse as gender discrimination in employment, unconstitutional conditions in jails, and unlawful policies in schools. These are court orders, but they are agreements in the nature of a contract with the power of contempt to enforce them. It is important for new managers in an organization to learn what kinds of contracts the unit has, what their status is, what obligations they impose, and whether or when they are due to expire or be reconsidered.

Fourth, there is the need to recruit, train, and retain in the public sector high-quality public contract managers. Hiring and retaining qualified and experienced contract managers is not cheap. They cost a good deal to train and develop. They must have a set of skills that will make them attractive to private sector employers, who can be counted on to try to hire them away from government with offers of substantial increases in salary. They must also be equipped with state-of-the-art management tools from computers to software to consulting advice. They cannot be expected effectively to manage relationships with private sector organizations that have up-to-date tools if they do not also have those tools.

Contract Oversight: Getting beyond the Audit Approach

One of the important responsibilities of contract administrators is the oversight of the contractor's operations. Traditionally, this has been described in terms of effective cost and quality monitoring, and that has in turn often been understood as auditing. Although these are important elements, the oversight of contracts is really a broader and hopefully more positive activity. Not only that, but as contracting for services (as opposed to the purchase of goods) has increased, new challenges have arisen that go well beyond the more traditional ideas of cost and quality auditing. The challenge is to move beyond a kind of law enforcement attitude in which the contract manager is viewed as the cop on the beat preventing bad things from happening and toward a more positive approach in which the object is to obtain the best performance possible in all the dimensions that together define a good deal for the public.

Historically, most of the discussion of cost and quality monitoring came out of the federal government, particularly the Pentagon's large weapons systems purchases. The Defense Contract Audit Agency (DCAA) became a leader in the development contract audit techniques, so much so that civilian agencies have been urged to use DCAA as an in-house consultant to improve their own practices. However, studies of problems in federal contracting continued to highlight shortcomings in contract monitoring in both defense and civilian contracts. Indeed, one of the problem areas to which critics return time after time is the poor quality cost analysis and control. These problems persist both in indirect cost estimates and in the ability to evaluate claims for direct cost reimbursements.[11] The SWAT Team report, for example, focused much of its attention on the ongoing tension between the need for timely payment of reimbursements that are due to a contractor and the importance of careful cost calculations and auditing.

Actually, three different kinds of audits have been done over the years to ensure that the contractor was actually performing the contract, that its financial practices met the contract and federal laws, and that it was in fact complying with the certifications that it had submitted concerning government labor standards, civil rights requirements, and other policies. These are generally known as performance, financial, and compliance audits. Efforts have been made in the recent past to combine these into a single audit to reduce the burdens and costs associated with all these audit programs where organizations receive multiple federal contracts.

However, as service contracting has increased, the level of complexity of contract oversight has also increased, and the effectiveness of that oversight has not been satisfactory. Thus, the General Accounting Office has found that "[w]hile we have seen the environment change considerably, what we have not seen is a significant improvement in federal agencies' management of service contracts. Put simply, the poor management of service contracts undermines the government's ability to obtain good value for the money spent."[12] Among the difficulties is the tendency to take the same kind of law enforcement attitude based on auditing that had been around for so long.

As if that were not enough, politicians love to paint many social service programs such as Medicare as particularly subject to abuse. The recipients of benefits under these programs and their service providers are often implicitly charged with seeking to defraud the government. To make the situation more complicated, what was then known as the Health Care Financing Administration contracted with various firms for claims administration under the program and assigned oversight duties for them to pursue.

Traditionally, HCFA's claims administration contractors performed most of Medicare's program safeguard functions. These five functions are intended to ensure that Medicare pays only appropriate claims for covered services performed by legitimate providers to eligible beneficiaries. They include:

- medical reviews of claims to identify claims for noncovered, medically unnecessary, or unreasonable services, conducted both before the claims are paid (prepayment review) and after payments are made (postpayment review);
- reviews to identify other primary sources of payment, such as private health insurers, that are responsible for paying claims mistakenly billed to Medicare;
- audits of cost reports submitted by institutional providers to determine if their costs are allowable and reasonable;
- identification and investigation of possible fraud cases that are referred to the Department of Health and Human Services Office of the Inspector General (HHS OIG) for investigation and possible prosecution by the Department of Justice; and

• provider education and training related to Medicare coverage policies and appropriate billing practices.

However, Congress added authority for HCFA to go further to contract with oversight specialist contractors who would be available to investigate any allegations of fraud, abuse, and waste. In 1999 HCFA contracted with thirteen Program Security Contractors (PSCs) to carry out these functions, either directly or through subcontractors. These are task order contracts and the agency triggered the services some fifteen times between 1999 and spring 2001. In some cases these were fixed-price contracts, whereas in others they were cost-reimbursement or performance contracts. Some aimed to assist existing HCFA contractors, others were designed to supplement or even supersede the claims contractors, and still others gave the PSCs the task of broad investigative or training work. Of course, in the end, these PSCs, which were to oversee the contract claims operation and the providers and patients they evaluated had themselves to be monitored and supervised by HCFA. By May 2001, the General Accounting Office concluded that "AHCFA has not yet developed clear, measurable criteria to evaluate PSCs' performance on the individual task orders."[13] This example alone should make clear that monitoring is a complex endeavor given the reality of today's public policies.

The situation at the state and local levels varies widely, depending, in part at least, on the capabilities of the agency or local government involved. In some instances, people who were in agencies and who were displaced as a result of the contracting out of programs end up as the people charged with monitoring those contracts.[14] In many instances, though, agencies have relatively limited capacity for this kind of work.

The purposes and techniques of financial, compliance, and performance audits and other oversight techniques should be integrated into a comprehensive program of contract management. Too often, these police-oriented approaches have driven the process and have tended to absorb energies that need to be directed toward service improvement and management innovation. One of the attractive characteristics of performance contracts that incorporate gain sharing is that they are intended to provide incentives for contractors to monitor their own operations and maximize their effectiveness. They also keep the focus on service to the public rather than on narrowly defined cost accounting issues. At the same time, it is essential to build the capacity for contract management teams in order to allow effective monitoring, since responsibility for oversight remains with the government agency or city that awarded the contract.

Mid-Course Corrections: The Use and Abuse of Change Orders

Even though it is not often described in this way, contract management is done by both the contractor and the government unit involved. Although government units seek to ensure that the services are effectively performed and costs do not escalate, contractors are on guard against efforts to change their obligations without compensation for increased work. The contract change order is the device that is used to address that problem.

There are legitimate reasons for government to issue change orders and also for contractors to seek them. Clearly, there are times when problems are encountered in the course of contract administration, when opportunities are detected for cost saving involving an appropriate change in performance standards, and when new technology is found that means that the service can be provided better, cheaper, or more responsively. Moreover, there are times when both the contractor and the government agree that assumptions made at the outset of a contract relationship simply need to be changed, such as when a contractor starts to perform a task only to find out that the problem it was hired to fix is greater than either party to the contract understood.[15] When any of these events occurs, it becomes necessary to issue change orders, instructions by the government to the contractor to change its tasks, standards, or methods.

However, change orders most often result in increased costs. The basic principle is that so long as the change fits within the general scope of the contract and is properly authorized by a contracting officer, the contractor, with some exceptions, has to make the change and seek an adjustment in payments as the work continues.[16] One of the important tasks of contract managers is to ensure that change orders are properly authorized and correct cost calculations are made to meet the new requirements. If performance contracts are involved, the use of change orders also means adjusting incentive targets and processes to meet the changed conditions. Such adjustments should address quality issues as well as other considerations.

Despite the comments above about the need to maintain a positive and constructive relationship with the contractor whenever possible, it is necessary to recognize a history of difficulty with change orders. Managing change orders can be a dangerous activity, since some contractors have sought change orders to raise reimbursements and reduce standards in cases where they provided unreasonably low bids and cost estimates in the beginning, or where they made excessive claims about performance during bid processes. Even if there was no inappropriate intent, change orders can place a public manager in a serious squeeze. Consider the following small example.

The manager of a small town contracted for repairs to two bridges. The winning bid totaled some $46,000. The manager applied for two types of grants to assist in financing the construction. One was a formula-based grant, but the other was a standard grant only offered once a year. He based his grant proposals on the $46,000 figure. However, no sooner had the work commenced than the contractor called the manager to the work site to inform him that the actual cost would be roughly twice the original estimate. There were few other available bidders in the area, and the community was at that point committed. Moreover, the community's dependence on a certain price and its significant assistance from grants created serious difficulties. It was possible to go back to increase the request from one grant source, but the other could not be refiled for another year. The amount may seem modest, but to a small community already facing financial stress, it was significant.

One other change order danger should be noted. There is a doctrine of "constructive changes" that has sometimes been invoked by courts to award increased costs for a contractor even where no formal and explicit change order was issued by the contracting officer. W. Noel Keyes explains it this way: "An express change takes place when a contracting officer purposely utilizes a changes article in the contract and issues a written order that is covered by it. A constructive change is a change that a contractor argues that he has to make even though he had not been issued a written order under a changes article."[17] Keyes points out that, although statutes and regulations call for express change orders, courts have in many instances recognized constructive change orders. In any case, he emphasizes that it is important for contracts to contain a changes clause that specifies how changes are to be authorized and issued, since a clearly expressed clause makes it difficult to claim constructive changes. Even so, he notes, "The 'Changes' clause has been one of the most litigated clauses in government contracts."[18] In large part because of the sensitive nature of change orders, it is critical that the project team and the contractor be absolutely clear as to who is authorized to issue change orders. Even so, agency employees must be warned that they must be careful in their communications with contractors so as not to be the source of what is later claimed to be a constructive change order.

Interventions by the Project Team

Beyond the idea of changing the work in a contract, one of the challenges that can arise in the management of contract operations, particularly in service contracts, is when and how to intervene in a contractor's operations. The nature, reach, and purpose of interventions by the project team present a dilemma for public managers. On the one hand, one of the purposes of contracting is to avoid micromanagement and to hire outside organizations to do a task based in part on their ability to manage themselves. At the same time, serious questions about a contractor's behavior may demand government action. Thus, if a church group contracted with government to provide child care and parents later complained about the effort of caregivers to influence the children with the religious beliefs of the church, to whom do parents complain? Is their recourse to be found in government or do they have rights with respect to the contractor directly? Is government constrained to wait until it is time for contract renewal or can it intervene immediately? Or, if there is a problematic employee in a contractor organization, can government or the individual client take action against him or her, or are there barriers against such intervention? In sum, the challenge is to prepare contract administrators with an ability to reach the internal management processes of contractors, to reach particular employees with contract organizations, to reach subcontractors, and to be able to intervene in service processes. The questions about providing the contractual foundation and contract manager competence to intervene when necessary become even more complex when the contractor is a nonprofit organization with substantial volunteer labor or where the organization is particularly sensitive to direct involvement, such as church groups.

At the same time, some commentators have suggested that for-profit firms in human service delivery contracts may require closer monitoring and more preparation to intervene simply because they are in the business of making a profit and because they may be national and not subject to some of the local scrutiny that would naturally apply to local nonprofits based in the community they serve.[19] Under 1996 legislation for-profit firms are permitted to subcontract for such services as the provision of foster care. Intervention in the operation of national firms working through subcontractors can present its own set of complex challenges. As this example suggests, the issue is complicated by the fact that many of the social service programs involve state contracts to for-profit or nonprofit organizations under federal funding. In such settings, the policy restrictions of both levels of government must be considered.

This area of contract management is very much a discussion in progress with few general prescriptions. The general cautions that are commonly offered are similar to advice often given with respect to contract management. First, attempt to address in the contract as clearly as possible the authority of the project team to intervene, the types of interventions that might be undertaken, and the manner in which disputes will be resolved in the event of disagreements between the contractor and the government. Of course, if the situation is extreme enough, the contract manager could claim a default of contract and seek to terminate the agreement, including possible sanctions against the contractor. However, there are many situations short of that in which the project team would want to intervene. The other approach is to provide in the contract for mechanisms by which the clients receiving services can present and have resolved complaints that they might have. In the end, the challenge is to maintain a balance between the need to intervene, if necessary, and the danger of a situation in which government pays a contractor in part at least to avoid hands-on delivery of services but then loses the benefit of the contract by being too closely involved in day-to-day operations.

CONTRACTS AS TRANSFORMATIVE AGENTS

Whether the public manager deliberately intervenes in day-to-day operations of the contractor or not, it is important to understand that the contract relationship is transformative. It affects both the city or agency that let the contract and the contractor. In some instances the effects of contracts with local nonprofit organizations are particularly obvious. Barbara Romzek and Jocelyn Johnston examined what happened when Kansas decided to contract out case management to the Area Agencies on Aging (AAA), only to find that the nonprofit was then faced with major challenges that affected its character and operations.[20] They point out that the organization had been a relatively small advocacy-oriented organization that faced the famous admonition that we should be careful what we wish for. The organization argued that it could provide a single point of entry to service system; using that approach, it would save money and improve service. However, to meet the challenge, the AAA had to expand significantly, acquire the necessary systems and equipment to manage across a large geographic area, and face the communications challenges needed to operate a larger organization. As they hired more people and grew organizationally to meet the challenge, they faced criticism for becoming more bureaucratic and exhibiting less of the "personal touch." Because of this need to grow and change along with their lack of experience as a major direct service provider, they underestimated their cost of service delivery. Romzek and Johnston concluded that in such a setting the "[o]rganizations involved can face serious stresses related to changes in organizational culture, not merely in artifacts, but in core values."[21] At the same time, many nonprofits have been affected by their increasing need to compete with for-profit firms.[22]

For-profit organizations, too, are often affected by the decision to undertake government contracts. Although it is known primarily for its aerospace work, largely growing as a result of defense contracting, Lockheed Martin has come to be a major vendor to state and local governments in various kinds of service contracts, ranging from social services to traffic enforcement programs. Companies like Lockheed Martin had to bring in significant numbers of executives with backgrounds and values very different from the values that had traditionally dominated the core businesses of the corporation.

The GAO found that over a six-year period twenty-one directors of state child support programs and state welfare programs left to go to work for social service contracting firms.[23] Of course, this practice also indicates that government agencies or cities that expand contract operations are themselves reshaped in the process. That is true in terms of both the internal and external operations of these organizations, and these changes are of increasing importance as agencies depend more on contract providers to carry out the agency's assigned responsibilities and are less able to do so on their own.

MANAGING RELATIONSHIPS AMID CHANGE

The changes that come with expanded contracting occur in a larger context that is itself changing in many ways, quite apart from the specific issue of expanded contracting. Demographic changes mean a need to pay more attention to cultural, racial, and gender differences even as we seek to attack discrimination and ensure equal opportunity. Issues of equity as well as equality must be addressed by every level of government. Demographic patterns are not, however, equally distributed. Thus, for example, the 2000 census showed that Arizona had grown 40 percent since 1990. Washington State has seen the creation of new cities as a growth industry during the same period. At the same time, however, northeastern states have witnessed population loss and an increase in the average age of their populations. All these factors affect service delivery and also the political context within which policy decisions are made.

The political context has also changed. There is an increasing tendency for citizens to view public policy as a fee-for-service idea. They are often described as customers and many come to think of themselves in that way. They want a greater voice in how their services are delivered and they want to customize those services to their individual taste. Thus, voucher programs are popular because they permit individuals to do their own contracting, in part at least with public money. In contrast, those taxpayers who do not see themselves benefitting directly from a particular program may oppose the very programs demanded by others. Many other consequences flow from this idea.[24]

These kinds of changes go on continually. Often, contracts are launched to serve particular clients when one set of political dynamics prevails, but wind up only a few years into the program in a different political setting. The expectations of a legislature conducting oversight five years into a policy and its implementing contracts may be different from the consensus on that same program when it was enacted.

The financial reality within which contract management takes place is also continually changing either incrementally or dramatically. For example, assumptions made about budgets at all levels in early to mid-2000 were turned on their heads within a matter of months.[25] Program coverage or services may be expanded when service expectations are high and there appear to be resources. However, although the resources may decrease as the economy changes, expectations may remain just as high. Moreover, in periods of economic downturn, service demands on government tend to increase.

In sum, when it operates as a market participant, government must deal with all the volatility that exists in that marketplace. In addition, it must face the dynamics of the political arena and the society that shapes it.

NETWORK MANAGEMENT: GOVERNING THROUGH CONTRACT SERVICE NETWORKS

Among the reasons public managers must be sensitive to these complexities is the fact that governments depend on service networks to accomplish their goals.

These networks are complex and sensitive operations that are very much affected by forces in their environments. Jurisdictions from the local level to the national often cannot meet their obligations through simple partnerships, a concept that conjures up a picture of two parties deciding to cooperate for a discrete purpose. Instead, they work through networks, collections of organizations, the parts of which depend on each other. Service networks can be effective and efficient mechanisms, but they pose special management challenges and require a commitment of resources to meet those realities. Beyond that, networks can have particularly significant impacts on the nonprofit organizations that are critical to the service systems.

What Are Networks and Why Does It Matter?

Popularized by international corporate operations, the idea of network operations has been to achieve maximum efficiency and minimum capitalization requirements by creating networks to produce and market a product or service rather than creating a single organization to do that job. This approach is also referred to in some settings as the concept of the "hollow corporation"[26] or, in a more recent manifestation, "the virtual corporation."[27]

A company using network operations contracts with a firm in one location to make a product, with another to handle distribution, with still another to do marketing, and with others to provide additional necessary services. One of the earlier and most commonly cited examples is Nike, the athletic shoe company.[28] Parts of a network may be spread across the country or around the world. In such a network, the manager must manage relationships not only each of the organizations in the network, sometimes referred to as nodes, but also the linkages among the nodes. If any unit in the network breaks down or if any of the relationships among units is blocked or fails, then the network manager must find a way to fill the gap and repair the system. Thus, the network is based on mutual interdependencies. The issue is not just the needs of the firm whose logo goes on the product, but also the interests of all the other participants in the process. The maintenance of the critical linkages among the units, as well as the skills that the managers have within each of the units, is essential to the success of the entire network and all those who participate in it.

Advocates claim two advantages of networks. First, this mode of operation allows the network builder to shed both operating costs and larger capital expenditures. The network is built with a series of contracts with each of the other units in the network. Each contractor is responsible for its own plant and equipment. More than that, it is responsible for the recruitment, training, management, and compensation of its people. Indeed, even if a firm had capabilities in-house, executives often choose to spin those units off into separate businesses to shed costs and management responsibilities. Taken far enough, this allows an organization to trim its costs to the minimum by slimming down internally to perform only those functions that cannot be contracted out. Hence the firm enhances its own productivity and efficiency by retaining and consuming only those resources absolutely necessary to its operation. The efficiencies for the other units in the system are achieved by using the marketplace to control contractor costs. This of course assumes the existence of a competitive market in whatever goods or services are required.

The second advantage cited by advocates for network operations is flexibility. At its best, the network relies on all its units to use their creativity to address problems as they arise, as opposed to an integrated organization, which must find solutions for all problems that come through the doors. If the contractors are unable to meet the new challenges, then the core organization can simply drop that contractor and enter into a contract with a new firm. Supply and demand would presumably generate new potential contractors with the necessary capabilities and with employees possessing the needed skill sets to deal with the changing environment.

The public sector counterpart of these developments is what has been referred to as the "Hollow Government" pushed by politicians around the world bent on cutting the size of government ministries and budgets, privatizing to the maximum, and employing as many private sector management tools as possible.[29] In slightly less dramatic terms, these are also known as service networks. With contracting having expanded to a point at which government no longer has the capability to deliver significant portions of many of the services it is mandated to make available,[30] the hope has been that these service networks will bring the same kinds of benefits to public organizations as to their private sector counterparts.

Network Management Is Different

Some of the early network advocates failed to recognize all the challenges that this approach entails. Even those in the private sector found that the model posed "real risks," including the loss of control, dependence on other organizations that might "drop the ball," the danger that a firm could become involved with organizations that could tarnish its reputation, and the need to share sensitive information. In addition, they realized that the more complex the network, the more likely it is that participating units might "stumble."[31] Above all, the network mode of operation meant "new challenges for management."[32]

If the networks posed difficulties for private sector groups, they meant even more complicated challenges for public service organizations. Looking back on early experiences with service networks, Robert Agranoff and Michael McGuire concluded: "One realization is becoming increasingly clear: the capacities required to operate successfully in network settings are different from the capabilities needed to succeed at managing a single organization. The classical, mostly intraorganizational inspired management perspective that has guided public

administration for more than a century is simply inapplicable for multiorganiza-
tional, multigovernmental, and multisectoral forms of governing."[33] They added:
"There are many more questions than answers in network management."[34] In
addition to the planning, organizing, staffing, budgeting, and other traditional
functions within their own organizations, managers in networks must also engage
in such specialized activities as "activation," "framing," "mobilizing," and "syn-
thesizing."[35] At a minimum, it is essential to recognize the level of sophistication
and capabilities needed for effective network management. However, many of the
organizations involved in networks do not even have really effective contract
management capabilities, let alone the more sophisticated requirements of network management. Building that kind of capability not only means assigning
people now attending to direct service or direct supervision to new tasks but also
requires the development of new skills or the hiring of people with the kinds of
specialized knowledge necessary to meet the evolving challenges posed by network operations.

There are, in addition, other challenges that are more complex for the public
sector networks. Since the programs involved are sometimes mandated services
for needy clients, network failures mean that someone must be able to step in
rapidly. Where government does not have the capability to do that, it must be
able to find alternate providers, which is not always easy. For one thing, statutes
and regulations concerning access to and use of confidential client information
must be met, particularly where public safety, children's programs, or health care
issues are involved.

The ability to take advantage of the claimed flexibility of networks requires the
availability of multiple suppliers. However, as networks become tighter and more
interdependent—some might say more efficient—often relatively few alternates
are available. This is one of the reasons that those who have studied the matter
have found that networks work best in resource-rich environments.[36] Resource-
poor environments can increase competition among some network participants, a
situation that can undermine the levels of trust that are so essential to the effective
operation of the network. Unfortunately, in recent years, despite claims of budget
surpluses, public service networks have often been anything but resource rich.

Clearly, networks in the public service arena are different from private sector
networks. They must respond to values other than economic efficiency, and their
success cannot be measured by profits. In addition to efficiency, public sector operations must meet the other criteria that make for a good deal for the public, including economy, effectiveness, equity, responsiveness, and responsibility.

Internal Impacts on Nonprofit Service Organizations

Apart from the government agency that seeks to build a service network, it is
common for many or even most of the other units in that network to be non-

profit service organizations. For example, typically a state agency will contract with nonprofits in each of several service areas of the state. A city will do the same with different types of nonprofits serving various neighborhood or interest groups. The federal government often builds such networks by using a prime contractor in various states or cities. That contractor then uses subcontracts to develop the network with other nonprofits in the service area. This is common in sectors as diverse as mental health services, refugee resettlement, and community development.

Nonprofits face special needs and special challenges in network operations that are different from those facing governments or for-profit firms. For one thing, the people who provide the human resources that are the very core of many service delivery programs are in a different situation from that of private sector employees. Many nonprofits still depend on volunteer programs to provide important elements of their services and also as a recruitment device for future employees. Development and operation of such volunteer programs requires significant investment of time and energy. Although a growing number of people in nonprofits are paid employees, they are often expected to provide far more hours and effort than a similar employee in a private firm. They often must do multiple duty in both direct service delivery and organizational maintenance and support. Moreover, they are frequently expected to devote significant amounts of time and effort to participation in community programs and projects.

The facts of life in service networks add stresses as nonprofit executives spend more time on boundary-spanning obligations and funding issues. Networks often expect that member organizations will, as one private sector network advocate recommends, "offer the best and brightest. Put your best people into these relationships."[37] However, doing so frequently brings stress inside the home organization, since those external demands take leaders away from the organization's primary mission, straining relationships with workers and sometimes with boards of directors.[38]

Even more than that, however, is the importance of the presence of leverage pressures in the networks. The use of grants and contracts with nonprofits is viewed in part at least as a way of leveraging greater impact from the same dollars than what could be developed in a government organization, and competition for resources makes it possible to leverage more.[39] That additional impact must come from the organization and its people. Because nonprofit service workers are so committed to their mission, they often willingly accept obligations to attend evening meetings, invitations to weekend events in the community, and emergency requests for help at virtually any time. However, there are costs to the service providers and their families for this commitment and responsiveness.

Unfortunately, there is often a tendency to underestimate these and other costs relative to actual revenue that comes into a service organization from grants and contracts. In addition to these costs are the costs associated with the preparation of proposals, administration of contracts, and contract renewals. Failing to incorporate the investments of time and energy required for proposal writing and contract administration in assessments of resource commitment for service delivery is a serious miscalculation of true cost. Another issue arises when some participants in service networks assume that other units of the network will make contributions that they are in reality unable to provide. These errors and constraints may produce overestimated resources and underestimated obligations. Just as agencies and local government agencies cannot contribute funds that they do not have, nonprofits cannot enter service commitments that they cannot support without damaging their people and their organizations.

Even assuming that a network participant is not overextended, it is still important that the people within the organization be equipped by training and support to deal with the stresses that the network is producing. It is particularly helpful if people from other parts of the network, including government units, can be trained together. Unfortunately, in organizations, both governmental and nongovernmental, that are under financial stress, training and professional development are often among the first areas to be cut—if, indeed, such support was ever available. Apart from training programs, few organizations in the network provide organizational renewal support. It should be no surprise to find that burnout is a problem even among committed service providers.

Of course, one of the dangers that can come from network stresses is a sense by service workers that the group has lost its identity. Many volunteers and employees come to particular organizations because of a strong commitment to what the group does. If the organization alters its direction or seeks to change its mission and character because of the demands of networks, there is a danger of internal conflict. The same is true if a board of directors, believing that it should focus primarily on the demands of the network, hires executives who are, or who are perceived to be, more committed to the network than they are to their own organization and the people it was designed to serve. If the executive decides to focus primary attention on entrepreneurial efforts to entertain new programs as opportunities for the organization, the message may be that the existing programs are not important. That can be devastating to paid employees or volunteers who have worked long and hard to develop the ongoing programs and make them work in the face of challenges.

Network Realities and Public Contract Managers

The challenges presented by networks noted to this point do not mean they should be abandoned. They are, for various reasons, facts of modern public life. Still, it is necessary to come to grips with what is required to lead and operate service networks. The ability of contract managers to meet this challenge includes the importance of network operations by design and not accident, the need to build capacity for all participants, the challenges of governance of the network, the need to address resources in the network, the critical importance of account-ability, and the internal impacts on nonprofit service providers in the network.

Networks as Deliberate Choices. If an agency or a city wants to provide serv-ices by a network instead of by many independent contractors, that decision is best made forthrightly and should not be the result of uncontrolled policy drift. On the one hand, networks cannot work well if the approach to their manage-ment is merely to seek to turn nonprofits into standard units of a state agency. Much of the strength and efficiency of networks is that they are made of different organizations, each with its own nature, function, and operation. On the other hand, the structure of networks and the processes by which they function mat-ter.[40] At some point, it becomes important for all the participants in network op-erations to understand what the networks of which they are a part are, who is in the network, how it is structured, and what formal or informal understandings guide the operation of the network. The object of an agency's attempting to be careful in operating networks is not to formalize them to the point where they lose their flexibility but to ensure that it is direct about the fact that there is a net-work and to be clear how it works, or for that matter does not work. Contracts provide much of that structure and function.

Creating the Foundation for Effective Service Network Operations. If the object is to create and rely on a network to provide public services, then it is essential to determine and specify clearly who will provide the resources for net-work maintenance and the management capabilities to ensure its effectiveness. It is also in everyone's best interest to ensure that all the units participating in the network have the requisite capabilities to function effectively, since, particularly in relatively tightly linked networks with high levels of interdependency, *the entire network is only as strong as its weakest component.*

This applies to networks with important interjurisdictional components as well as nonprofits or for-profits. For example, one modest-sized but growing community entered into an agreement with two other small communities to pro-vide first-response emergency medical capability. A nonprofit was formed with representation on the board from all three communities and from the volunteers who provided the service. The group relied primarily on volunteers for its day-to-day leadership and operation. However, groups like this often experience turnover, and its volunteers have varying levels of energy and commitment. At the same time, the communities involved relied on the services, but the level of service they received ultimately depended on the strength of the nonprofit.

Several factors, in particular, require attention in network operations. First, public service network management requires a fairly high degree of sophistica-tion. The backbone of most networks is a set of contracts, but few organizations have substantial contract management capabilities. Beyond that, although each participant in the network must manage its own internal operations, each must also participate in the management of the network; and networks, for reasons noted earlier, are subject to a host of uncertainties and contingencies.[41]

The resources needed to function in networks must come from somewhere. Although provider organizations can support some of the work, it is clear that government must accept responsibility for a significant part of the capacity-building effort. Just as the government must provide resources for network management, so public managers must themselves be provided with the types and amounts of resources needed to perform their roles. It is not possible to push more demands and large amounts of resources through agencies or city departments that have been cut to the point at which they no longer have the capacity to perform their base functions, let alone new obligations.

Governance: A Critical Fact of Life whether Recognized as Such or Not. Attention must also be paid to the governance and not simply the management of such networks. The numbers of organizations involved in network decision making and the limits on the ability simply to control operations requires increased effort. As H. Brinton Milward puts it:

> The fact that a hollow state relies on networks is a weakness as well as a strength. . . . Networks, the mainstay of the hollow state, are inherently weaker forms of social action. Because of the need to coordinate joint production, networks are inherently unstable over time. Managers continually are faced with problems that can lead to instability—negotiating, coordinating, monitoring, holding third parties accountable, and writing and enforcing contracts.[42]

Networks do not respond well to simple overhead controls. Besides, the creativity and drive that make nonprofits such constructive partners for the provision of public services can easily be lost if they are not afforded an active role in the governance of the network.

Still, there are power relationships among the units of a network, and not simply from government to nonprofits. Those who have studied the matter find that governance issues relating to power are often overlooked because it is assumed that the very idea of networks implies mutual cooperation and that special interests are to be "checked at the door."[43] The simplistic assumption that it is the government's contract and therefore control is left to the agency that awarded the contract is equally unrealistic. Networks in which a government unit contracts with one organization as a prime contractor and depends on the prime contractor to build and control the network can be just as problematic. Anyone who has participated in meetings involving city or county officials, state authorities, and nonprofit service providers knows that the representatives of each of these organizations comes to the meeting with a sense of their specific mission and of the interests of the organization they represent in addition to their concern for the common goal of the network.

Although the lessons of the private sector networks may be of some assistance, such issues as accountability and the critical importance of high levels of trust between clients and service providers make the public service context different. For all these reasons, it is important to consider how the networks in which one operates are governed. That means not only a consideration of cooperative efforts but also a willingness to consider what happens when conflicts arise. It also requires thought about the kinds of concerns that each of the participants in the service network brings to the table.

The Nagging Problem of Resource Scarcity and Interdependence. One of the serious problems facing service networks is the difficulty of resource shortages amid increasing demands for services. Efforts to offer expanded services, often with the same or less support from the federal and state governments, have presented precisely the kinds of circumstances that those who study networks suggest are counterproductive. They are counterproductive in part because they provide incentives for nonprofits to compete with one another for resources in the form of a more limited number of contracts.

Where the funds for existing grants or contracts are reduced, providers are faced with a need to seek a larger number of grants or contracts to yield the same level of funding, which is essential if those organizations are to be able to support their paid staff and their operations. Of course, each of those grants or contracts comes with administrative costs and reporting obligations as well as the need to perform the specific activities set forth in the funding agreement. Thus, the nonprofit is leveraged to produce more for the same amount of funding or less. Not only that but the organization must find a way to release officers to do the additional work on the contract applications as well as administration of the additional programs if the applications are successful.

There is the additional problem that the issue of resources in a network context is not simply a question of the resources available to a particular service provider organization. It also has to do with the cumulative resources available to the network as a whole in relation to the service demands that it must address. It is in part for this reason that networks are so sensitive to fluctuations in their environments.

The Accountability Challenge. The question of accountability in contract management will be a focus of attention in Chapter 5. In the present context, it is worth noting that virtually everyone who has studied networks agrees that accountability in such settings is particularly difficult. There are several reasons. It has been argued that "[t]he leakage of accountability in the hollow state and the lack of government capability or willingness to effectively manage its contracts with nonprofits is a major problem."[44] This issue of "leakage" is a concept popularized by Eugene Bardach and Cara Lesser. They have argued that the "leakage of authority" that occurs when networks are created and operated collaboratively offers flexibility, but it also makes accountability much more complex.[45] Because authority and responsibility are parceled out within the network, it is difficult to get a clear picture of how well the network is performing as well as the effectiveness of individual units within the network. The nonprofits within the network are accountable not only to the governments and private agencies at all levels who provide resources but also to their boards of directors, to the other member units of the network, and ultimately to the clients they serve for whom the entire system was created in the first place. The government units, in turn, face other accountability requirements for the operation of the network. And, of course, the accountability is not simply about authority and reporting requirements but is very much about performance standards.

CONCLUSION

Despite the reality that most of the life of a contract relationship is spent in the operations stage, too little attention is paid to it. Major studies of contract management have found that many agencies do not place emphasis on contract management during this phase and the tools they use are often inadequate to ensure that the deal turns out to be as good in practice as it appeared during the integration stage. Indeed, final contract negotiations and the start of the working relationship marks the beginning of contract operations.

That contract alliance must then be managed, which requires more than simply an audit and control approach in which the contract manager plays police officer on the beat. Done properly, management of contract operations should be a positive effort not only to ensure that the people get what they pay for, but also that providers will want to bid on contract opportunities in the future. That, in turn, requires creative use of such devices as performance contracts, careful handling of change orders, maintenance of effective working relationships within the project team, and the ability to adapt to changing circumstances, economic, technical, and political.

In the contemporary environment, management of contract operations involves the development, management, and, in a larger sense, even governance of provider networks. That said, network management is acknowledged by virtually all who have studied it to be different in many important respects from organizational management internally or even the management of a simple two-party relationship. Network management requires special skills and adequate resources that are often not fully appreciated by those who advocate the network approach. Like all other aspects of contract management, networks and the environments within which they operate change, and network management must be adaptable enough to change with them.

Environmental factors do change and so do agencies, cities, nonprofits, for-profit vendors, and the need for contract services or goods. That means in turn that contracts change or are terminated. However, the termination or transformation stage of contract management is as essential as the operation stage and as closely tied to it as the operation phase is to integration. Yet, contract termination or transformation often receives surprisingly little attention apart from concern with dispute resolution that flows from the ending of a contract relationship. It is to that part of the contract management enterprise that we turn in Chapter 5.

Notes

1. See *Reinventing Federal Procurement: Accompanying Report of the National Performance Review* (Washington, D.C.: Government Printing Office, 1993).
2. U.S. Office of Management and Budget, *Summary Report of the SWAT Team on Civilian Agency Contracting* (Washington, D.C.: Office of Management and Budget, 1992), i–ii.
3. Id., at 11.
4. Arthur S. Link, ed., *The Papers of Woodrow Wilson* (Princeton: Princeton University Press, 1968–1969), 5: 689–690.
5. Interview with Hassam Khan, the Executive Director of FCOS, The Fiji Coalition of Social Service Organizations, Suva, January 18, 1996.
6. Ben Wildavsky, Jeff Pelline, and Jamie Beckett, "I-5 Closed—Freeway System Devastated," *San Francisco Chronicle,* January 18, 1994, A1.
7. Paul Jacobs, "CalTrans Chops Down Red Tape to Put Up Concrete," *Los Angeles Times,* February 16, 1994, S6.
8. See SWAT Team report, supra note 2.
9. David N. Ammons, ed., *Accountability for Performance: Measurement and Monitoring in Local Government* (Washington, D.C.: International City/County Management Association, 1995).
10. *Edmonds Institute v. Babbitt,* 42 F. Supp. 2d 1 (D.D.C. 1999).
11. See SWAT Team report, supra note 2, and U.S. General Accounting Office, High Risk Series (Washington, D.C.: GAO, 1997).
12. U.S. General Accounting Office, *Contract Management: Trends and Challenges in Acquiring Services* (Washington, D.C.: GAO, 2001), 5. See also U.S. General Accounting Office, *Contract Management: Taking a Strategic Approach to Improving Service Acquisitions* (Washington, D.C.: GAO, 2002).
13. U.S. General Accounting Office, *Opportunities and Challenges in Contracting for Program Safeguards* (Washington, D.C.: GAO, 2001).
14. Barbara S. Romzek and Jocelyn M. Johnston, "Reforming and Privatizing Medicaid: The Nexus of Policy Implementation and Organizational Culture" (paper presented at the Fourth National Public Management Research Conference, University of Georgia, Athens, October 1997). Later published in revised form as "Reforming Medicaid through Contracting: The Nexus of Implementation and Organizational Culture," 9 *Journal of Public Administration Research and Theory* 107 (1999).
15. Id.
16. See W. Noel Keyes, *Government Contracts under the Federal Acquisition Regulation,* 2d ed. (St. Paul, Minn.: West Publishing, 1996), chap. 43.
17. Id., at 929–930.

18. Id., at 917–918.

19. Susan Vivian Mangold, "Welfare Reform and the Juvenile Courts: Protection, Privatization, and Profit in the Foster Care System," 60 *Ohio State Law Journal* 1295 (1999). See also U.S. General Accounting Office, *Welfare Reform: Interim Report on Potential Ways to Strengthen Federal Oversight of State and Local Contracting* (Washington, D.C.: GAO, 2002).

20. Romzek and Johnston, supra note 14.

21. Id., at 15.

22. Paul C. Light, *Making Nonprofits Work* (Washington, D.C.: Brookings Institution Press, 2000), 13–17. See also Burton A Weisbrod, "The Future of the Nonprofit Sector: Its Entwining with Private Enterprise and Government," 16 *Journal of Policy Analysis and Management* 541, 543–544 (1997).

23. U.S. General Accounting Office, *Social Service Privatization: Ethics and Accountability Challenges in State Contracting* (Washington, D.C.: GAO, 1999), 2.

24. See Jon Pierre, "The Marketization of the State: Citizens, Consumers, and the Emergence of the Public Market," in *Governance in a Changing Environment,* ed. B. Guy Peters and Donald J. Savoie (Ottawa: Canadian Center for Management Development and McGill-Queens University Press, 1995).

25. See, for example, John Buntin, "Budget Shocks," 14 *Governing* 28 (2001).

26. H. Brinton Milward, "The Changing Character of the Public Sector," in *Handbook of Public Administration,* 2d ed., ed. James Perry (San Francisco: Jossey-Bass, 1996), 77.

27. John A. Bryne, "The Virtual Corporation," *Business Week,* February 8, 1993.

28. H. Brinton Milward, "Implications of Contracting Out: New Roles for the Hollow State," in *New Paradigms for Government: Issues for the Changing Public Service,* ed. Patricia W. Ingraham and Barbara S. Romzek (San Francisco: Jossey-Bass, 1994), 41.

29. See generally Paul M. Tellier, *Public Service 2000: A Report on Progress* (Ottawa: Ministry of Supply and Services, 1992); David Osborne and Ted Gaebler, *Reinventing Government* (New York: Plume/Penguin, 1993); Al Gore, *From Red Tape to Results: Creating a Government That Works Better and Costs Less,* report of the National Performance Review (Washington, D.C.: Government Printing Office, 1993).

30. See Donald F. Kettl, *Sharing Power: Public Governance and Private Markets* (Washington, D.C.: Brookings Institution, 1993).

31. All quotes in this paragraph are from Byrne, supra note 27.

32. Id.

33. Robert Agranoff and Michael McGuire, "Big Questions in Public Network Management Research" (paper presented at the 1999 National Public Management Research Conference, Texas A&M University, George Bush Presidential Conference Center, December 3–4, 1999), 1.

34. Id., at 1.

35. Id., at 3.

36. H. Brinton Milward and Keith G. Provan, "Governing Networks, Managing Networks: Principles for Controlling Agents" (paper presented at the 1999 National Public Management Research Conference, Texas A&M University, George Bush Presidential Conference Center, December 3–4, 1999), 12.

37. Byrne, supra note 27, at 98.

38. See Judith R. Saidel and Sharon Harlan, "Contracting and Patterns of Nonprofit Governance," 8 *Nonprofit Management and Leadership* 243 (1998); Judith R. Saidel, "Resource Interdependence: The Relationship between State Agencies and Nonprofit Organizations," 51 *Public Administration Review* 543 (1991); Saidel, "The Dynamics of Interdependence between Public Agencies and Nonprofit Organizations," 3 *Research in Public Administration* 201 (1994).

39. Laurence O'Toole discusses a variation on the concept of leveraging, but one that is quite different from the refugee services case, in "Hollowing the Infrastructure: Revolving Loan

Programs and Network Dynamics in the American States," 6 *Journal of Public Administration Research and Theory* 225, 233 (1996).

40. Laurence J. O'Toole Jr., "Different Public Managements? Implications of Structural Context in Hierarchies and Networks," in *Advancing Public Management: New Directions in Theory, Methods, and Practice,* ed. Jeff Brudney, Laurence J. O'Toole, and Hal Rainey (Washington, D.C.: Georgetown University Press, 2000).

41. "In brief, network contexts increase the range of potentially manipulable variables subject to influence by public managers thus apparently enhancing the importance of management. At the same time, however, networks also increase uncertainty and decrease institutional fixedness for all actors in the setting. Managers have more levers available, but so do others." Id.

42. H. Brinton Milward, "Introduction to Symposium on the Hollow State: Capacity, Control, and Performance in Interorganizational Settings," 6 *Journal of Public Administration Research and Theory* 194 (1996).

43. Agranoff and McGuire, supra note 33, at 18.

44. Milward, supra note 26, at 87.

45. Eugene Bardach and Cara Lesser, "Accountability in Human Service Collaboratives—For What? And to Whom?" 6 *Journal of Public Administration Research and Theory* 197 (1996).

Separation or Transformation: Ending or Remaking Relationships

In August 2001, national news media announced that several United States Marine Corps officers, including a major general, had been charged in connection with the falsification of operations and maintenance records for the V-22 Osprey aircraft.[1] The $40 billion program created an aircraft that could fly like an aircraft and also function like a helicopter. The Osprey has been a troubled program, with twenty-three servicemen killed in accidents concerning the airplane in 2000. The alleged motive for the falsification of Osprey records was to prevent termination of the program. In another large-scale defense-related case some years ago, a senator from New York used federal appropriations processes to force the U.S. Navy to purchase F-14 fighter aircraft when that service did not want more of that kind of plane.

At an entirely different level, consider the case of the city manager in a small town who concluded that it was time to change the contract and hire a different firm to provide legal services to the community. The area had few law firms and the change would clearly make waves, not only within the local legal establishment but also perhaps politically. The firm that lost the contract would still be practicing in the area and, presumably, representing clients challenging the city. Then there was the problem of the confidentiality of records. How exactly would case files be handled when the city shifted its business to another firm?

Consider one final example. A school district in a growing upper-middle-class community issued an invitation for bids for its school bus contract. Everyone was perfectly satisfied with the service provided by the current contractor, and no one was complaining about the price of that service. Even so, the community was required to rebid the contract on a regular basis. To everyone's sur-

124

prise, a competitor submitted a bid that was significantly lower than the present contract and seemed to be the obvious winner of the competition. The new bid would be some $44,000 lower on a five-year contract than the bid submitted by the current provider.

There was a flurry of protest. One parent's comments reflected the community view: "I like the bus driver we have now. I'm very happy with the service. Who knows what we'd get with a new one."[2] After the vote to change to the new contractor, drivers from the losing firm wrote an open letter in the local community newspaper reminding everyone that although the savings may have seemed dramatic, they amounted to only 1.8 percent on the total contract. The drivers added: "Do not sell us out for so little money, when all of your savings will come from our pockets and break a working system." To underscore that point, their letter concluded that their firm had recently received national recognition as "Best School Bus Contractor."[3] In a poignant farewell to his riders and their families, one driver wrote in a separate letter: "In my thirteen years of driving . . . , I have seen the children grow. Sometimes I felt like a parent to each and every one of them. I will miss them all."[4]

The process of termination of a contract or transformation of existing agreements is, as these examples indicate, as complex and dynamic as the other aspects of the contracting process. That is true even if the changed agreements remain with the same contract partners. To someone who views contracts as simple purchases, that may seem odd. After all, a contract is about a product or service purchased in a particular time frame for a given amount of money. It would seem obvious that once those conditions have been satisfied, the contract ends and it is time to move on to rebid the contract if there is a desire to continue purchasing a service. Doing so is the way that public managers can continue to test the market to ensure the best deal for the public. Terminating a contract is also an important way to get the public out of a bad deal. Surely it makes no sense to pressure public managers into renewing or expanding a contract to purchase aircraft or anything that is no longer needed, or for that matter wanted, by a branch of the armed services or a community.

By this point, though, two important realities should be clear. First, many contracts are not simple purchases, but alliances, many involving critically important interdependent relationships between government and its contractors. That is why, in many instances, the real option may not be to terminate completely a contractual relationship but rather to seek to transform it into a more functional situation. Second, it matters, in this stage as in the others, that the public manager operate at the intersection between the horizontal contract model driven by negotiation and influenced by important business-related considerations and the vertical, authority-based model driven by the political complexities of modern democracy. Whether the forces influencing that vertical model are high-stakes national debates over defense policy (and the congressional constituencies that stand to gain or lose from the outcome) or local decisions driven by a host of values that extend well beyond economy and efficiency, they are critically important facts.

Public managers who seek to get and maintain a good deal for the public must function within those realities. Even so, they will sometimes find it necessary to terminate contracts or to transform them over time. This chapter addresses these challenges and considers (1) the decision to challenge the status quo; (2) the need for recognition of the dynamics that tend to resist contract termination; (3) the issues associated with dispute resolution at termination; (4) the problems of contract close out; and (5) the challenge of accountability. As with the previous phases in the contract management process, the separation or transformation, operation, and integration phases are strongly interrelated. What happens during the separation or transformation phase, the way this phase is handled, or even the threat that a contractual relationship may reach this phase affects the behavior of all the participants in the contractual relationship throughout the process. It may also affect the willingness of potential contractors to bid on future contracts and therefore influences not only whether the public gets a good deal out of the current contract but also what opportunities there might be for good deals in the future.

THE DECISION TO CHALLENGE THE STATUS QUO

There are legitimate reasons for challenging current working relationships and also unacceptable grounds. But whatever happens, the early stages of contracting can shape in important ways how the last phase will work.

Reasons for Challenging the Relationship

Clearly, if problems that arise during contract administration become significant enough, if the needs of the government change, if new opportunities for better ways to deliver services arise, or if there are opportunities to rebid the contract to save money, it may be time to end the contractual relationship. Obviously, the most serious situation is one in which the contractor actually defaults on the contract. That can happen for many reasons, including sheer incompetence, undercapitalization, management inadequacies, subcontractor lapses, or bankruptcy. In some settings, the contractor may actually inform the government agency of its inability to deliver on the contract. In other cases, the public manager will have to monitor the contract services and initiate adverse actions if required. Normally, the ability to terminate will require formal notice to the contractor with an opportunity for the contractor to respond.

Short of a complete default, the situation becomes more complex. In the case of the federal government, for example, and in general terms, "the government has the right to terminate the contract completely, or partially, for default (1) if the contractor fails to make delivery of the supplies, perform the services within the time specified in the contract, perform any other provision of the contract, or make progress and (2) that failure endangers performance of the contract."[5] Also, there may be a technical default if the contractor fails to provide the promised security, such as the performance bond.[6] A default can also be partial rather than complete. A default remains a default even if it is the result of the failure of a subcontractor hired by the prime contractor.

Of course, it is normally the case that the defaulting contractor will be responsible unless the default occurred for reasons that could not have been anticipated or controlled by the contractor. However, there may be a serious dispute about a default in situations in which the government has changed the requirements of the goods or services involved. That is another reason why it is important to take change orders seriously and to deal with them fully and formally when they are issued. Informal understandings are of no help if things break down later.

The question often is where the signals for termination originate and who can spot problems. Rehfuss has a relatively simple but useful list. Contractor reports, inspections, and complaints are often the basis for action. As explained in Chapter 4, the effort to ensure effective contract operations entails more than auditing, although performance, financial, and compliance audits are clearly tools that can be useful.[7] In addition to observations by the contract manager, Rehfuss explained, the reports that bring termination may come from line personnel (sometimes called whistleblowers), outside inspectors, or the citizens who are supposed to receive the services.[8]

The issue is frequently more complex than the question whether a nonprofit or a for-profit firm is in violation of the terms of its contract such that the contract should be terminated and sanctions imposed. The effort these days is to seek performance-based contracts that, as earlier chapters explained, are focused on the accomplishment of the real goals of the working relationship and not on narrow technical issues of compliance or narrow points of procedure. Since they are based on sets of incentives and disincentives for various levels of performance, the determination of when and how to terminate or transform the relationship can often be complex.

David Ammons, one of the leading authors on performance management, has suggested a list of factors essential to an effective performance-monitoring system:

• Careful development of suitable performance measures
• Use of appropriate data collection techniques
• Timely reporting of performance information
• Relevant context for performance measurement
• Suitable opportunities for operating officials to explain especially favorable or unfavorable results (i.e., the use of explanatory notes)

• Timely feedback to reporting units
• A demonstrated linkage between the performance monitoring system and important decision-making processes [9]

As this list clearly indicates, most of what is needed to ensure appropriate decisions when it is time to terminate or transform a contract relationship must be prepared in the integration stage and developed during the operation stage.

The Ending Starts with the Beginning: Early Phases Set the Framework for Termination or Transformation

Ensuring that the public gets a good deal throughout the contractual relationship requires that the standards for termination or transformation, the processes that will govern critical decisions, and the protections that will be in place in the event that the relationship breaks down are laid out at the outset of the contract. It also requires that the monitoring process and effective communications be developed and maintained during contract operation.

Many of these issues are addressed in clauses placed in the contract, whereas others are managed by the contracting agency or community. The former includes criteria and processes for termination. In order to allow some degree of flexibility for the public side, contracts often include provisions permitting change orders and others allow reduction in service levels or termination in case the legislature cuts funds or terminates the program. Related to these is a set of processes for the settlement of disputes arising from these decisions.

Contracts also generally include protections in the event of default or inadequate levels of performance. In general, these involve statements about the level of liquidated damages that can be assessed if the contractor falls short of required performance levels. Liquidated damages allow the government to avoid overpaying by withholding a reasonable portion of the payment due the contractor in case of substandard performance.[10] (Technically, although it sounds illogical, liquidated damages are not the same as penalties, but the full explanation as to why goes beyond what is needed for the present discussion.)[11] Contracts also commonly contain requirements for performance bonds or other kinds of financial guarantees against default that are administered by a third party. These guarantees and the firms that stand behind them are sometimes referred to as sureties.

Notwithstanding all this negative language about termination and possible charges against a contractor, it is important to remember that the goal is to maintain as positive and constructive a relationship as possible. Although the point is to ensure a good deal for the public, in order to achieve that purpose it is important to convince potential service providers that working with the government is a good deal for them as well. Thus, performance contracting is not focused primarily on threats but rather on incentives to enhance performance beyond mini-mums whenever possible.[12] If it does become necessary to deal with problems, as is true at some point in virtually any relationship, the idea is, as much as possible, to avoid a law enforcement attitude and instead use a problem-solving approach unless and until it becomes clear that harsher steps are required. With that in mind, Donald Harney suggests that: "If a performance problem occurs, the con-tract administration team should address the problem immediately; deal with it in a calm, rational, and orderly manner; and strive to resolve it at the lowest man-agement level possible."[13] More specifically, he suggests five steps in escalating or-der of severity.

> In the first step, the field manager attempts to resolve the problem by working directly with the contractor's on-site supervisor. If this is unsuccessful, the sec-ond step follows in which the field or contract manager calls the contractor. The third step is more formal, involving meetings of the contract manager, field manager, and contractor. If the problem is still not resolved, the process moves to the fourth step, in which liquidated damages or similar provisions of the contract are put into effect. If enforcement does not produce the desired re-sult, the process moves to the fifth step: cancellation. All attempts to resolve the problem have failed, and action is taken to cancel the contract.[14]

If the process moves beyond the initial levels, the contract administration team usually provides what is called a cure letter, informing the contractor about the deficiencies and what must be done to remedy the situation.[15] If default is in the offing, the bonding firm is also notified.

Regardless of how cautious the agency or city involved tries to be in the devel-opment of the contract, there may be a service gap. While the contract adminis-trators deal with the failed contractor, there is still a need to step into the breach and ensure continued service delivery. Here again, the time to prepare for that problem is at the outset of the contracting process. More will be said about those options later in this chapter in the discussion of shutting down operations and moving on.

Unacceptable Reasons for Terminating or Failing to Renew

It is also important to be aware that there are some unacceptable reasons to ter-minate a contractual relationship or even to refuse to renew a contract. There are generally three reasons that bar an action that a contracting agency or community might wish to take. If its actions are beyond its authority or jurisdiction; if it be-haves in a manner that is arbitrary and capricious or abuses its discretion; or if it violates the Constitution, statutes, or properly issued administrative rules, it faces serious difficulties in court. Some contract administrators have found themselves, or their principals, in trouble because political leaders sometimes believe that they can choose to do business or not with anyone they wish. This is another of those areas in which people often fail to recognize the differences between public and private contracts.

Contracting organizations as well as individuals can assert legal rights in situations in which they have been refused contracts or refused renewal of existing public contracts unlawfully. Two broad doctrines of constitutional law apply with respect to this question of protected rights. The first is a rejection of the so-called right versus privilege dichotomy. Under this old idea, some courts concluded that one may have a right to talk politics but not to be a police officer.[16] In other words, because a government job was a privilege and not a right, a city could place any restrictions it chose on the job and the applicant could accept them or refuse the employment contract. Although there are some judges who would like to reimpose it,[17] the right/privilege dichotomy has long been rejected by the U.S. Supreme Court.[18] Indeed, the Court established, through a series of precedents beginning in the 1950s, a principle known as the doctrine of unconstitutional conditions.[19] It holds that although one may not have a right to a government job, contract, or program benefit, once the government has undertaken to provide them, it cannot force a citizen to trade away constitutional rights in order to receive them.[20]

As surprising as it may seem, the boundaries of the constitutional protections to be afforded contractors are still the subject of judicial discussion. As contract operations increase, these debates are likely to continue to do so. Consider just three cases.

The first came from Kansas and concerned a contract issued by the Board of County Commissioners of Wabaunsee County in 1981 to a Mr. Umbehr to be the exclusive hauler of solid waste for the county's communities.[21] Any of the cities could opt out of the contract, but only one did. The contract was automatically renewed every year but was renegotiated in 1985. Umbehr was a constant, outspoken critic of the county board and its members. In 1990 the board voted to terminate the contract, but that decision was overturned on procedural grounds. The following year the board terminated the contract. However, five of the six cities that Umbehr had served negotiated continuation agreements with him.

The Supreme Court was asked to determine whether the First Amendment freedom of speech protected public contractors from retaliatory termination. It found that the protection does apply and prevents termination in retaliation for public criticism. Speaking for the Court, Justice O'Connor started from the basic constitutional protections that would be available to any public employee. She found that government may terminate an employee for "poor performance, to improve the efficiency, efficacy and responsiveness of service to the public and to prevent the appearance of corruption."[22] In fact, if there is no contract, then employment can be terminated at will. Notwithstanding that broad range of discretion, she said, the Court had long ago made the determination that the government may not condition government jobs or benefits on the surrender of constitutional rights.

The First Amendment protects government employees from termination because of their speech on matters of public concern. Government could prevail if it demonstrated that it would have taken the same action without regard to the protected speech or if it could convince the Court that the government's interests outweighed those of the employee. Even greater protections from government abuse would be available where government seeks to impose conditions on citizens for the receipt of government benefits or grants. "Independent contractors appear to us to lie somewhere between the case of government employees, who have the closest relationship with the government, and our other unconstitutional constitution precedents, which involved persons with less close relationships with the government."[23]

The Court concluded that a balancing test could be applied to protect the contractor while simultaneously attending to the legitimate interests of the government unit involved. "[T]he Board exercised contractual power, and its interests as a public service provider, including its interest in being free from intensive judicial supervision of its daily management functions, are potentially implicated. Deference is therefore due to the government's reasonable assessments of its interests as contractor."[24] Even with its recognition of the government's legitimate concerns, the Court nevertheless concluded: "However, we recognize the right of independent government contractors exercising their First Amendment rights."[25]

A second case, *O'Hare Truck Service v. Northlake,*[26] was decided at the same time as *Umbehr.* The O'Hare Truck Service company was qualified as one of the towing services used by the city of Northlake, Illinois, and had been on the list since 1965. A new mayor came to office in 1989, kept O'Hare on the list, and indicated that he was pleased with the work. However, it was alleged that after the company's owner refused to make a campaign contribution to the major's reelection campaign at the request of the campaign committee, his firm was removed from the list. He had also displayed a campaign poster of the opposition candidate.

The case sounds similar to *Umbehr,* but it raised a question not about free speech but freedom of association. The Court was asked to determine whether conditioning a contract on providing political support violates the First Amendment freedom of association as applied to the states through the due process clause of the Fourteenth Amendment. Justice Anthony M. Kennedy, writing for the Court, found that it does. "A State may not condition public employment on an employee's exercise of his or her First Amendment rights."[27] The same applies to government benefits with respect either to speech or association.

As in the *Umbehr* case, the Court recognized that the government is in a somewhat different position as a contractor than an employer would be, and yet the Court found that there were elements of both situations that were similar enough to require constitutional protection. Thus, when government is dealing with a contractor, the Court will ask:

> whether the affiliation requirement is a reasonable one, so it is inevitable that some case-by-case adjudication will be required even where political affiliation is the test the government has imposed. . . . This case by case process will allow the courts to consider the necessity of according to the government the discretion it requires in the administration and awarding of contracts over the whole range of public works and the delivery of governmental services. . . .

> [W]e fail to see a difference of constitutional magnitude between the threat of job loss to an employee of the State, and a threat of loss of contracts to a contractor.[28]

While the Court was clear that contractors have these constitutional protections against unlawful termination or failure to renew their contracts, the opinions do leave considerable ambiguity about just how contractors will be treated as compared with government employees or citizens. The Court clearly acknowledged the significant public interest that government has in managing the contracts and overseeing those who operate public programs under contract. And it is also clear that although organizations, whether nonprofits or for-profit firms, are treated like individual citizens for some constitutional purposes, they are different. They are creatures of the state in that they exist by virtue of charters or, in the case of nonprofits, enjoy special benefits such as tax-exempt status. The laws that create and support such organizations also constrain them with special regulations.

Among the special challenges posed by these conflicting tendencies are issues related to religious organizations. On the one hand, church-affiliated groups and institutions have long provided services under a host of charters and public grants and contracts around the country. Many medical, educational, social, and community development programs were developed and staffed by church groups. At the same time, the separation of church and state is a long-standing tradition and a firm constitutional principle under the First Amendment. The Court has ruled that the prohibition against establishment of religion means:

> Neither a state nor the Federal Government can set up a church. Neither can pass laws which aid one religion, aid all religions, or prefer one religion over another. Neither can force nor influence a person to go to or remain away from church against his will or force him to profess a belief or disbelief in any religion. No person can be punished for entertaining or professing religious beliefs or disbeliefs, for church attendance or non-attendance. No tax in any amount, large or small, can be levied to support any religious activities or institutions, whatever they may be called, or whatever form they may adopt to teach or practice religion. Neither a state nor the Federal Government can, openly or secretly, participate in the affairs of any religious organizations or groups and vice

versa. In the words of Jefferson, the clause against establishment of religion by law was intended to erect "a wall of separation between church and state."[29]

The Court has repeatedly held that the standard to be applied to government policies is that "[f]irst, the statute must have a secular legislative purpose; second, its principal or primary effect must be one that neither advances nor inhibits religion; finally, the statute must not foster an excessive government entanglement with religion."[30]

Of course, at the same time, under the other religion clause of the First Amendment, protecting the free exercise of religion, government is not to impose substantial burdens on the exercise of religious belief, although it may regulate behavior if there is a compelling interest and if the means chosen to attain that end are narrowly tailored. This tension was presented to the Supreme Court in *Rosenberger v. University of Virginia* in 1995.[31] This case arose from the operation of student organizations at the university. In order to have bills paid from the student activity fund through the university, the student groups were chartered as Contracted Independent Organizations (CIOs). They were required to meet certain minimum requirements for recognition and make clear in their activities and materials that they were not part of the university as such, but independent student organizations. Some students formed a group called Wide Awake Productions, the major activity of which was publication of a newspaper entitled *Wide Awake: A Christian Perspective at the University of Virginia*. The student association refused to release student activity funds to pay the printing bill for the paper. The university was concerned that payment of support for the publication would constitute establishment of religion, a position accepted by the United States Court of Appeals for the Fourth Circuit.[32] However, the Supreme Court reversed the decision, concluding that the university's refusal to make the third-party payments through the contracted independent organizations was a viewpoint-based discrimination in violation of the First Amendment. In the process, it concluded that the establishment clause neither required the university to block the contractor payments, nor justified the violation of freedom of expression.

Thus, there is considerable ambiguity about which situations involving contracts with religiously focused or affiliated groups will be permissible and which will not. The secular purpose, content neutrality, and no excessive entanglement criteria remain, but the Virginia case shows that their application can be confusing in the contemporary context.

These matters are all the more complex because of statutes that have sought to insulate religious organizations from government regulation on grounds of free exercise of religion. The case law is still very much evolving in this regard, but there are interesting questions about the degree to which compliance with standard contracting policies can be enforced when the contractor is a religiously affiliated group. Many jurisdictions, including the federal government, seek to ensure that contractors are in compliance with standard worker protection legislation. However, there are cases holding religious employers exempt.

For example, the United States Circuit Court of Appeals for the District of Columbia Circuit rejected a Title VII enforcement action for sex discrimination brought by the Equal Employment Opportunity Commission (EEOC) on behalf of Sister Elizabeth McDonough. Sister McDonough had filed the sex discrimination complaint against Catholic University, claiming that she had been denied tenure based on her gender in violation of the Civil Rights Act of 1964. The district and circuit courts found that the application of Title VII to her case would be a violation of the university's free exercise of religion and that the investigation of the complaint by the EEOC constituted excessive government entanglement in religion in violation of the establishment of religion clause of the First Amendment.[33]

The following year the Supreme Court struck down the Religious Freedom Restoration Act (RFRA), maintaining that "neutral, generally applicable" laws are not generally subject to free exercise challenges.[34] In that case, the Court rejected efforts to exempt a church project from local zoning laws that apply to everyone else. In contrast, the Supreme Court has refused to permit the National Labor Relations Board (NLRB) to assert jurisdiction over lay teachers in religiously affiliated schools, largely because to do so suggested the likelihood that serious constitutional issues of religious liberty would be raised.[35]

Lower courts have upheld federal and state statutes that provide religious exemption from state unemployment compensation taxes for the Salvation Army in a case brought by a former social worker for the organization.[36] However, the United States Circuit Court of Appeals for the Ninth Circuit upheld NLRB jurisdiction over employment practices at a detoxification center operated for the county of Los Angeles under contract by Volunteers of America (VOA). Although the VOA is a recognized church that claimed that its social service programs were an integral part of its religious mission, the court concluded that the detoxification center operation was secular and therefore unlike the situation in the Supreme Court ruling on the Chicago church-affiliated schools.[37] The question of just how much entanglement of government in the operation of religious institutions is too much, whether they are operating public contracts or being affected by laws generally applicable to secular organizations, continues to be a matter of debate and uncertainty.[38] It is clear that care is called for in making decisions to terminate contracts with religiously affiliated groups. Even investigations or audits must be approached with care and concern for the risk of a finding that there has been excessive entanglement of government and religion.

These examples suggest a host of difficult issues that are in the offing when government decides, as the administration of George W. Bush did, to emphasize contracting with faith-based groups. That is particularly true where those groups intend to incorporate elements of their faith into the services they deliver under contract. Just how significant the challenges can be was made clear in early 2002, when a federal district court in Wisconsin struck contracts by the state's Department of Corrections and Wisconsin Works program that had been developed during the administration of Gov. Tommy Thompson, later secretary of health and human services in the George W. Bush administration.[39] The court found the contracts and establishment of religion in violation of the First Amendment.

Other constitutional doctrines also limit the choices of states or local governments in their contracting decisions. These involve federal preemption, the so-called "dormant commerce clause," and the privileges and immunities clause. Under the supremacy clause (see Chapter 2) the federal government is supreme with respect to the areas in which it has authority, and state actions that are contrary to federal law fall. The Massachusetts effort to limit contracting with any firms doing business with Myanmar fell because it conflicted with federal foreign affairs actions. The federal government, of course, has the power to regulate interstate commerce, and states that place a burden on that commerce violate what has come to be known as the dormant commerce clause. Thus, state or local governments that discriminate against firms or nonprofit organizations from other states are in trouble.

However, as explained in Chapter 2, some state and local governments have argued that they stand in a different position when they are not seeking to regulate commerce but come into the marketplace as direct participants, buying or selling goods or services. The Supreme Court has accepted that argument in some cases, but it has rejected it in others. For example, when Alaska tried to place conditions in its contracts to sell state timber that required the first milling operations on the logs to be performed in the state, the Supreme Court struck it down. The Court warned that governments would not be permitted to regulate interstate commerce in the guise of contracting.

Although the Court has agreed that states and local governments are exempt from the normal constraints of the interstate commerce clause in many cases, other constitutional provisions still apply. Thus, when Camden, New Jersey, tried to require some contractors to use local workers, the city was found to have violated the privileges and immunities clause of the Constitution.[40] The right to travel freely and pursue a lawful calling is protected by that clause against state or local discrimination.

In addition to these constitutional limitations, of course, many statutes make it clear that discriminatory practices are prohibited. Various state statutes also place boundaries on the kinds of organizations that cannot be excluded.

CONTRACT TERMINATION AND PROBLEMS OF MOMENTUM AND HOSPICE CARE

Whatever the causes, a decision to end a contract relationship—particularly a long-standing agreement, a complex service delivery system, or a large contract

involving a considerable amount of money—often triggers three sets of challenges. They include the problem of momentum, the difficulties of administering
the phase just before the end of a contract, and the task of shutting down and
moving on.

Momentum Pressures: Fiscal and Political Separation Anxieties

Of all the stages of the policy process and of public management, termination of
a program, organization, or process is the one that has received the least attention.[41] It is not difficult to understand why. For one thing, as the examples provided at the beginning of the chapter indicate, termination usually signifies a failure, although there is no reason why it necessarily should be seen in that way.
After all, it is perfectly normal to recognize a changed reality and alter administrative and policy directions to meet the new situation. For that matter, ending a
contract may simply be an effort to test the market to see if new savings and better service can be realized. That is rarely how service contract terminations are
perceived. They are most often publicly described, not in terms of efficiency or effectiveness, but in terms of the types of adverse effects they are expected to have
with respect to lost employment or elimination of services. That may be due in
part to the fact that programs have sometimes been terminated primarily to save
money or for political reasons when everyone involved recognized that the services were probably still needed.

It is not at all unusual for political figures to come forward in an attempt to res-
cue a contract on behalf of a constituent group or an important employer as former
senator Alfonse D'Amato of New York did in the fighter plane example cited at the
beginning of the chapter, as then House Speaker Newt Gingrich did for Lockheed's advanced C-130 cargo aircraft program, and as Senate majority leader Trent
Lott did for Mississippi's shipbuilders. Nonprofit groups sometimes see the loss of
a service agreement as a death warrant for the organization or at least as a reason to
remake significantly their organization and its mission. These pressures can be particularly intense if the contractor is a dominant employer in the district or if the
secondary effects on the economy from the loss of wages may be significant.

Quite apart from the fears or frustrations of the contractor and other constituents, the separation phase may raise anxieties for the agency involved as well.
The termination of a contract means a possible breakdown in service delivery if a
replacement contractor cannot be found and services replaced quickly. It can also
result in interorganizational tensions if the termination significantly disturbs a
service network.

For all these reasons, there can be a strong momentum not to end a contractual relationship. That pressure can cause contract managers simply to avoid contract termination and let the contract run out if the time is sufficiently short, the
balance of the work to be provided is modest, or the costs are limited.

Hospice Care: Trying to Ensure the
Best Care at a Time Few Want to Face

One reason that the termination of contract services has been viewed in such overwhelmingly negative terms is because it is not always managed well, at least at the organizational level. It is not surprising to find that insufficient managerial attention has been provided in the separation stage. The analogy to end-of-life medical care, hospice care, is an appropriate one.

Once physicians have diagnosed patients with a terminal illness, they may find it difficult to give them their full attention and to concentrate their energies on providing the most innovative and creative care possible. The same is true for those who must administer the end of contracts. The situation is not made easier by the common tendency to transform what had been a working partnership into something more confrontational and less cooperative during this stage of the process. Few managers in the government agency or the contracting organization are likely to see presiding over the ending and separation of a contract relationship as an activity that will be valued. Fewer still are likely to see it as a positive career-building activity.

However, one way to reduce tensions is to improve the tone and quality of contract administration during this phase of the process. That requires that contract managers be encouraged to see that good work in this portion of the process is just as essential as any other aspect of their obligations, efforts for which they will be recognized and rewarded. The first tendency of experienced managers, public or private, in a termination stage of any effort is to get away so that they will not be associated with what is seen to be a losing operation. One method of addressing this problem is to provide assurances that effective management of the separation stage of the current contract will result in a future assignment to positive and desirable opportunities. Another comparison with the hospice care situation is worth noting. Hospice nurses and other staff who are called on to work closely with patients during this difficult period are sometimes provided periods of time off for recharge or reassignment. A recognition of the special stresses present in contract termination and a commitment to renewal for those called on to manage the process can help to keep people with valuable skills and to add recognition that this is an important activity. Another key signal is sent when management is seen by others to be assigning valued staff to administer the separation stage.

It is also important to prevent the contract manager from being moved, formally or informally, into the role of chief adversary and head flak-catcher in a contentious set of exchanges. The manager must be provided with some degree of insulation from at least a portion of those interactions. Just as there is a contract team up to the point of termination, there should be a team or at least supporting personnel during separation. That is not limited to lawyers or auditors.

Indeed, if the goal is not punitive but is one that seeks simply to make adjustments in service delivery so as to provide better service at a better price in the public interest, then the challenge is to execute contract separation in as positive a manner as possible that causes all parties to emerge with optimism and new directions for the future. If the last dealings that a contractor has with a city or an agency are negative, those events not only can influence future interactions with that contractor but will be watched by other potential contract partners as well.

The task of separation is not only concerned with ending the relationship between the city or agency and the contractor. It is also about easing the consequences of the separation and working to build for a positive future. Thus, the process of shutting down and moving on is not only about problem solving in the present but building for the future.

Shutting Down and Moving On: Contract Management as Juggling

That said, the final steps in the separation process can resemble a skilled juggling act, particularly if the separation was unanticipated or particularly difficult. That means that it is generally necessary to launch the new contract integration process while the separation phase of the old contract is still under way. This is another of those times when there is a danger that attention can be diverted from ongoing contract administration to the new process. Ideally, the closeout and re-contracting process should be transparent to the service recipient, but that requires careful coordination by contract managers, particularly in cases in which there may be several subcontractors as well as a lead prime contractor.

As with other aspects of the separation phase, the public manager's ability to address possible service gaps is significantly shaped in the integration and operation phases. Part of the challenge is to build in contingencies in the integration stage and to manage during the operation phase with an awareness of the contractor's capabilities, those of other contractors working with the community, and the city's own internal capacity. These contingencies often include performance bonds, contract interruption insurance, contingency contracts, partial contracting or multiple award contracting, and partial service by government providers or at least limited reserve capacity for direct government service. Rehfuss and Harney have suggested what are relatively common lists of options that can be used to address service gaps.[42] They include the use of other contractors presently performing other work; an interjurisdictional agreement, such as from a county government, to assist a city; interagency cooperation to cover until other arrangements can be made; hiring additional contractors for short-term work to fill the gap; or a full-blown rebidding process. Of course, it is important that contracts include the authority to terminate for poor performance; the requirement of a guarantee—whatever form it might take; the right to assess liquidated damages; the authority to rebid; as well as a dispute resolution clause explaining how actions will be taken in the event of a problem. Government agencies and communities have a balancing problem in setting out these kinds of protections in their contracts. On the one hand, firms that have the capability are often required to have a surety in some form against the danger of a default. If, however, significant levels of bonding or other security are made a precondition for bidding, then many smaller local organizations, particularly many nonprofit providers, may be frozen out of the process. What we can say with some confidence is that risk assessment and risk management are important, although sometimes overlooked, elements of contract administration.

It is particularly important to keep these issues in mind throughout the contracting process, including in the presolicitation portions, the very earliest planning for a contract. One reason is that agencies and communities called on to shrink the size of their public sector workforce are increasingly dependent on contractors for essential services. In such settings, service gaps are simply unacceptable.

That has led some governments, like that of Sweden, to maintain a limited amount of internal capacity. Thus, it retains capabilities at the county level such that government can step in if there are service problems during a contract, so that the direct government service can be used for comparison with contractor services and costs, and to train government contract administrators by providing them hands-on experience in direct service. Indeed, some local governments, for example the city of Phoenix, Arizona, in the United States, have encouraged public/private contract competition in which government departments, like public works, are permitted to bid against private sector service providers. The Region IV office of the U.S. Environmental Protection Agency in Atlanta, has, in the past, used a practice of breaking in new people by having them work together to do a remedial investigation and feasibility study (RI/FS) for the cleanup of toxic sites covered by the Superfund program. This both builds in-house capacity to do work that is generally done by contractors and also trains the agency's cleanup site coordinators so that they can be more effective in supervising contractors performing that same kind of task. Thus, when techniques are used to reduce complete government dependence on contractors, the separation process becomes less anxiety provoking and service gaps can be less traumatic.

Transformation: The Other Change of Life for Contract Relationships

Contract termination is not the only option for changing a contract relationship. If the contract is written to allow processes for change in level or type of service and for process or standards changes within the general scope of the existing contract, based on a reasonable process of negotiation, it is possible to make midcourse corrections. In fact, this flexibility, plus contract extension or contract renewal options, can allow for a constructive transformation of the contractual relationship. As Kelman has argued, private sector firms learn to value good suppliers and service providers over time and seek to maintain their relationships while meeting new needs or changing conditions. There is no real reason, he notes, why government should not do the same.[43]

Transformation can be traumatic or hardly noticeable, depending on the nature of the changes required, the reasons that brought it about, and the personalities and attitudes of the players. Momentum seeks to keep change to a minimum, which can be destructive, since it might mean a Band-Aid® solution to a serious problem. Even after a contract has been renegotiated, it can be difficult to ensure that the personnel involved in the operation of the agreement really understand and accommodate to the new relationship. After implementation, there may be a tendency to drift slowly and quietly back to the old relationship. These inertial tendencies can be especially difficult where the same managers are in charge in the new relationship as in the old. Here again, though, there is a danger that a change in key people if done in the wrong way can be discouraging. If the transformation process is used more strategically with a view toward doing even better in the future, and less emphasis is put on focusing solely on problem solving from past behavior, these negative signals can be minimized.

SETTLEMENTS FROM PLEASANT TO CONFRONTATIONAL

One of the common tasks during separation is the resolution of disputes. The methods and climate of such settlements vary depending in part on the causes for contract separation and the techniques used to resolve disputes. Obviously, if a contract ends because goods are delivered or because it is time for a required periodic rebid of a service contract and the parties have a good working relationship, settlements are often relatively technical and negotiations to solve minor difficulties are generally positive. If, however, the termination stems from allegations of illegal behavior or default of the contract by the service provider such that disciplinary actions may follow, then the interactions are inevitably adversarial.

A third type of separation is used in many jurisdictions, known as termination for the convenience of the government. It is a deliberate decision by the government to break a contract and involves a settlement process to determine how much the government should pay for having terminated the contract before its normal conclusion. As explained in Chapter 2, this concept was developed with respect to federal contracts long before statutes were in place to justify it. Such terminations are done in situations in which government makes a decision that a service is no longer needed or in which dramatic changes in law or policy require a change in programs. Technically, termination for convenience of the government, where a clause authorizing that kind of termination is in the contract, is not a breach of contract. Thus, for example, a contractor in this kind of situation does not have a right to collect anticipated profits.[44] As long as the contract contains a breach for convenience clause,[45] the contractor seems likely to be treated and compensated fairly, and is not prevented from entering into other kinds of working agreements with government, these processes can be relatively positive. They can certainly be less problematic than a badly pieced together patchwork of change orders that seek to maintain a contract that is no longer viable. In any case, terminations for convenience must be managed carefully.[46]

Of course disputes do not arise only at the separation stage in a contract. They may very well arise with respect to change orders, with payments required during contract implementation, or with respect to compliance with national goals clauses at any point during the contract. For these reasons, as well as to deal with settlements during termination, it is important to pay close attention to dispute resolution clauses at the time of contract drafting.

Although the parties generally have recourse to courts and government contract law to settle disputes, most parties prefer to provide in the contract for alternative dispute resolution techniques in order to save time, reduce costs, and, it is hoped, avoid adversarial interactions.[47] Within the confines of law, contracting parties are free to specify the techniques that are to be used to resolve disputes from mediation to binding arbitration. At the federal level, in fact, the Alternative Dispute Resolution Act favors the use of these alternatives to litigation.[48] Lisa Bingham has noted that the point is not merely to find ways of settling disagreements but to seek to avoid them in the first place.

> In the area of procurement and government contracting, many agencies have begun to use a process called partnering. This process is intended to build a strong, collaborative working relationship between contracting parties before disputes arise, and to set up channels of communication that parties will use immediately upon the first sign of a dispute. The chief executive officer or top management of the contractor and the top public administrators responsible for the project go on a retreat, generally lasting for several days, during which they discuss their expectations for the contract and the means through which it will be executed. They set up avenues of communication and processes for handling disputes as soon as they arise. In addition, they simply get to know each other better. After the retreat, they have regular troubleshooting meetings to catch any problem early in its development. The process is one of dispute avoidance.[49]

Even if a contract does not specifically set forth alternative dispute resolution techniques, such approaches are commonly used to avoid the costs of formal litigation and the costs to ongoing working relationships that flow from pitched legal battles.

Of course, it is also important to pay attention to the formal dispute processes. Contracts generally specify what law will apply and in which jurisdiction or tribunal action can be taken. At the state and federal levels, contract statutes and regulations often specify the institutions that will have jurisdiction over disputes and the processes by which they will be adjudicated.

Three general points are worth remembering in discussions about settlements and dispute resolution. First, public managers often deal not with one or two contracts but often with several or perhaps many contracts of several different kinds. A common example is the city manager who may have half a dozen or more bargaining units within the city organization, all represented by different unions, each of which has its own contract. It is normal for such collective bargaining agreements to contain a set of informal processes to be used for personnel actions and other decision making. Although it is certainly the desire of managers to avoid the problem, it is not at all uncommon for several contracts in one organization to require different kinds of processes for different purposes. The same is true for other kinds of contracts. In an earlier time, efforts were made at the federal and state levels to impose boilerplate language in all contracts mandating a particular type of process. However, in an attempt to improve public/private partnerships and to enhance flexibility, the effort has been made to open contract processes to negotiation. The number and variations among contract dispute resolution processes are now an important fact of life for managers, particularly those at the state and local levels.

Second, all the factors about the differences among the three types of contract partners—for-profit, nonprofit, and governmental—can present different kinds of challenges and behavior in the separation phase just as they do in the integration and operation stages. For one thing, the issue of differences in negotiating cultures discussed in Chapter 3 is very important in understanding how the various types of organizations will approach settlement.

Third, some situations may be better resolved formally than through alternative dispute resolution. Although the Alternative Dispute Resolution Act speaks to administrative agency disputes generally and not to contract disputes in particular, it does contain a useful set of suggested situations that call for more formal processes for the resolution of disputes.

An agency shall consider not using a dispute resolution proceeding if

1. a definitive or authoritative resolution of the matter is required for precedential value, and such a proceeding is not likely to be accepted generally as an authoritative precedent;
2. the matter involves or may bear upon significant questions of Government policy that require additional procedures before a final resolution may be made, and such a proceeding would not likely serve to develop a recommended policy for the agency;
3. maintaining established policies is of special importance, so that variations among individual decisions are not increased and such a proceeding would not likely reach consistent results among individual decisions;

4. the matter significantly affects persons or organizations who are not parties to the proceeding;

5. a full public record of the proceeding is important, and a dispute resolution proceeding cannot provide such a record; and

6. the agency must maintain continuing jurisdiction over the matter with authority to alter the disposition of the matter in the light of changed circumstances, and a dispute resolution proceeding would interfere with the agency's fulfilling that requirement.[50]

If government must take action for disciplinary reasons, then there must not only be assurance of proper contract law processes, but also provision of due process in any administrative or judicial action that might be taken to suspend or debar the contractor (that is, to prohibit the organization from seeking to do business with the government again). It is helpful if there can be a range of responses to problem situations in order to avoid a highly polarized process while allowing for corrective actions to be taken where necessary.

THE ACCOUNTABILITY CHALLENGE: PUBLIC AGENCIES, FOR-PROFIT FIRMS, AND NONPROFIT ORGANIZATIONS

In many ways, of course, the discussion throughout this chapter is about the responsibility of contractors to their government contract partner and the mechanisms by which they can be held accountable. However, the subject of accountability in public contract management is considerably more complex than dispute resolution, settlement, or even administrative adjudication. In fact, one of the most important problems of government contracting, whether for goods or services, is accountability, and it is one of the most complex and perhaps the least-well-understood dimension of the process. Some Canadian officials have referred to it as the "missing hole in the doughnut" of modern public management and warned that "unless we can make progress on this front other reform measures are always likely to fall short of expectations."[51] Certainly the effort to ensure accountability is very much about the point at which the vertical and horizontal models meet, and it is quite literally at the center of many of the tensions over contracting.

The Emergence of a New and Expanded Discussion of Accountability

The good news is that the discussion of accountability in public administration in general, and in contemporary contract operations as well, has been reinvigorated in recent years in several important respects. That discussion includes the perspectives of those actually making decisions,[52] those concerned with management for performance,[53] and those concerned with more traditional, though updated assessments of responsibility for official conduct.[54]

Although contemporary discussions of accountability emphasize the characteristics of twenty-first century public management, most of the ideas at the heart of the current conversations can be traced back to an ongoing debate over responsibility that took place more than half a century ago, originating with an argument between Carl Friedrich and Herman Finer. Finer asserted: "It is most important clearly to distinguish a 'sense of duty' or 'a sense of responsibility' from the fact of responsibility, that is, effective answerability."[55] A "sense of duty" or responsibility means that an administrator accepts and is guided by an obligation. This is a subjective form of responsibility as opposed to legal answerability, an internal check. The second type, "effective answerability," is an external type of responsibility, a constraint imposed by others, whether the public manager feels an obligation internally or not.

Friedrich rejected reliance on external accountability and responded: "Responsible conduct of administrative functions is not so much enforced as it is elicited."[56] The only real way to ensure responsibility, he said, was to recruit people with the values of public service and then socialize them into the profession of public administration in a way that reinforces those values. Friedrich added that there is a danger that externally imposed responsibility tends to discourage initiative when the problem is often to get public agencies to move on something.

> Too often it is taken for granted that as long as we can keep government from doing wrong we have made it more responsible. What is more important is to insure effective action of any sort. . . . An official should be as responsible for inaction as for wrong action; certainly the average voter will criticize the government as severely for one as for the other.[57]

Be that as it may, Finer said,

> My chief difference with Professor Friedrich was and is my insistence upon distinguishing responsibility as an arrangement of correction and punishment even up to dismissal both of politicians and officials, while he believed and believes in reliance upon responsibility as a sense of responsibility, largely unsanctioned, except by loyalty to professional standards.[58]

Certainly in the area of contracting, the public and elected political leaders have shown little interest in whatever internal checks there might be or with the importance of the public manager's own perception of appropriate types of accountability. As explained by the history discussed in Chapter 2, ongoing criticisms of public contracting have continued a negative focus with uncharitable assumptions about public servants and the agencies or local governments for which they work. The emphasis on the vertical, authority-based model and externally imposed mechanisms of accountability have, as Steven Kelman argued so vigorously, made it difficult to take advantage of marketplace opportunities, discouraged firms from contracting with the government, and driven up costs. If we are going to do more contracting for more types of services at all levels, then there must be a reasonable balance between the Friedrich and Finer perspectives. Some of the innovative techniques discussed in earlier chapters have been about exactly that challenge.

For the present, there are several types of internal and external mechanisms that operate to address accountability concerns across the spectrum of public administration. As to internal checks, public managers feel the pressures of professionalism, an obligation for representativeness in a broad sense, and, of course, ethical precepts. At the same time, most of the attention has been focused on external forms of responsibility, including internal organizational controls, executive branch regulation, legislative oversight, and judicial mechanisms. The judicial devices include judicial review of agency actions, the use of injunctions to stop illegal action or to command public officials to respond to their obligations, damage suits against officials or local governments for damages that resulted from violation of citizens' rights, possible criminal prosecutions, and, of course, contract actions brought against agencies or communities by contractors. Most of the devices have been in place for a long time now, and none of them appears likely to go away any time soon.

It must also be said that these complexities are not adequately resolved by the traditional use of an audit approach to accountability in public contracts. If the contractor demonstrates to the satisfaction of government auditors that it has not improperly sought or expended public resources, the contract operation is often considered accountable. While that criterion has been tacitly accepted as important over the years, virtually no one would argue that it is sufficient to ensure accountability. For one thing, the audit model of contract accountability is very much at the heart of the criticism that government contracts in the past have had far more to do with not doing things wrong than with expectations about doing things better and more effectively.[59] However, for reasons developed in earlier chapters, the contemporary challenge in contract administration has to do with the need to simultaneously ensure economy, efficiency, effectiveness, equity, responsiveness, and responsibility.

Convergence and Tension among Political, Legal, and Market Approaches

Two factors have become increasingly important with respect to accountability in public management in general, and contract management in particular. They concern the growing importance of market accountability and the significance of an international dimension, in no small part related to the increasing importance of the market in so many areas.

The international factor has been partly a function of globalization, under-written by the free trade policies of the United States and many other countries as well as important international lending agencies such as the World Bank and the International Monetary Fund. Globally, the United States and other industrial countries have joined to reduce trade barriers, to prohibit the creation of new ones, and, with international donor institutions, to press developing nations to move toward free trade and away from regulation or other market controls as a condition of loans and other forms of assistance. Of course, some of the most vis-ible efforts have been the North American Free Trade Agreement (NAFTA) and the General Agreement on Tariffs and Trade (GATT), which created the World Trade Organization (WTO). With governments encouraged to become not merely market regulators but market participants, public contract managers have increasingly found themselves dealing with some of the kinds of forces constrain-ing other market players that come from globalization. The Massachusetts effort to block business deals with contractors doing business with Myanmar discussed earlier provides a clear example. In addition, if a state or local government faces a challenge in the WTO from other countries or regional trade groups like the Eu-ropean Union (EU) or the Association of Southeast Asian Nations (ASEAN) be-cause of environmental constraints or labor restrictions in contracts, it is the U.S. government that will decide whether and how to defend the practices, not the state or local governments whose policies are challenged.

These international dimensions are not limited solely to state and local con-tracting. The federal government found itself in an interesting situation not long ago when the army decided to issue black berets to all its forces, a distinctive uni-form accessory previously reserved for its elite Ranger units. Not surprisingly, there was an outcry from Rangers past and present, but that was not the end of the story.

The federal government had decided to contract with several different firms for the hats. One contract went to a U.S. firm that had the berets manufactured in Arkansas. The other firms had the hats made in the People's Republic of China, Romania, Sri Lanka, and South Africa. In order to meet the deadline, the army waived the so-called Berry Amendment requiring all military uniforms to be made in the United States from American materials and paid a higher price for them than it would have in a competitive market.[60] These facts alone might have been enough to create criticism, but there was more. It happened that this deal was in progress at a time when relations between the United States and China had been in decline, so much so that a Chinese fighter jet forced down a U.S. recon-naissance aircraft, costing the life of a Chinese pilot and jeopardizing the lives of more than a dozen crew members aboard the American plane. Once on the ground, Chinese officials delayed the return of the crew and the aircraft. In the face of all this, the U.S. contract was cancelled, Chinese-made berets already is-sued to troops were recalled, and a U.S. supplier was found.

This is not the only time that a foreign purchase has raised concerns. Thus, when the military replaced the venerable .45 automatic pistol, manufactured by the U.S. firm Colt Arms, with the Italian 9 mm. Beretta, there was considerable concern, notwithstanding the fact that the sidearms were manufactured by Beretta at its U.S. plant. Far less visible contracts have engendered criticism, as when, in 1988, a U.S.-based subsidiary of a Dutch firm won a contract to manage the National Oceanic and Atmospheric Administration (NOAA) library.[61] In that same year an Israeli firm won a $150 million contract in the Bush administration's continued work on the Star Wars program.[62] In fact, the discussions under the GATT produced an Agreement on Government Procurement that now covers some twenty-two countries. The U.S. government has not yet acceded to the agreement.[63] In addition to the relatively obvious questions raised by these contracts, there is the problem that government may contract with one firm only to see that firm acquired by foreign firms, as in the case of Daimler/Benz acquisition of Chrysler. Additionally, domestic contractors may have work performed by divisions or subcontractors that may be located offshore.

Clearly, the Chinese beret situation involved a kind of political accountability that had absolutely nothing to do with the quality of the product under purchase and was not really about the price. Indeed, for reasons discussed earlier in this chapter, political accountability has been invoked many times quite apart from, and sometimes in conflict with, the criteria that we use to determine whether a contract is a good deal for the public. It is important to recall that government contracts have long been viewed as policy instruments that serve a wide variety of purposes, from civil rights to environmental protection and military doctrine.

Actually, we have seen in recent decades calls for a movement away from traditional legal approaches to accountability and toward more political accountability, even in some cases with respect to contracting. The reinventing government efforts of the Clinton administration consistently criticized traditional legally oriented approaches to accountability. In this, the administration echoed the argument by Osborne and Gaebler, whose book gave its program its name and guiding principles.[64] However, the stronger argument was that too often the legal approach has been narrowly focused on winning recompense for an individual or company allegedly harmed by some administrative practice rather than on fixing a problem so that the entire nation would benefit from better public management in the future.

Ironically, at the same time that the United States was reacting against traditional legal accountability and moving more toward political accountability, other societies, including both industrial and developing countries were moving away from their political approach and toward the legal. Thus, several European countries created or strengthened their constitutional courts with dramatic results, striking down important policies on constitutional grounds very much in the model of the U.S. Supreme Court.[65] Closer to home, the Canadian Supreme

Court was applying the Charter of Rights to do exactly that kind of thing. Moreover, Canadians were more often seeking recompense to remedy individually felt injuries, as opposed to the tradition of ministerial responsibility. Under the British-inspired Westminister parliamentary form of government, ministers have traditionally answered in public for the misdeeds of their ministries and offered the corrections that would be undertaken to see that the problem at issue would not be repeated. Yet questions have arisen about whether ministerial responsibility is working today in its traditional form and whether a tendency is growing to look for somewhere to place blame and seek recompense, more in line with the American legal model.[66]

In the midst of this interesting dynamic the tendency arose during the 1980s and 1990s to inject market accountability into the mix. Of course, market accountability is quite different from either political or legal accountability, and the combination of all three in varying degrees makes for a challenging mix. The core value in the market perspective is efficiency, which has several dimensions.

Often, the market approach assumes that that which costs less is more responsible. Of course, in reality that is an economy judgment rather than an assessment of efficiency, but that distinction is often missed by market advocates.[67] Then there is a cost-benefit view, which holds that public action is responsible if, and only if, it is based on a positive cost-benefit calculation. The more we work with cost-benefit calculations in public policy, the more we learn that, despite increasing sophistication, their use has many difficulties and limitations.

These kinds of market-oriented arguments rarely acknowledge that although many actions that agencies or communities take may not be considered cost effective, they are mandated by legislation. The administrator is responsible to the law whether the required action makes sense in market terms or not. For reasons discussed earlier in this volume, market approaches often emphasize performance standards. At heart that means that public managers and their agencies should not be accountable primarily for the inputs to their programs, such as the numbers of people or dollars involved, or to outputs, as in the number of contracts processed, but to outcomes in the sense of actual improvements in service for which the contracts were let in the first place. Still, questions continue to arise about whether market measures are the right way to determine accountability for some kinds of services. Continuing debates over contracts for correctional services provide an ongoing example.[68]

There is often an effort to address accountability from a market perspective in terms of customer satisfaction. It assumes that if the clients receive adequate levels of quality service at a good price, then the agency is acting responsibly. There is much to be said for including measures of citizen satisfaction with services in accountability assessments, but we are coming to understand with time that implementing such an approach is far more complicated than describing it. In any case, it is also clear that citizens and customers are not the same thing. This approach views citizens or subjects as consumers or customers.[69] One variation on this customer satisfaction approach is the market choice perspective, typified by voucher programs. The idea is that, if given choices, consumers will select the better services and those organizations, whether public or private, which provide them. Those service providers that win customers will prosper, and poor performers will fade away. This is based on the idea discussed earlier of public policy as a fee-for-service operation. If the direct customers of an organization's services are satisfied, then presumably the organization is behaving responsibly. This approach has many problems, discussed in earlier chapters, starting with the assumption that, for example, the entire society should be bound by the choices of parents who happen to have children in school at a particular moment in time as opposed to considering the views of all those who support public education. This kind of limitation is not a significant issue in the marketplace, since decisions are discrete and involve individual parties without regard to the well-being of others. That is usually not true in the public contracting arena.

Whatever one thinks of the market approach as it is commonly presented, its proponents sometimes ignore the fact that people have legal rights and legislation imposes legally enforceable obligations on administrators and their agencies. Ironically, advocates of market-oriented approaches to accountability often forget that, even in the private sector, important legal issues are frequently the focus of tensions and conflict. Contracts themselves define and confer legal rights on the parties, which they often choose to exercise whether doing so makes market sense or not. Finally, there is no question that the larger issues of political responsibility, which may or may not have anything to do with market considerations, are continuously present, as in the black beret example.

Another controversial example of the presence of legal and political issues came in the hotly contested 2000 presidential voting in Florida. Florida contracted out the management of lists of ineligible voters. In its postelection investigation of complaints of civil rights violations, the U.S. Commission on Civil Rights found:

> Similarly, while the duty for developing and maintaining a "centrally maintained database" containing voter registration information for the entire state is placed upon the state, the responsibility for verifying that the database is accurate is delegated. Florida state law shifted the responsibility for identifying individuals to be purged from this list initially to a private contractor and then placed it on the shoulders of the county supervisors of elections. Yet, this law provided no requirement to ensure the accuracy of the data provided in these purge lists. Florida state law ultimately placed the burden of ensuring the accuracy of these purge lists on the voter.[70]

Clearly then, there are tensions among these three approaches to accountability. Although each of the three has useful contributions to make in our effort to get a good deal for the public, no one of them will displace the others. Despite all the criticism of legal mechanisms, legal accountability will continue to be an important element in maintaining responsible contract operations and ensuring accountability, not only among the parties to a contract, but also in the broader sense of public responsibility for proper governance.

New and Challenging Issues of Legal Accountability

The evolving and expanding ways in which public contracts are being used are producing new legal issues such that we now have unanticipated problems without clearly established answers. Even so, it is important to take notice of some of the types of problems that are emerging even as courts and legislatures are working through them. These evolving areas of inquiry include questions as to (1) the kind of contractor that will be treated as a state actor for purposes of legal accountability to affected citizens; (2) the types and limits of immunities available to government contractors to protect them from legal vulnerability; (3) complexities that stem from the use of contracts in regulatory contexts; (4) legal accountability in contracting for social services; and (5) potential difficulties of legal accountability in interjurisdictional relationships. These are in addition to many constitutional concerns raised earlier in the chapter with respect to religious organizations. The state action doctrine provides that there are some instances in which a for-profit firm or a nonprofit organization acts on behalf of the state in such a way that it is to all intents and purposes behaving as a government agency. In that situation, citizens dealing with that organization can commonly assert the kinds of legal rights and demand the legal protections that would be available if they were dealing with the government. However, although the Supreme Court has provided some case law guidance on the subject,[71] in many cases it is not at all clear just what rights someone dealing with the organization may have with respect to a government contractor either at the time of service or later. For example, the Court has held that a doctor providing medical care under contract to the state corrections department is a state actor.[72]

In contrast, the Court rejected the assertion that a claimant was entitled to due process where a Pennsylvania worker's compensation statute permitted the insurers under the state program to refuse payment pending a utilization review by another private program participant without notice or an opportunity for the claimant to be heard.[73] In this case, the Court held that, although the insurer acted "with knowledge of and pursuant to the state statute," that does not make it a state actor.[74] The Court said:

> [The actor] will not be held to constitutional standards unless there is a sufficiently close nexus between the State and the challenged action of the regulated

entity so that the latter may be fairly treated as that of the State itself. . . . Whether such a close nexus exists . . . depends on whether the State has expressed coercive power or has provided such significant encouragement, either overt or covert, that the choice must in law be deemed to be that of the state.[75]

Most attorneys have difficulty understanding exactly what the Court means by that statement (and other cases about what is to be considered a state actor), let alone the average citizen who is concerned with maintaining his or her rights and the accountability of the contractor. Even much simpler cases are not necessarily clear to most citizens. Indeed, some people are surprised to learn that a nonprofit corporation that was responsible for designing, operating, and promoting a municipal festival is not a state actor,[76] but a volunteer fire department is.[77]

Assuming that a contractor is found to be a state actor, is it liable for violations of civil rights and does it, or its employees, enjoy the same immunities from suit as a government agency or public official? The answer appears to be yes and no. The Supreme Court concluded, for example, that prison guards working for the Corrections Corporation of America operating a facility under contract to the state of Tennessee could be sued for alleged abuse of a prisoner under the same civil rights law under which a guard working as a civil servant in a state prison could be challenged. However, the Court then rejected the claim by the guards working for the contractor that they should enjoy the same immunity from suit that would be available to their public sector counterparts.[78] In reaching its decision, the Court made a fundamental point about the difference between contractors and civil servants.

> This is not to say that government employees, in their efforts to act within constitutional limits, will always, or often, sacrifice the otherwise effective performance of their duties. Rather, it is to say that government employees typically act within a *different* system. They work within a system that is responsible through elected officials to voters who, when they vote, rarely consider the performance of individual subdepartments or civil service rules that, while providing employee security, may limit the incentives or the ability of individual departments or supervisors flexibly to reward, or to punish, individual employees.[79]

In addition, the Court found that contractors are in a different position from public sector employers precisely because of the dynamics of the marketplace.

> First, the most important special government immunity-producing concern— unwarranted timidity—is less likely present, or at least is not special, when a private company subject to competitive market pressures mean not only that a firm whose guards are too aggressive will face damages that raise costs, thereby threatening its replacement, but also that a firm whose guards are too timid will face threats of replacement by other firms with records that demonstrate their ability to do both a safer and a more effective job.[80]

The United States Circuit Court of Appeals for the Ninth Circuit applied this prison ruling in a case in which Lockheed Information Management Systems was sued for violations of the same civil rights law as the prison guards. Lockheed operated the parking ticket management system under contract to the city of Los Angeles. A law firm and several vending machine service fleet operators sued, claiming that Lockheed was violating their constitutional rights in the way that it controlled the process for challenging tickets. The contractor responded that it should be immune, but the court, citing the prison case, rejected its request.[81]

The civil rights statute involved in both the prison and traffic ticket cases speaks to violations of rights by state and local officials.[82] Federal officials are sued for constitutional violations under a doctrine created by the Court in a case called *Bivens v. Six Unknown Named Agents of the Federal Bureau of Narcotics*.[83] Such suits are known as *Bivens* actions and at least two U.S. Court of Appeals circuits held that contractors "acting under color of federal law" are subject to such *Bivens* suits.[84] However, the Supreme Court rejected that conclusion, refusing to extend *Bivens* liability to a federal corrections contractor.[85]

There are other complexities in determining just when a contractor is accountable in court. Consider the case of a physicist hired to work at the U.S. Department of Energy's Lawrence Livermore Laboratory operated by a contractor in California. The scientist, who was ultimately denied the position in a dispute concerning his security clearance, sued in federal court for breach of contract. The contractor claimed immunity and the Supreme Court agreed. In this case, the contractor was the University of California and it was held immune from suit under the Eleventh Amendment to the Constitution even though the contract specifically provided that the federal government would indemnify the University of California for any losses due to liability, a clause that seemed clearly to indicate that the federal government expected the contractor to be liable.[86]

Apart from these immunity issues, there is another rather confusing area of the law, known as the government contractor defense, that makes it unclear whether contractors can be held to account by citizens affected by the contractor's actions. The Supreme Court has said, "Liability for design defects in military equipment cannot be imposed, pursuant to state law, when (1) the United States approved reasonably precise specifications; (2) the equipment conformed to those specifications; and (3) the supplier warned the United States about the dangers in the use of the equipment that were known to the supplier but not to the United States."[87] As one court put it, when a contractor claims the government contractor defense, it is saying that "the Government made me do it."[88] The idea is not new that if a contractor does what it is required by the government to do, it should not be responsible for problems that result. The Court held in 1918 that "if the contractor is bound to build according to plans and specifications prepared by [the government], the contractor will not be responsible for the consequences of defects in the plans and specifications."[89]

That does not mean that "the Government made me do it" defense will cover all ills. Companies that joined a voluntary settlement in litigation brought by Vietnam veterans and their families because of exposure to the defoliant Agent Orange tried that defense with surprising results. One of the companies that settled the case wanted the government to reimburse it for the cost of the settlement, claiming that it was really the government's liability under the government contractor defense. The company was taken aback when the Supreme Court held that the government contractor defense would have protected the companies involved if they had litigated the case, but the defense does not apply in a settlement situation.[90]

Another area has led to some surprising results in regard to the federal government's use of contracts and the question of responsibility for injury. In the past two decades efforts have been made to negotiate resolutions to thorny regulatory problems, and few have been more complex or difficult than the federal government's attempt to deal with the failure of a host of savings and loan institutions. The savings and loans got into trouble for a variety of reasons but in no small part because of deregulation and growing interest rates. These realities caused some of them to undertake risky loans in an effort to earn the money necessary to attract deposits in a volatile money market. To make matters worse, the federal government's efforts to fix the problem through its Federal Savings and Loan Insurance Corporation (FSLIC) created more problems. The federal government wanted to encourage stronger institutions to acquire the weaker ones, but these institutions feared that taking on weaker firms would place them in jeopardy from regulators, who might turn around and go after them for failing to meet capitalization requirements.

Their fears were well founded and that is exactly what happened. However, the firms sued the federal government for breach of contract on grounds that they had a contract under which special accounting mechanisms would be used for the firms trying to help in order to avoid regulatory problems. There never was a contract in the formal sense of the word, but the Supreme Court found that the regulatory understandings communicated from the federal government to the savings and loans amounted to an enforceable contract whether there was a written agreement in the normal form of a government contract or not and the federal government had breached that contract.[91]

Of course, most of the service contracts are not federal but state and local. Moreover, the situation at that level is very dynamic, not only because so much has been contracted but also because federal programs have been changing to permit state and local governments more latitude in contracting out federally funded services. The welfare reform legislation mentioned in Chapter 1 has permitted a great deal more discretion as to the range and nature of contracting under federal funds. However, there are real questions about the degree to which accountability issues have been adequately addressed in the rush to contract out even more aspects of the programs.[92]

Consider the following challenge under a different federal program, the Individuals with Disabilities Education Act (IDEA). A small community did not have a high school but contracted with a local private academy for the education of its children. One of the families had a son with significant disabilities who was qualified to receive services under IDEA. The parents and their clinicians agreed on what should be included in the individual education plan (IEP), but the academy disagreed with some of the services called for in the plan. The parents sued under IDEA, but the academy answered that the parents had no cause of action against it, since it was not a government unit but a contractor. The United States Circuit Court of Appeals for the Second Circuit agreed.[93]

The court found the implementation of the requirements of IDEA rested with the local education agency, which, it concluded, meant the school district in this case. However, the school district did not have any mechanism other than sending the student away to ensure the services it acknowledged were required for the student. The court made it clear that the school district could make the contractor responsible in the contract for services, but it was very likely that the private institution would not enter into a contract with those provisions.

Beyond that, not all issues of accountability, even those involving the law, are about recovering money. Consider the case of a North Carolina volunteer fire department. The department was a nonprofit organization with a service agreement with the county. However, the volunteer fire department had met with difficult times, and it ultimately informed the county that it was no longer able to operate effectively and could not provide fire protection coverage. The county reallocated coverage left open by the volunteer department's problems. In the meantime, the volunteer group reorganized and went back to the county seeking to be reinstated. The county agreed but insisted that the service contract include a provision that neighborhoods that wanted to opt into another department's service area could do so and that the department would waive the veto that it could otherwise exercise under state law. The department signed reluctantly but later challenged the agreement. The U.S. Circuit Court of Appeals rejected the department's challenge and upheld the agreement as a valid contract, waiving the option for a constitutional challenge.[94]

Another fire department found itself in the midst of a quite different difficult situation as a result of a contract. Rye Brook, a New York suburb, had been part of the Port Chester fire protection program. After a dispute over costs, Rye Brook decided to break off its participation in Port Chester and hired an Arizona-based for-profit firm to provide fire protection. Neighboring volunteer and paid departments were upset for a variety of reasons, including the new firm's differences in training practices and its employment of nonunion firefighters.[95] The crunch came when a major residence fire resulted in a call for mutual aid to the Port Chester fire department. The union firefighters would not assist and the fire destroyed a $1 million home. An investigation ensued and the Rye Brook city council terminated its controversial fire protection contract.[96] The discussion is ongoing about how to deal with accountability in a setting in which one community uses a contract in a new way that upsets traditional service and mutual support patterns.

CONCLUSION

Clearly, the separation or transformation stage of the contracting process is as dynamic and important as the other stages, not only in regard to gaining recompense for contract failures or filling service gaps but for many other reasons. Perhaps the most important reason is that the steps taken by public managers in this stage of the process are likely to control whether they will be able to get good deals for the public in the future. For that to happen, it must be clear that the public sector will terminate or transform contracts and not merely let them ride. It is also necessary that these stages be managed in ways that will ensure that nonprofits, for-profit firms, or other governmental units will want to enter into future agreements.

At the same time, the public manager's success or failure at this stage depends mightily on steps taken in the integration and operation stages. Just what will trigger a termination, the process by which it will be conducted, and the way that service gaps or other difficulties will be managed must be developed long before those events actually transpire. Equally important, the right kinds of management incentives must be in place at this critical stage so that the level of creativity and dedication needed to obtain a good deal for the public is as high as it was when the contract was launched and during its operation.

Finally, the challenge of understanding issues of accountability in public contracting is growing. New kinds of service contracts and new applications of existing agreements in changing circumstances require a careful consideration of accountability. Of course, a contract is in its nature a legal instrument, and legal mechanisms of accountability, although only one dimension of the subject, are still very important. But even in this area, things are changing, and new issues concerning the nature of accountability and who can trigger it continue to emerge.

It is precisely because public contract management is being done in new ways by different kinds of contract participants that it is essential to consider the need for capacity building to meet the challenge of the years ahead. The fact that virtually no level of government can claim adequate contract management capability presently and many are facing a loss of key people over the coming decade only adds to the importance of this capacity-building effort. This challenge is addressed in Chapter 6.

Notes

1. Christopher Marquis, "Eight Marine Officers Are Charged in Osprey False-Records Case," *New York Times*, August 18, 2001, A10.

2. "School Board to Decide Bus Contract," *Burlington Free Press,* January 17, 2000, 4B.

3. School Bus Drivers, "Bus Contract Switch a Mistake," *Essex Reporter,* January 27, 2000, 4.

4. John Bombard, "Will Miss the Kids on the Bus," *Essex Reporter,* January 27, 2000, 4.

5. W. Noel Keyes, *Government Contracts under the Federal Acquisition Regulation,* 2d ed. (St. Paul, Minn.: West Publishing, 1996), 1007.

6. Id.

7. John A. Rehfuss, *Contracting Out in Government* (San Francisco: Jossey-Bass, 1989), 87–94.

8. Id.

9. David N. Ammons, ed., *Accountability for Performance: Measurement and Monitoring in Local Government* (Washington, D.C.: International City/County Management Association, 1995), 11–12.

10. Donald F. Harney, *Service Contracting: A Local Government Guide* (Washington, D.C.: International City/County Management Association, 1992), 56–57.

11. John D. Calamari and Joseph M. Perillo, *Contracts,* 3d ed. (St. Paul, Minn.: West Publishing, 1987), 639–641.

12. Id., at 57.

13. Id., at 170.

14. Id., at 171.

15. Keyes, supra note 5, at 1026–1028.

16. This theory is generally traced to an opinion written by Justice Oliver Wendell Holmes while he was a member of the Massachusetts Supreme Court. *McAuliffe v. Mayor of New Bedford,* 155 Mass. 216, 220 (Mass. 1892).

17. See *Rutan v. Republican Party of Illinois,* 497 U.S. 62, 97 n.2 (1990), Scalia, J., dissenting; *Cleveland Bd. of Ed. v. Loudermill,* 470 U.S. 532, 563 (1985), Rehnquist, J. dissenting.

18. See generally, William Van Alstyne, "The Demise of the Right-Privilege Distinction in Constitutional Law," 81 *Harvard Law Review* 1439 (1968).

19. *Slochower v. Board of Higher Education,* 350 U.S. 55 (1956); *Speiser v. Randall,* 357 U.S. 513 (1958); *Sherbert v. Verner,* 347 U.S. 398 (1963); *Keyishian v. Board of Regents,* 385 U.S. 589 (1967); *Pickering v. Board of Education,* 391 U.S. 563 (1968); *Shapiro v. Thompson,* 394 U.S. 618 (1969); *Goldberg v. Kelly,* 397 U.S. 254 (1970); *Perry v. Sinderman,* 408 U.S. 593 (1972); *Mt. Healthy Board of Education v. Doyle,* 429 U.S. 274 (1977); and *Givhan v. Board of Education of Western Line Consolidated School Dist.,* 439 U.S. 410 (1979).

20. Ironically, in the same period in which the Supreme Court has been announcing new applications of the doctrine of unconstitutional conditions in contracting, it has been constraining it with respect to public employees. See *Waters v. Churchill,* 511 U.S. 661 (1994); *Connick v. Myers,* 461 U.S. 138 (1983); *O'Connor v. Ortega,* 480 U.S. 709 (1987).

21. *Board of County Commissioners, Wabaunsee County, Kansas v. Umbehr,* 135 L.Ed.2d 843 (1996).

22. Id., at 851.

23. Id., at 855.

24. Id., at 853–854.

25. Id., at 858.

26. 518 U.S. 712 (1996).

27. Id., at 717.

28. Id., at 719–722.

29. *Everson v. Board of Education,* 330 U.S. 1, 15–16 (1947).

30. *Agostini v. Felton,* 521 U.S. 203, 218 (1997). See also *Committee for Public Education v. Nyquist,* 413 U.S. 756 (1973); *Tilton v. Richardson,* 403 U.S. 672 (1971); *Lemon v. Kurtzman,* 403 U.S. 602 (1971); *Walz v. Tax Commission,* 397 U.S. 664 (1970); *Epperson v.*

Arkansas, 393 U.S. 97 (1968); *School District of Abington Township v. Schempp,* 374 U.S. 203 (1963); *McGowan v. Maryland,* 366 U.S. 420 (1961).

31. 515 U.S. 819 (1995).

32. 18 F.3d 269, 281 (4th Cir. 1994).

33. *EEOC v. Catholic University,* 83 F.3d 455 (D.C. Cir. 1996).

34. *City of Boerne v. Flores,* 521 U.S. 507, 513–514 (1997), reaffirming a similar position taken in *Employment Div., Department of Human Resources of Oregon v. Smith,* 494 U.S. 872, 885 (1990).

35. *NLRB v. Catholic Bishop of Chicago,* 440 U.S. 490, 507 (1979).

36. *Rojas v. Fitch,* 928 F. Supp. 155 (D RI 1996).

37. *Volunteers of American v. NLRB,* 777 F.2d 1386 (9th Cir. 1985).

38. *Wilder v. Bernstein,* 848 F.2d 1338, 1349 (2d Cir. 1988).

39. *Freedom from Religion Foundation v. McCallum,* 179 F.Supp.2d 950 (WDWI 2002).

40. *United Building & Construction Trades Council of Camden County v. City of Camden,* 465 U.S. 208 (1984); *Hicklin v. Orbeck,* 437 U.S. 518 (1978).

41. Peter deLeon, "Public Policy Termination: An End and a Beginning," 4 *Policy Analysis* 369 (1978).

42. See Rehfuss, supra note 7, at chap. 6, and Harney, supra note 10, at chap. 12.

43. See, generally, Steven Kelman, *Procurement and Public Management: The Fear of Discretion and the Quality of Government Performance* (Washington, D.C.: AEI Press, 1990).

44. *G. L. Christian v. United States,* 312 F.2d 418, 423 (Ct. Cl. 1963).

45. In the *G. L. Christian* case, id., the Court of Claims found that the government could terminate in this way even though there was no specific clause in the contract because the regulations in place at the time governing armed services procurements required such a stipulation.

46. See generally, Keyes, supra note 5, at 1036–1045.

47. Lisa Bingham, "Alternative Dispute Resolution in Public Administration," in *Handbook of Public Law and Administration,* ed. Phillip J. Cooper and Chester A. Newland (San Francisco: Jossey-Bass, 1997), 548–549.

48. 5 U.S.C. §571 et seq.

49. Bingham, supra note 47, at 552.

50. 5 U.S.C. §572(b).

51. B. Guy Peters and Donald J. Savoie, eds., *Governance in a Changing Environment* (Ottawa: Canadian Center for Management Development and McGill-Queens University Press, 1995), 326.

52. Barbara S. Romzek and Melvin J. Dubnick, "Accountability in the Public Sector: Lessons from the Challenger Tragedy," 47 *Public Administration Review* 227 (1987).

53. Ammons, supra note 9; Robert D. Behn, *Rethinking Democratic Accountability* (Washington, D.C.: Brookings Institution Press, 2001).

54. I have addressed these in more detail in Phillip J. Cooper, *Public Law and Public Administration,* 3d ed. (Itasca, Ill.: F. E. Peacock, 2000), chap. 13.

55. Herman Finer, "Better Government Personnel: America's Next Frontier," 51 *Political Science Quarterly* 569, 582 (1936).

56. Carl Friedrich, "Public Policy and the Nature of Administrative Responsibility," in *Public Policy,* ed. C. J. Friedrich and E. S. Mason (Cambridge: Harvard University Press, 1940), 19.

57. Id., at 4.

58. Herman Finer, "Administrative Responsibility in Democratic Government," 1 *Public Administration Review* 335, 335 (1941).

59. See Al Gore, *From Red Tape to Results: Creating a Government That Works Better and Costs Less,* report of the National Performance Review (Washington, D.C.: Government Printing Office, 1993).

60. U.S. General Accounting Office, *Contract Management: Purchase of Army Black Berets* (Washington, D.C.: GAO, 2001).

61. Bill McAllister, "Foreign Control of NOAA Library? Amid FBI Warnings, Dutch-Owned Firm Wins Management Contract," *Washington Post,* April 4, 1988, A15.

62. "Israeli Firm Wins Bid," *Washington Post,* July 26, 1988, C1.

63. See Paul J. Carrier, "Sovereignty under the Agreement on Government Procurement," 6 *Minnesota Journal of Global Trade* 67 (1997).

64. David Osborne and Ted Gaebler, *Reinventing Government* (New York: Penguin, 1992).

65. See C. Neal Tate and Torbjorn Vallinder, eds. *The Global Expansion of Judicial Power* (New York: New York University Press, 1995).

66. I have explained this trend and provided documentation in "Accountability and Administrative Reform: Toward Convergence and Beyond," in Peters and Savoie, supra note 51.

67. See Henry Mintzberg, "A Note on that Dirty Word 'Efficiency,'" 5 *Interfaces* 101 (1982).

68. U.S. General Accounting Office, *Private and Public Prisons: Studies Comparing Operational Costs and/or Quality of Service* (Washington, D.C.: GAO, 1996).

69. See Jon Pierre, "The Marketization of the State: Citizens, Customers, and the Emergence of the Public Market," in Peters and Savoie, supra note 51.

70. U.S. Commission on Civil Rights, *Voting Irregularities in Florida during the 2000 Presidential Election* (Washington, D.C.: U.S. Commission on Civil Rights, 2001), chap. 3, http://www.usccr.gov/vote2000/stdraft1/ch3.htm, December 9, 2001.

71. See generally, *Lugar v. Edmondson Oil Co.,* 457 U.S. 922 (1982); *Blum v. Yaretsky,* 457 U.S. 991 (1982); *Rendell-Baker v. Kohn,* 457 U.S. 830 (1982).

72. *West v. Atkins,* 487 U.S. 42 (1988).

73. *American Mfrs. Ins. Co. v. Sullivan,* 526 U.S. 40 (1999).

74. Id., at 50.

75. Id., at 52.

76. *United Auto Workers v. Gaston Festivals, Inc.,* 43 F.3d 902 (4th Cir. 1995).

77. *Goldstein v. Chestnut Ridge Volunteer Fire Co.,* 984 F.Supp. 367 (NDMD 1997).

78. *Richardson v. McKnight,* 521 U.S. 399 (1997).

79. Id., at 410–411.

80. Id., at 409.

81. *Ace Beverage Co. v. Lockheed Information Management Services,* 144 F.3d 1218, 1220 (9th Cir. 1998).

82. 42 U.S.C. §1983.

83. 403 U.S. 388, 389 (1971).

84. *Malesko v. Correctional Services Corporation,* 229 F.3d 374, 380 (2d Cir. 2000). See also *Hammons v. Norfolk Southern Corp.,* 156 F.3d 701 (6th Cir. 1998).

85. *Correctional Services Corp v. Malesko,* 534 U.S. 1 (2001).

86. *Regents of the University of California v. Doe,* 519 U.S. 425 (1997).

87. *Boyle v. United Technologies, Corp.,* 487 U.S. 500, 512 (1988).

88. *In re Joint Eastern and Southern Dist. New York Asbestos Litg.,* 897 F.2d 626, 632 (2d Cir. 1990).

89. *United States v. Sperin,* 248 U.S. 132 (1918), quoted in *Hercules Incorporated v. United States,* 516 U.S. 417, 424 (1996).

90. *Hercules Incorporated v. United States,* 516 U.S. 417 (1996).

91. *United States v. Winstar Corp.,* 518 U.S. 839 (1996).

92. Susan Vivian Mangold, "Welfare Reform and the Juvenile Courts: Protection, Privatization, and Profit in the Foster Care System," 60 *Ohio State Law Journal* 1295 (1999); Michele Estrin Gilman, "Legal Accountability in an Era of Privatized Welfare," 89 *California Law Review* 569 (2001); Clayton P. Gilette and Paul B. Stephan III, "Constitutional

Limitations on Privatization," 46 *American Journal of Comparative Law* 481 (1998); Panel Discussion, "Public Oversight of Public/Private Partnerships," 28 *Fordham Urban Law Journal* 1357 (2001).

93. *St. Johnsbury Academy v. D.H.,* 240 F.3d 163 (2d Cir. 2001).

94. *Lake James Community Volunteer Fire Department v. Burke County,* 149 F.3d 277 (4th Cir. 1998).

95. Monte Williams, "Judge Tells Village to Keep Fire Department It Replaced," *New York Times,* February 1, 1996, B5.

96. Elsa Brenner, "Fire Department Out," *New York Times,* March 22, 1998, C7.

6

Capacity Building for Contract Management: Developing Hybrid Institutions for a Complex State

From the outset of the contracting process through separation of the parties from their working relationship, two things should be clear with respect to efforts to ensure a good deal for the public. First, contract management is a pervasive fact of modern public policy and administration and will continue to be. The evidence shows that contracts are growing in quantity and expanding in scope. Second, since virtually every serious study that has considered the matter has found a lack of capacity for effective contract management, good government in the contemporary environment requires capacity building. That will require changes in both the vertical, authority-based model that drives and directs contracting from above and in the horizontal, negotiation-driven model that operates when public agencies or local governments enter the marketplace.

REINFORCING THE FOUNDATION FOR PUBLIC CONTRACT MANAGEMENT: THE VIEW FROM THE VERTICAL MODEL

Before turning to more specific recommendations for enhancing contract management capability, however, it is essential to consider five basic principles. First, successful contract operations require institutions that embody and reinforce the multiple values discussed throughout this volume. As Michael Sandel has pointed out, institutions are not merely instruments for governing. They embody important political ideas, and the way those institutions are structured affects the way in

160

which those values are advanced or inhibited in the development and implementation of public policy.[1] Strong and effective institutions are necessary, and neither policy process nor modern management techniques have eliminated the need for them.[2] There has been a tendency to argue that indeed it is the institutions of government that stand in the way of effective governance and that process and management can facilitate problem solving.[3] In fact, these were among the arguments in favor of increased contracting out, often termed "privatization," and that were important to the new public management movement.[4] However, government contracting by weak institutions is hardly likely to obtain a good deal for the public.

Second, the United States is a constitutional republic that operates under the rule of law, and public contracts are legal instruments that function as a part of that public law structure. For that reason, it is essential to understand the public law foundations of public contract management. That may seem obvious, but like the discussion about public institutions, it has been increasingly common to argue that contracting and other entrepreneurial practices were necessary alternatives to avoid the constraints and burdens of public law. Thus, if we could just deregulate and privatize we would eliminate the dreaded "red tape" and be free to fashion whatever kinds of policies were helpful to solve any problem that presented itself.[5] In truth, however, government agencies and public managers do not exist and have no authority except insofar as they are created and empowered by law.[6] Furthermore, the use of contracting does not, in general at least, ensure that there will be less "red tape," and it is certainly not a way to support deregulation. Each contract is in itself a set of binding rules for the parties to the agreement, and enforcement may be triggered by any of the parties, unlike most administrative rules, which leave enforcement discretion to the agency involved. Moreover, as should be apparent by this point, numerous federal and state statutes regulate public contracting and administrative rules as well. Effective public contract management requires both an understanding and appropriate use of public law and the application of well-developed management techniques. The public will not get a good deal if either of these critical components is not adequately considered.

Third, effective contract management requires that we move beyond negative assumptions and toward a more positive attitude in contracting. We do not ensure a good deal for the public merely by preventing corrupt bidding practices or adding more statutes and regulations to control the participants in the contract process. A respect for the role of public law does not mean that more laws and more restrictions are always to be preferred. Steven Kelman was absolutely correct in arguing that it is essential to change the general view that every public servant or contractor is corrupt and to build contracting processes intended to achieve something and not merely to prevent evils.[7] Although Kelman was specifically speaking to the federal contracting process, his admonition to take a more positive view is important for all levels of government.

Fourth, the contemporary efforts at reform of public policy and public management have produced a situation in which governing must be accomplished through hybrid institutions staffed by appropriately qualified professionals. Public agencies and local government organizations are hybrids in that they must accomplish both traditional requirements of administrative agencies and also market-oriented, contract-driven service delivery programs. Successful management of this new workforce and its organizations presents new techniques and new challenges. For example, the kinds of people who can perform these functions are extremely attractive to the private sector, and the public sector will have to compete for their services. At the same time, the vertical model always ensures that these contract-oriented and negotiation-driven operations will always be conducted alongside authoritative policy. There often seems to be a tendency to speak as though public managers operate in the traditional mode or the entrepreneurial mode but not both.

Finally, it is important to engage elected officials in the conversation about improving public contract management. Too often elected officials have taken little responsibility in this area and have become involved only to protect a constituent—whether it is a good deal for the public to protect them or not—or to serve as Monday morning quarterbacks who use problems in contracting as a way to get headlines. When contracting promises are not met, the political leaders have too often attempted to make political capital out of chastising agencies and public managers for not achieving a good deal for the public, when it was an impossible situation from the beginning, in no small part because of the politicians' behavior. The corollary to that difficulty is that the media and some elected leaders have a symbiotic relationship in which both get attention from cheap shots at contract managers. For example, Sen. William Proxmire of Wisconsin used his so-called Golden Fleece awards to get headlines about what he regarded as operations that fleeced the public. However, he was known to attack completely legitimate programs and people in very damaging ways.[8]

Besides, merely concluding that a contract had cost overruns or was delayed does not solve any problems. It is perfectly appropriate for elected officials to identify contracting problems, but the officials, too, are part of the contracting system and are at least partially responsible for many of the difficulties. Recently, one of the major television networks broadcast a segment on its evening news program with a title referring to "fleecing" very similar to Proxmire's gimmick and with quick, attention-grabbing, and always negative commentary. The media network has no obligation to improve the public contracting system, but members of the legislature and elected executives do. That means in part that any effort to improve public contract management needs to involve and engage those elected leaders.

Congress and Contract Management

Legislators can do many things to help improve contract management. For one thing, Congress could and should address the disconnect between the law of government contracting and administrative law. Traditionally, these two bodies of law have been separated, at least in part, by government contracting law's primary focus on prevention of corruption and administrative law's emphasis on administrative procedure. It would be particularly helpful if contracting laws could be better integrated with existing administrative law. The more that agencies administer their programs through contracts and operate traditional administrative programs side by side with contract operations, the less tenable the distinction between administrative law and government contract law. The Federal Property and Administrative Services Act, the Armed Services Procurement Act, and the Administration Procedure Act were adopted in the 1940s before the dramatic increases in social service programs, the expansion of contracting for services, and the increasingly complex interdependency of the systems for implementing policy. Although it may make sense from an attorney's point of view, the attempt to treat general administration and contract administration as completely distinct activities simply does not reflect modern governance.

At the same time, it is important for Congress to take a careful look at what has happened to government contract statutes in the years since the Federal Procurement Commission Report in 1972. As explained in Chapter 2, we have witnessed a veritable blizzard of legislation from the late 1970s through the 1990s dealing with all aspects of contracting. Some of these statutes were overreactions to particular problems, aimed more at threats and punishment than improvements in contract management. The Acquisitions Streamlining Act of 1994 was a step in the right direction, but the landscape is still strewn with legislation. Much of this legislation could at least be consolidated and perhaps pared down to make contracting more attractive to potential contractors and to public managers who might not want to become more involved in contract management for fear of tripping over punitive statutory constraints. It is important, too, that if and when these kinds of revisions are undertaken, Congress should not take a narrow purchasing perspective to contract operations but should consider the full scope of contracting done today.

It is also important for Congress to consider ways to check abuses in the appropriations process. The practice of hanging appropriations for constituents on various pieces of legislation has become too much of a habit. The same legislators who one day attack pork barrel spending by a colleague often push for appropriations bills for their districts the next. This is very much the kind of problem that emerged as the federal government tried to close military installations. It may be necessary to find some vehicle that will permit the institution to block programs that promise bad deals for the public and yet allow individual members to argue on behalf of the folks back home. The present system creates contract disasters waiting to happen.

Speaking of disasters, another lesson from history is that emergency situations such as wars, civil unrest, or natural disasters often lead to efforts to waive standard contract management tools in order to get fast action. A long history of such expedited operations, however, suggests that it is often necessary to clean up messes later created in the name of a temporary emergency. It would be useful to consider legislation aimed at how to handle such emergencies without simply abandoning contract management policy.

Oversight of contracting also needs a fresh look, but it faces two difficulties. First, and in general, it can be difficult to interest legislators in investing the time and resources necessary to do careful and effective oversight unless there is a highly visible scandal or disaster, like the explosion of NASA's space shuttle *Challenger.* It requires legislators to learn the techniques of oversight so that they can design and execute oversight processes well and efficiently.[9] This process also requires staff support. Fortunately, the U.S. General Accounting Office, an agency responsible to both political parties, has a long history of investigating contract management and providing useful information. The GAO, however, is too often called in at the behest of a member of Congress who has an axe to grind with an executive branch agency or who would like to receive some media publicity. Some members of Congress have long records of calling for studies and perhaps even holding hearings with little serious effort to enact any constructive legislation. If legislators really want to improve contracting and to attract and retain talented public managers to work in the field, it is essential that more effort be dedicated to oversight that is intended to help and build capacity rather than to grab headlines on the evening news in the home district.

White House Leadership

The challenge of making enhanced contract management a priority has also been difficult at the other end of the avenue. To its credit, the Clinton administration implemented many of the policy recommendations that came out of the National Performance Review study of federal contracting. Steven Kelman, as head of the Office of Federal Procurement Policy, was in a position to put into action some of the important concerns about which he had been writing before coming to office. The administration of George W. Bush has announced that expanded and improved contracting is a priority,[10] although it is as yet unclear just what direction its efforts will take beyond its desire to implement its so-called faith-based initiative.[11] That initiative poses its own difficulties for reasons indicated in Chapter 5.

The White House can take three obvious steps that really are not about partisan or ideological positions. First, it is not necessary to reinvent the wheel.

Numerous studies have been made of the contracting process and its problems dating back to the Federal Procurement Commission Report of the early 1970s, and each administration since has undertaken some kind of examination of that same process. It is important to monitor the development and implementation of policies that address recommendations that are worthy of action. Once that is done, it is important to use the available mechanisms, led by the Office of Federal Procurement Policy, to set agendas for future studies. The OFPP effort during the 1990s to develop annual publications on best practices is a useful approach.

Second, two issues concerning the availability and capability of the people required for effective contract management can and should be important to any administration. As indicated in the previous chapters, we are very nearly at crisis conditions in regard to the loss of trained and experienced contract managers in the federal government. It is problematic when an administration, without regard to workloads, measures success by the number of jobs it can eliminate. That has been the case under both Democratic and Republican presidents in recent history. The more complex the contracting that is done and the more pervasive that kind of activity is across the range of agencies, the more important it is to recruit, train, and, above all, retain a talented workforce. Failing to do that will almost guarantee that the public will not get a good deal in most of what government seeks to do.

Making adequate staffing and education for contract management a priority evokes an even wider concern. It is important for the White House, as well as for Congress, to begin to pay more attention to the relationship between the roles of market regulator and market participant that state and local governments are being asked to play and ensure federal support for those roles. That includes a need to pay attention to federal preemptions that interfere with state and local ability to deal with their obligations, many of which are created and controlled by federal government funding or substantive mandates.

Finally, it is important for the chief executive to be overt, realistic, and candid in his or her assessments of the trade-offs that must be made in contracting (see Chapter 3). It is ultimately self-defeating for an administration to develop slogans or management programs that promise to maximize all dimensions of contracting at once. The hearings on a series of dramatic failures by NASA in the late 1990s provided a case in point. Early in the 1990s NASA adopted a program known as "Faster, Better, Cheaper." However, it became clear that an unwillingness to recognize important trade-offs and to be realistic about how many goals could be achieved simultaneously led to serious problems in the end.[12] Trade-offs must also be made among the elements that go into defining a good deal for the public, as explained in Chapter 1. Claims by the White House, or other political leaders, that a complex group of sometimes conflicting criteria can all be simultaneously maximized help no one.

States: Key Players in the Effort

Of course, most of the public contracts in this country are not done by the federal government but by state and local governments, albeit often using federal funds. States, too, can play critically important roles in building capacity for contract management. It is true that states differ from one another, and it is entirely likely that each has special concerns that are important in the way it manages its contracts. Still, state and local governments operate within the constitutional framework discussed in Chapter 2, which places limits on how far states can go in carving out special policies before they run afoul of the interstate commerce clause or the privileges and immunities clause. Also, many federal statutes partially or completely preempt state or local discretion. It is therefore useful to have a statewide public contract council, consisting of representatives from state agencies, the state attorney general's office, the county, the city, and both nonprofit and for-profit firms, to provide recommendations and support for contract management policy.

It is obvious that some of the concerns expressed about the role of the White House in the process also apply to that of the governor. In addition, it is important for governors to reconsider seriously the role that contract operations play in the state. Although contract operations have been growing and changing in recent decades, many states have failed to give careful consideration not just to policies but to the way they manage contracts. Contract operations are not often clearly understood as a central part of the management of the state.

In particular, it is imperative that this attention be devoted to the entire process and not merely to the bid portion. Many states have gone to on-line invitations and bid acceptance. A growing number announce awards and the results of bid protests on the World Wide Web. However, that is obviously only part of the overall process.

In some cases, general contract management issues are assigned to a state secretary of administration or the head of a state-level general services agency. That may be appropriate in regard to staff support for projects and for the generation of reports, but it is not enough to ensure adequate attention to contracting. To be taken seriously, state cabinet members must see this subject as on an equal footing with all other key management and policy initiatives on the governor's agenda.

Similarly, state legislatures would do well to consider some of the recommendations made for Congress. They can certainly check for potentially conflicting legislation or guidance and enhance oversight. States also might benefit from consideration of legislation to cover emergency contract operations, since it is not uncommon for state agencies to find themselves seeking to remedy flooding or other storm damage, even if they do not reach a full-blown state of declared emergency involving federal assistance.

However, the situation is somewhat more complex at the state level than it is for Congress, since most states have part-time legislatures, often with limited staff. It is possible to have the existing fiscal committees, which do often have the most staff of any state legislative committees, take on some aspects of contracting within their area of concern. Still, it is not necessarily the best idea to place over-sight and responsibility for contracting in that committee. The demands of sup-porting the appropriations process are usually difficult, and these pressures may well mean that attention to contracting would be limited and largely negative in character. The committee would get to it when a problem had to be solved and not necessarily otherwise. But whether it is housed in the fiscal committee or in another part of the legislature, it is important to ensure that contracting be given appropriate attention while recognizing the limitations of the state legislature.

At the same time, it is important to ensure that legislation controlling or regu-lating local governments provides sufficient flexibility to allow those governments to get a good deal for the public. It is also important that state legislation recog-nize that much of the contracting done in the state is intergovernmental in char-acter. In addition, states have increasing numbers of interjurisdictional agree-ments. The intergovernmental reality also means that much of what is done in the state works through contracting under federal grants to the states and through the states to nonprofit or for-profit organizations.

Another part of state government that is often ignored in discussions of con-tracting must be included. The attorney general is in most instances an inde-pendently elected official. In many states, the attorney general has nearly com-plete control over legal resources in the state. It is very important for the governor, the legislature, and state agencies to seek cooperation with the attorney general in the development of contract management policy. The attorney general will be in-volved in many ways in contract disputes, and it is well to include that office throughout the process. This is true despite the fact that in some states there may be tension, partisan or otherwise, between the attorney general and other execu-tive branch officials.

IMPROVING THE PROCESS AND
SUPPORTING THE PEOPLE: REFORMS ON
THE HORIZONTAL MODEL

A variety of steps can be taken on the horizontal level of the contract process as well as in the vertical model portion of the process.

Building Capacity at the Integration Stage

Public managers need assistance to ensure that their organizations are able to avoid a purely reactive approach, the public administration equivalent of running to the store when one runs out of food. Many organizations simply see contracting as one more task to be carried out rather than as a major area of endeavor for which planning and support are needed. The capacity for forecasting and market analysis is critical. Rare is the business of any size that would fail to staff and support these activities in order to spot good business opportunities, but rare is the public agency that does so.

Many organizations do not seek to provide additional staff to address contract management burdens. That usually means excessive burdens during the presolicitation and bid process on already stressed managers and clerical staff. It also means that once the bid is awarded, attention to contract operation will relax unless there is a significant breakdown in service. That is a serious problem for reasons explained in the preceding chapters.

Accounting and legal support are also important, but not with a largely audit or legal protection attitude. Risk management is important but only part of the decision calculus that positions an organization to know when and how to engage the market for the best deal. Best value contracting requires cost accounting support that will help a manager know when and whether it will cost less to contract work out or do it in-house.

What all these requirements mean is that to ensure a good deal for the public, it is essential to build effective practices for budgeting for contract management. For reasons indicated above, little attention has traditionally been accorded to this issue, which is one reason why contract management is usually understaffed and why what appear to be important opportunities at the beginning result in repeated tales of failure and abuse. If, for example, a city manager is expected to manage a contract process directly as part of his or her duties, it is important to understand, as part of the true costs of the contract, the cost of the time that he or she dedicates to that task. The manager cannot meet two responsibilities at the same time, although many seem to try. Any contract process beyond simple purchasing that does not consider the true costs of contract operations makes it almost impossible to determine whether or not the public is getting a good deal.

Finally, even if the organization has people to support contract operations, they cannot ensure effective management unless they are adequately trained. This is not just a challenge for those specifically charged to be contract officers. Federal and state programs are no more effective than the capability of the other participants in the contracting process. Wise firms, nonprofits, or agencies will always seek out the most capable contract partners. It may be possible to get an advantage over a weaker partner in regard to costs or work on the front end, but over the long term weak partners produce problems that carry costs. It is therefore essential for the federal government to support states and for states to support localities in training for contract management. Including nonprofit officers and for-profit managers in the process can only help in the long term to get the best deal for the public. Unfortunately, to this point at least, university programs have not generally done a very good job of educating for public contract management. Courses on privatization and nonprofit management are sometimes long on the politics of contracting out but not necessarily effective in addressing contract management specifically. One of the purposes of this book is to help in that regard.

It is very helpful if people who work in this field also have some exposure to administrative law. Because agencies and communities often operate traditional administrative programs and standard management functions along with their contract operations, there is a clear and important overlap. Due process requirements and agency rules clearly affect contract operations. However, adjudications are in some cases contracted out. This parallel system, along with the essential legal character of contracting, suggests that foundation education in both areas is important. This type of education is important for all public managers and not just for those specifically charged with contract management. It should be just as clear that education and training in this area need to reach beyond a narrow purchasing approach.

The Operation Stage: An Often Ignored Portion of the Process

If contract management is to improve, the SWAT Team noted, it is essential to overcome the traditional tendency to view contract administration as somehow tangential to core agency mission.[13] It is extremely dangerous to have top management believe that one can contract something out and forget it. Contract management is as intensive as any other public management enterprise. Indeed, the key to recruiting and retaining top quality contract managers is to ensure that they are made to feel central to the life and performance of the city organization or state agency when they are managing contracts.

That means that it is important to keep a priority on management after the integration stage. Chapters 3 and 4 discussed the importance of ensuring that contract operations management not be an activity limited to the contract officer. It is, rather, a continuation of the project team or management team that should be in place even before the contract is put out to bid and should be maintained throughout the working relationship of the contract. Thus, fully integrating contract management into public management is essential.

Contract operations involve more than a mere audit and control operation. Today, for reasons discussed throughout this book, the emphasis is on performance contracting. Those who are responsible for the management of performance contracts need to be involved in the early discussion of how the contract will be negotiated, including the way in which incentives are structured and the means built into the contract for performance monitoring. By the same token, incentive provisions in contracts cannot be effective unless they can be adequately administered during contract operations. Gain-sharing arrangements, in which both parties are intended to benefit from strong performance and creativity by the contractor, must be structured to include quality issues as well as cost. That means that contract managers must be trained to understand the nature and operation of incentive systems. Like the integration stage, management of contract operations costs money. If it is approached as a free good that will be taken care of as one more duty of an already busy manager, the results will very likely reflect that lack of commitment. It has been estimated that a reasonable assumption for the cost of performance monitoring and management may be as much as 25 percent of the value of the contract.[14]

Training for performance monitoring, for the management of mid-course corrections through change orders, and for the management of service networks is essential for successful managers in contract operations. It is particularly necessary in those situations in which the agency or community involved is dependent on the contractor because there is no internal direct service capability for backup and in situations in which there are limited alternative suppliers in the immediate environment. Here again, it is essential not only that the contracting officer be trained but that the generalist manager or the project team, if one is involved, be sufficiently familiar with this work. Inadequate understanding beyond the contracting officer can lead to communications difficulties or limited understanding of the overall management situation.

Separation and Transformation: Adequate Capacity for Active Engagement throughout the Process

The requirements for success in the separation or transformation stage were discussed in some detail in Chapter 5. Capacity building for this portion of the process requires sufficient support to ensure that managers involved in administering the separation or transformation stage do not view themselves in a dead-end position. They must be encouraged to understand that the city or agency views this portion of the process as being as important as any other and the key to good deals in the future. That also means that they must have the training and staff support to address the challenges of this stage. A message that one's work is important but that no resources required to do the job are forthcoming is a contradiction in terms.

Beyond support for the manager and his or her team, though, is the large need to have in place contingency resources to ensure that service gaps can be filled. A public/private service mix is one mechanism, but several additional suggestions were provided in Chapter 5. Direct service can be used as a training tool to assist in building skills and knowledge and also can serve as an emergency service gap response technique.

Although settlement or dispute resolution is a normal part of contract termination, it should not be viewed as the sole or dominant mode, just as audit and control is not all that is involved in the operation stage. It does mean that if alternative dispute mechanisms are to be used, the infrastructure and resources to take advantage of them must be available, such as legal support, available lists of mediators, and clear policies with regard to the use of techniques such as arbitration. It is also essential to know when and how to use these devices, and when to avoid them.

A great deal more work is needed on accountability in contracting by both practitioners and academics. This will require both broad discussions of the sort that are in progress presently in public administration and more focused discussions aimed at contracting. Accountability for contracting includes all the parties to the contract, including the intended recipients of services, and all the elements of a good deal. It is not simply an issue of the signatories to the contract. As indicated in Chapter 5, there is a range of issues particularly concerned with the rights of citizens under contracted service operations. Some of these are relatively narrow, but many of them are complex constitutional and statutory issues.

Above all, the separation or transformation stage should be a learning experience that is treated as a way to learn how to get better deals for the public in the future. Therefore, consideration must be given to the vehicles that will be used to ensure that those lessons are not lost and do in fact make it back into the overall performance assessment of the organization as well as into the integration considerations for future contracts.[15] Such mechanisms as a facilitated debriefing, even for what may seem relatively routine but significant contracts, can yield useful learning. This is as important for contracts viewed as a success as it is for those considered to be failures.

Learning is not limited to contract managers or the organizations for which they work. Elected officials need to be apprised of the lessons that are being learned about contract operations. Judges and lawyers also need to be kept informed. They are frequently brought into troubled situations, but it can be helpful for them to have more general knowledge to provide context when specific issues come before them.

CONCLUSION

As is true of all the elements of public contract management considered in this book, there is no magic to understanding how to build capacity. It does require commitment to the enterprise measured by a willingness to invest resources in contract management in order to realize the return of good deals for the public over the long term. It also requires a candor about contracting, its strengths and its weaknesses. The choice is not whether we deal with the challenge of public contract management. Given our contemporary reality, the only real question is whether we are prepared to do what is necessary, to do it well, and to get that good deal for the public measured by economy, efficiency, effectiveness, responsiveness, responsibility, and equity.

Notes

1. Michael Sandel, *Democracy's Discontent* (Cambridge: Harvard University Press, 1996), 8.

2. See Sandel, supra note 1, and James G. March and Johan P. Olsen, *Rediscovering Institutions: The Organizational Basis of Politics* (New York: Free Press, 1990). I have laid out this argument in some detail in Phillip J. Cooper, *Public Law and Public Administration,* 3d ed. (Itasca, Ill.: F. E. Peacock, 2000), 574–578.

3. See, for example, David Osborne and Ted Gaebler, *Reinventing Government* (New York: Penguin, 1992). See also Al Gore, *From Red Tape to Results: Creating a Government That Works Better and Costs Less,* report of the National Performance Review (Washington, D.C.: Government Printing Office, 1993).

4. See generally, Christopher Pollitt, "Management Techniques for the Public Sector: Pulpit and Practice," in *Governance in a Changing Environment,* ed. B. Guy Peters and Donald J. Savoie (Ottawa: Canadian Center for Management Development and McGill-Queens University Press, 1995).

5. See Barry Bozeman, *All Organizations Are Public* (San Francisco: Jossey-Bass, 1987); "Exploring the Limits of Public and Private Sectors: Sector Boundaries as Maginot Line," *Public Administration Review* 48 (March/April 1988): 672–674.

6. See Ronald C. Moe and Robert S. Gilmour, "Rediscovering Principles of Public Administration: The Neglected Foundation of Public Law," 55 *Public Administration Review* 135 (1995); Ronald C. Moe and Thomas H. Stanton, "Government–Sponsored Enterprises as Federal Instrumentalities: Reconciling Private Management with Public Accountability," 49 *Public Administration Review* 321 (1989); Ronald Moe, " 'Law' versus 'Performance' as Objective Standard," 48 *Public Administration Review* 675 (1988); "Exploring the Limits of Privatization," 47 *Public Administration Review* 453 (1987).

7. Steven Kelman, *Procurement and Public Management: The Fear of Discretion and the Quality of Government Performance* (Washington, D.C.: AEI Press, 1990).

8. See *Hutchinson v. Proxmire,* 443 U.S. 111 (1979).

9. See Morton Rosenberg, *Investigative Oversight: An Introduction to the Law, Practice, and Procedure of Congressional Inquiry* (Washington, D.C.: Congressional Research Service, 1995).

10. See, for example, "The President's Management Agenda, Fiscal 2002," http://www.whitehouse.gov/omb/budget/fy2002/mgmt.pdf, September 6, 2001.

11. Executive Order 13198, "Agency Responsibilities with Respect to Faith-Based and Community Initiatives," 66 FR 8497 (2001); Executive Order 13199, "Establishment of White House Office of Faith-Based and Community Initiatives," 66 FR 8499 (2001).

12. See *Report on Project Management in NASA,* Mars Climate Orbiter Mishap Investigation Board, March 13, 2000, ftp://ftp.hq.nasa.gov/pub/pao/reports/2000/MCO_MIB_Report.pdf, September 11, 2001; *NASA FBC Task Final Report, Spear Report,* ftp://ftp.hq.nasa.gov/pub/pao/reports/2000/fbctask.pdf, September 1, 2001.

13. U.S. Office of Management and Budget, *Summary Report of the SWAT Team on Civilian Agency Contracting* (Washington, D.C.: Office of Management and Budget, 1992), 11.

14. John A. Rehfuss, *Contracting Out in Government* (San Francisco: Jossey-Bass, 1989), 95.

15. U.S. General Accounting Office, *NASA: Better Mechanisms Needed for Sharing Lessons Learned* (Washington, D.C.: GAO, 2002).

Bibliography

Ammons, David N., ed. *Accountability for Performance: Measurement and Monitoring in Local Government.* Washington, D.C.: International City/County Management Association, 1995.

Appleby, Paul. *Big Democracy.* New York: Knopf, 1945.

Ball, Howard, and Phillip J. Cooper. *Of Power and Right.* New York: Oxford University Press, 1992.

Bardach, Eugene, and Cara Lesser. "Accountability in Human Service Collaboratives—For What? And To Whom?" 6 *Journal of Public Administration Research and Theory* 197 (1996).

Beard, Charles A. *An Economic Interpretation of the Constitution.* New York: Macmillan, 1935.

Behn, Robert D. *Rethinking Democratic Accountability.* Washington, D.C.: Brookings Institution Press, 2001.

———. "Strategies for Avoiding the Pitfalls of Performance Contracting," 22 *Public Productivity and Management Review* 470 (1999).

Beveridge, Albert J. *The Life of John Marshall.* New York: Houghton Mifflin, 1916.

Bingham, Lisa. "Alternative Dispute Resolution in Public Administration." In *Handbook of Public Law and Administration.* Edited by Phillip J. Cooper and Chester A. Newland. San Francisco: Jossey-Bass, 1997.

Bornet, Vaughn Davis. *The Presidency of Lyndon B. Johnson.* Lawrence: University Press of Kansas, 1983.

Bozeman, Barry. *All Organizations Are Public.* San Francisco: Jossey-Bass, 1987.

———. "Exploring the Limits of Public and Private Sectors: Sector Boundaries as Maginot Line," 48 *Public Administration Review* 672 (1988).

Burton, Lloyd. "Ethical Discontinuities in Public-Private Sector Negotiation," 9 *Journal of Policy Analysis and Management* 23 (1990).

Calamari, John D., and Joseph M. Perillo. *Contracts.* 3d ed. St. Paul, Minn.: West Publishing, 1987.

Carrier, Paul J. "Sovereignty under the Agreement on Government Procurement," 6 *Minnesota Journal of Global Trade* 67 (1997).

Chubb, John E., and Terry M. Moe. *Politics, Markets, and America's Schools.* Washington, D.C.: Brookings Institution, 1990.

Cibinic, John, Jr., and Ralph C. Nash. *Administration of Government Contracts.* 3d ed. Washington, D.C.: George Washington University Press, 1995.

Cooper, Phillip J. *By Order of the President: The Use and Abuse of Presidential Direct Action.* Lawrence: University Press of Kansas, 2002.

———. "Crise de Coordenação e Governance No Século 21: Compreendo as Tendências Centrais." In *Sociedade e Estado: Superando Fronteiras.* By Fundação do Desenvolvimento Administrativo (FUNDAP). Sao Paulo: FUNDAP, 1998.

———. "Ejecución de la politica social en tiempos de crisis de coordinatión," 7 *Reforma y Democracia* 99 (1997).

———. "Government Contracts in Public Administration: The Role and Environment of the Contracting Office," 40 *Public Administration Review* 459 (1980).

———. *Public Law and Public Administration.* 3d ed. Itasca, Ill.: F. E. Peacock, 2000.

———. "The Wilsonian Dichotomy in Administrative Law." In *Politics and Administration.* Edited by J. Rabin and J. Bowman. New York: Marcel Dekker, 1984.

deLeon, Peter. "Public Policy Termination: An End and a Beginning," 4 *Policy Analysis* 369 (1978).

DeMoss, Douglas P. "Procurement during the Civil War and Its Legacy for the Modern Commander," 1997 *Army Lawyer* 9 (1997).

Deming, W. Edwards. *Out of the Crisis: Quality, Productivity and Competitive Position.* Cambridge: Cambridge University Press, 1988.

Donahue, John. *The Privatization Decision.* New York: Basic Books, 1989.

Douglas, William O. *Democracy and Finance.* Port Washington, N.Y.: Kennikat Press, 1969.

Downs, George W., and Patrick D. Larkey. *The Search for Government Efficiency.* New York: Random House, 1986.

Finer, Herman. "Administrative Responsibility in Democratic Government," 1 *Public Administration Review* 335 (1941).

———. "Better Government Personnel: America's Next Frontier," 51 *Political Science Quarterly* 569 (1936).

Fisher, Louis. *Constitutional Dialogues.* Princeton: Princeton University Press, 1988.

Fitzgerald, A. Ernest. *The High Priests of Waster.* New York: Norton, 1972.

Frederickson, H. George, ed. *Ideal and Practice in Council-Manager Government.* 2d ed. Washington, D.C.: International City/County Management Association, 1994.

Freidel, Frank. *Franklin D. Roosevelt: A Rendezvous with Destiny.* Boston: Little, Brown, 1990.

Friedrich, Carl. "Public Policy and the Nature of Administrative Responsibility." In *Public Policy*. Edited by C. J. Friedrich and E. S. Mason. Cambridge: Harvard University Press, 1940.

Gilette, Clayton P., and Paul B. Stephan III. "Constitutional Limitations on Privatization," 46 *American Journal of Comparative Law* 481 1998.

Gilman, Michele Estrin. "Legal Accountability in an Era of Privatized Welfare" 89 *California Law Review* 569 (2001).

Gore, Al. *From Red Tape to Results: Creating a Government That Works Better and Costs Less*. Report of the National Performance Review. Washington, D.C.: Government Printing Office, 1993.

————. *Reinventing Federal Procurement: Accompanying Report of the National Performance Review*. Washington, D.C.: Government Printing Office, 1993.

Gulick, Luther, and Lyndal Urwick. *The Papers on the Science of Administration*. Fairfield, N.J.: Augustus M. Kelley, 1977. Originally published by the Institute of Public Administration, New York, 1937.

Guttman, Dan. *Making Reform Work: Contracting for Government*. Washington, D.C.: National Academy of Public Administration, 1997.

Hamilton, Alexander, James Madison, and John Jay. *The Federalist Papers*. New York: Mentor, 1961.

Hansen, Shirley J., and Jeannie C. Weisman. *Performance Contracting: Expanding Horizons*. Lilburn, Ga.: Fairmont Press, 1998.

Harney, Donald F. *Service Contracting: A Local Government Guide*. Washington, D.C.: International City/County Management Association, 1992.

Holifield, Chet. "Federal Procurement and Contracting Reform," 41 *Brooklyn Law Review* 479 (1975).

Hoogland DeHoog, Ruth. *Contracting Out for Human Services*. Albany: State University of New York Press, 1984.

John, Richard R. *Spreading the News: The American Postal System from Franklin to Morse*. Cambridge: Harvard University Press, 1995.

Joy, James. "Eli Whitney's Contracts for Muskets," 8 *Public Contract Law Journal* 140 (1976).

Kelman, Steven. *Procurement and Public Management: The Fear of Discretion and the Quality of Government Performance*. Washington, D.C.: AEI Press, 1990.

Kettl, Donald F. *Government by Proxy*. Washington, D.C.: CQ Press, 1988.

————. *Sharing Power*. Washington, D.C.: Brookings Institution, 1993.

Keyes, W. Noel, *Government Contracts: Under the Federal Acquisition Regulation*. 2d ed. St. Paul, Minn.: West Publishing, 1996.

Kotz, Nick. *Wild Blue Yonder: Money, Politics, and the B-1 Bomber*. New York: Pantheon Books, 1988.

Light, Paul C. *Making Nonprofits Work*. Washington, D.C.: Brookings Institution Press, 2000.

Maine, Sir Henry. *Ancient Law*. London: Dent, 1972.

Mangold, Susan Vivian. "Welfare Reform and the Juvenile Courts: Protection, Privatization, and Profit in the Foster Care System," 60 *Ohio State Law Journal* 1295 (1999).

March, James G., and Johan P. Olsen. *Rediscovering Institutions: The Organizational Basis of Politics*. New York: Free Press, 1990.

McCullough, David. *Truman*. New York: Simon and Schuster, 1992.

Milward, H. Brinton. "The Changing Character of the Public Sector." In *Handbook of Public Administration*. 2d ed. Edited by James Perry. San Francisco: Jossey-Bass, 1996.

———. "Implication of Contracting Out: New Roles for the Hollow State." In *New Paradigms for Government*. Edited by Patricia W. Ingraham and Barbara S. Romzek. San Francisco: Jossey-Bass, 1994.

———. "Introduction to Symposium on the Hollow State: Capacity, Control, and Performance in Interorganizational Settings," 6 *Journal of Public Administration Research and Theory* 194 (1996).

Moe, Ronald. "Exploring the Limits of Privatization," 47 *Public Administration Review* 453 (1987).

———. " 'Law' Versus 'Performance' as Objective Standard," 48 *Public Administration Review* 675 (1988).

Moe, Ronald, and Robert S. Gilmour. "Rediscovering Principles of Public Administration: The Neglected Foundation of Public Law," 55 *Public Administration Review* 135 (1995).

Moe, Ronald C., and Thomas H. Stanton. "Government-Sponsored Enterprises as Federal Instrumentalities: Reconciling Private Management with Public Accountability," 49 *Public Administration Review* 321 (1989).

Morgan, Ruth. *The President and Civil Rights: Policy-Making by Executive Order*. New York: St. Martin's, 1970.

Morstein Marx, Fritz, ed. *Elements of Public Administration*. New York: Prentice Hall, 1946.

Nagle, John F. *A History of Government Contracting*. 2d ed. Washington, D.C.: George Washington University School of Law, Government Contracts Program, 1999.

Nalbandian, John. *Professionalism in Local Government: Transformations in the Roles, Responsibilities, and Values of City Managers*. San Francisco: Jossey-Bass, 1991.

———. "Tenets of Contemporary Professionalism in Local Government." In *Ideal and Practice in Council-Manager Government*. 2d ed. Edited by H. George Frederickson. Washington, D.C.: International City/County Management Association, 1994.

Nash, Ralph C. *Formation of Government Contracts*. Washington, D.C.: George Washington University School of Law, Government Contracts Program, 1998.

National Commission on the Public Service (Volcker Commission). *Leadership for America: Rebuilding the Public Service*. Washington, D.C.: Government Printing Office, 1989.

National Commission on the State and Local Public Service (Winter Commission). *Hard Truths/Tough Choices: An Agenda for State and Local Reform.* Albany, N.Y.: The Nelson A. Rockefeller Institute of Government, 1993.

National Partnership Council. *A Report to the President on Implementing Recommendations of the National Performance Review.* Washington, D.C.: Government Printing Office, 1994.

Osborne, David, and Ted Gaebler. *Reinventing Government.* New York: Penguin, 1993.

O'Toole, Laurence J. "Different Public Managements? Implications of Structural Context in Hierarchies and Networks." In *Advancing Public Management: New Directions in Theory, Methods, and Practice.* Edited by Jeff Brudney, Laurence J. O'Toole, and Hal Rainey. Washington, D.C.: Georgetown University Press, 2000.

————. "Hollowing the Infrastructure: Revolving Loan Programs and Network Dynamics in the American States," 6 *Journal of Public Administration Research and Theory* 225 (1996).

Pach, Chester J., Jr., and Elmo Richardson. *The Presidency of Dwight D. Eisenhower.* Lawrence: University Press of Kansas, 1991.

Peters, B. Guy, and Donald J. Savoie, eds. *Governance in a Changing Environment.* Ottawa: McGill/Queens University Press, 1995.

Pollitt, Christopher. "Management Techniques for the Public Sector: Pulpit and Practice." In *Governance in a Changing Environment.* Edited by B. Guy Peters and Donald J. Savoie. Ottawa: Canadian Center for Management Development and McGill-Queens University Press, 1995.

"Public Oversight of Public/Private Partnerships" (Panel Discussion), 28 *Fordham Urban Law Journal* 1357 (2001).

Randall, Willard Sterne. *George Washington: A Life.* New York: Henry Holt, 1997.

Rehfuss, John A. *Contracting Out in Government.* San Francisco: Jossey-Bass, 1989.

Richards, Craig E., Rima Shore, and Max B. Sawicky. *Risky Business: Private Management of Public Schools.* Washington, D.C.: Economic Policy Institute, 1996.

Romzek, Barbara S., and Melvin J. Dubnick. "Accountability in the Public Sector: Lessons from the Challenger Tragedy," 47 *Public Administration Review* 227 (1987).

Romzek, Barbara S., and Jocelyn Johnston. "Reforming and Privatizing Medicaid." Paper presented at the Fourth National Public Management Research Conference, Athens, Georgia, October 1997.

Saidel, Judith R. "The Dynamics of Interdependence between Public Agencies and Nonprofit Organizations," 3 *Research in Public Administration* 201 (1994).

————. "Resource Interdependence: The Relationship between State Agencies and Nonprofit Organizations," 51 *Public Administration Review* 543 (1991).

Saidel, Judith R., and Sharon Harlan. "Contracting and Patterns of Nonprofit Governance," 8 *Nonprofit Management and Leadership* 243 (1998)

Salamon, Lester M., ed. *Beyond Privatization: The Tools of Government Action.* Washington, D.C.: Urban Institute, 1989.

Sandel, Michael. *Democracy's Discontent.* Cambridge: Harvard University Press, 1996.

Savas, E. N. *Privatization.* Chatham, N.J.: Chatham House Publishers, 1987.

Schein, Edgar. *Organizational Culture and Leadership.* 2d ed. San Francisco: Jossey-Bass, 1992.

Schulman, Bruce J. *Lyndon B. Johnson and American Liberalism.* Boston: Bedford Books, 1995.

Sherry, Suzanna. "The Founders' Unwritten Constitution," 54 *University of Chicago Law Review* 1127 (1987).

Tate, C. Neal, and Torbjorn Vallinder, eds. *The Global Expansion of Judicial Power.* New York: New York University Press, 1995.

Tellier, Paul M. *Public Service 2000: A Report on Progress.* Ottawa: Minister of Supply and Services, 1992.

U.S. Commission on Civil Rights, *Voting Irregularities in Florida during the 2000 Presidential Election.* Washington, D.C.: U.S. Commission on Civil Rights, 2001, http://www.usccr.gov/vote2000/stdraft1/ch3.htm, December 9, 2001.

U.S. Commission on Government Procurement. *Report of the Commission on Government Procurement.* Washington, D.C.: Government Printing Office, 1972.

U.S. Environmental Protection Agency. *A Study of State and Local Government Procurement Practices that Consider Environmental Performance of Goods and Services.* Washington, D.C.: Environmental Protection Agency, 1996.

U.S. General Accounting Office. *Acquisition Reform: Purchase Card Use Cuts Procurement Costs, Improves Efficiency.* Washington, D.C.: General Accounting Office, 1996.

―――. *Contract Management: Purchase of Army Black Berets.* Washington, D.C.: General Accounting Office, 2001.

―――. *Contract Management: Taking a Strategic Approach to Improving Service Acquisitions.* Washington, D.C.: General Accounting Office, 2002.

―――. *Contract Management: Trends and Challenges in Acquiring Services.* Washington, D.C.: General Accounting Office, 2001.

―――. *Cooperative Purchasing: Effects Are Likely to Vary among Governments and Businesses.* Washington, D.C.: General Accounting Office, 1997.

―――. *Department of Energy Contract Management.* Washington, D.C.: Government Printing Office, 1997.

―――. *High Risk Series.* Washington, D.C.: General Accounting Office, 1997.

―――. *NASA: Better Mechanisms Needed for Sharing Lessons Learned.* Washington, D.C.: General Accounting Office, 2002.

―――. *Opportunities and Challenges in Contracting for Program Safeguards.* Washington, D.C.: General Accounting Office, 2001.

―――. *Private and Public Prisons: Studies Comparing Operational Costs and/or Quality of Service.* Washington, D.C.: General Accounting Office, 1996.

————. *Privatization: Lessons Learned by State and Local Governments*. Washington, D.C.: General Accounting Office, 1997.

————. *Public-Private Competitions*. Washington, D.C.: General Accounting Office, 1998.

————. *Small Business: Trends in Federal Procurement in the 1990s*. Washington, D.C.: General Accounting Office, 2001.

————. *Social Service Privatization: Ethics and Accountability Challenges in State Contracting*. Washington, D.C.: General Accounting Office, 1999.

————. *Worker Protection: Federal Contractors and Violations of Labor Law*. Washington, D.C.: General Accounting Office, 1995.

U.S. Office of Federal Procurement Policy. *A Guide to Best Practices for Performance-Based Service Contracting*. Washington, D.C.: Office of Management and Budget, 1996.

U.S. Office of Management and Budget, *Summary Report of the SWAT Team on Civilian Agency Contracting*. Washington, D.C.: Office of Management and Budget, 1992.

Van Alstyne, William. "The Demise of the Right-Privilege Distinction in Constitutional Law," 81 *Harvard Law Review* 1439 (1968).

vom Bauer, F. Trowbridge. "Fifty Years of Government Contract Law," 29 *Federal Bar Journal* 305 (1970).

Waldo, Dwight. *The Administrative State*. New York: Ronald Press, 1948.

Weisbrod, Burton A. "The Future of the Nonprofit Sector: Its Entwining with Private Enterprise and Government," 16 *Journal of Policy Analysis and Management* 541 (1997).

Wheaton, Kelly D. "Spycraft and Government Contracts: a Defense of Totten v. United States," 1997 *Army Lawyer* 9 (1997).

Whelan, John W. "Reflections on Government Contracts and Government Policy on the Occasion of the Twenty-Fifth Anniversary of the Public Contract Law Section," 20 *Public Contract Law Journal* 6 (1990).

White, Leonard D. *The Federalists*. New York: Macmillan, 1956.

————. *Introduction to the Study of Public Administration*. 4th ed. New York: Macmillan, 1955.

Wilson, Woodrow. "The Study of Administration," 2 *Political Science Quarterly* 209 (1887).

Wright, Deil S. *Understanding Intergovernmental Relations*. 3d ed. Pacific Grove, Calif.: Brooks/Cole, 1988.

Opinions Cited

Index